EVALUATION ESSENTIALS

EVALUATION ESSENTIALS
—— From A to Z ——

MARVIN C. ALKIN

Anne T. Vo
Research and Editorial Assistant

THE GUILFORD PRESS
New York   London

©2011 The Guilford Press
A Division of Guilford Publications, Inc.
72 Spring Street, New York, NY 10012
www.guilford.com

Printed in the United States of America

This book is printed on acid-free paper.

Last digit is print number: 9   8   7   6   5   4   3   2   1

Library of Congress Cataloging-in-Publication Data
Alkin, Marvin C.
    Evaluation essentials: from A to Z / Marvin C. Alkin.
        p.   cm.
    Includes bibliographical references and index.
    ISBN 978-1-60623-898-1 (pbk. : alk. paper)
    ISBN 978-1-60623-899-8 (hardcover : alk. paper)
    1. Evaluation research (Social action programs)   I. Title.
    H62.A45675 2011
    001.4—dc22

                                                2010022239

Acknowledgments

First, my most sincere thanks to Anne Vo for her important assistance in preparing this book. Anne prepared early drafts of portions of several sections of the book and provided valuable research and editorial assistance at all stages of the writing. However, Anne's most important contribution was as a trusted colleague who was a thoughtful sounding board for all my ideas. Anne is among the very best doctoral students that I have had, and she will excel in the academic world.

Nicole Eisenberg, a former doctoral student of mine, is a superb evaluator currently working in the Seattle area. Her case study demonstrates a clear understanding of the context in which evaluators work and provides excellent fodder for discussion. Nicole is a wonderful writer and a clean thinker, and I am grateful for her contributions to this volume.

Several people read early versions of the whole book and offered helpful advice. An early version of the book was pilot tested on two people to obtain comments on content and readability. Rebecca Luskin, a doctoral student in my Social Research Methodology Division, was meticulous in her examination and offered a host of insightful comments. Allison Taka, an undergraduate student (and member of the UCLA women's basketball team), provided very helpful comments about understandability. I am also grateful to William E. Bickel, Ben Charvat, Chris Ethimiou, and Gary Galluzzo, who did blind reviews of the book and offered many helpful suggestions. Finally, my colleague

Tina Christie reviewed the "almost final" manuscript and provided wise and helpful advice.

A number of others offered substantive comments that most certainly improved the book. Eric Barela offered suggestions on the qualitative methods chapters. My UCLA colleagues Felipe Martinez and James Catterall made suggestions related to the sections on quantitative methods and cost analysis, respectively. Kyo Yamashiro, Tarek Azzam, and Annamarie Francois reviewed material as well. Assistance was also provided by several of my doctoral students: Lisa Dillman, Mark Hansen, and Jessica Robles.

As with each of my other books, it has been a delight working with my editor, C. Deborah Laughton. Deborah spent several years trying to persuade me to write this book and provided encouragement throughout the process. I am grateful for all of her assistance.

Last, but certainly not least, let me express deep gratitude and love to my wife, Marilyn. She had to live with me day by day as I obsessed with getting this book "right" (in my mind). Thank you, thank you, for putting up with me.

MARVIN C. ALKIN

To the Reader

HELLO

I think we should get acquainted, since we will be carrying on a conversation—a long conversation. I'm Marv Alkin. I've been a professor at UCLA for more than 40 years. Many years ago, I founded and directed the Center for the Study of Evaluation. Since then, I've written books on evaluation, done research on the field, and written many journal articles and chapters. But don't get me wrong—I'm not some ivory-tower type. My work has always been based on engaging in real evaluations and learning from doing. I probably have done more than 100 evaluations—mostly small- and middle-size scale.

I view evaluation skills as very cross-disciplinary. I have done many school program evaluations, both K–12 and higher education. I've also conducted evaluations of a psychiatric residence training program, a state's juvenile detention facilities, a self-actualization program for campesinos in Ecuador, an agricultural extension program in eight Caribbean countries, and many others. I love evaluation, and I'm happy that I fell into it. I hope you come to appreciate evaluation as well.

Now, a few comments about my personal life. I am married, with two children and six marvelous grandchildren (as determined by my unbiased evaluation). My avocational passion is college basketball, particularly UCLA basketball. I rarely miss a UCLA game, and go to some basketball practices as well. I never played on a basketball team, but when my son was very young, I coached his Junior Hi-Y team to two undefeated seasons—and then I retired from coaching.

Well, that's much too much about me. What about you?

WHO ARE YOU?

Actually, you are a number of different people. You might be a program administrator taking an introductory evaluation course (or a unit on evaluation) in your field. This course might be taught at the master's-degree level. This book is relevant to you because you use evaluations, you commission evaluations, and you are often engaged in ongoing evaluation of your program's development.

Perhaps, also, you are a member of a program staff reading this book at the suggestion of an evaluator. Some evaluators consider the most effective kind of evaluation to be one that obtains active participation from those who have a stake in the program. In reading this book, you might be able to participate more fully as a partner in the evaluation.

You might also be a beginning (or would-be) evaluator who is using this book in a first-course overview to the field. Furthermore, you might be using this book in a doctoral-level course as an accessible introduction to the field, supplemented by another text or by a variety of original source readings creatively selected by your instructor.

I welcome all of you to our conversation. For the first of you, reading this book will provide the eye-opening experience you desire. You will gain some understanding of evaluation and the processes involved. Your ability to potentially conduct evaluations will be enhanced by the opportunity to examine a case study (following Section B) and to apply newly acquired skills to that case example.

For the potential professional evaluators, this book is a start. You'll gain a foundation in evaluation, which can certainly be enhanced by examining the suggested further readings at the end of each section. You will, however, need other courses to expand on some of the technical aspects of evaluation.

And so join me, and let's have a talk.

Contents

Contents

Overview

Do you remember when in the fifth grade you were asked to learn all of the presidents and vice presidents (in order)? And then, most certainly, you were asked to memorize the state capitals. (Do you still remember them?) The question that I ask is whether these activities provided you with a real understanding about each of these states or about how government works.

In this book, I will not pepper you with the names of evaluation "capitals"—the names of evaluation theorists. After many years in the field as an evaluation researcher and theorist, I know the literature, and it is reflected in the writings of this book. Instead, I want to provide you with concepts—the ability to engage in evaluation. When people talk, when people converse, they don't stop after every second sentence and say something like "Jones, 2009." Let us converse about the process of evaluation so that you can "walk the walk" instead of just "talk the talk."

However, let me point out that some people might, at the conclusion of a conversation, express further interest in a topic and the desire to learn more. Thus, at the end of each section, I have provided some items for "further reading." Each of these suggested readings was selected because I felt that they were easily understood and not overly esoteric. Moreover, I generally have not recommended long articles or books. Finally, each "further reading" is accompanied by a statement consisting of a sentence or two indicating why I think it might be worthwhile to read.

Another means for further reinforcing evaluation understandings is provided by a case study scenario (the RUPAS case) to be found after Section B of this book. This case involves education, social welfare, community building, health, and so forth. It is potentially applicable to many fields. At the end of each of the subsequent sections there are questions to be answered or suggested group activities related to the RUPAS case. A group leader or instructor might further modify or adapt the case study questions to fit your field of study. (Note: Gaining Additional Understanding "Case Study Exercise/Resources/Further Reading" appear at the end of each section, starting with Section C. Only "Further Reading" suggestions appear at the end of Sections A and B.)

STRUCTURE

You might have guessed from the title that I am going to follow through with the "A-to-Z" theme. Yes, indeed. There are 26 sections in this book designed to teach you, sequentially, how to do an evaluation. I selected A–Z as a mnemonic device and as a way to break the sections into manageable pieces. However, let me point out that evaluation is not some mechanical, step-by-step valuing procedure. Furthermore, program site contingencies might alter the sequence and perhaps leave out steps. Evaluation involves people and interrelationships, and this is highlighted throughout the book.

Sections A and B provide some general understandings about evaluation: what is evaluation, why do evaluation. Section C is a "Who is the evaluator?" section. This is both general understanding and an important aspect in defining evaluation. The logic of this book is presented in the accompanying overview table. Then there are 13 evaluation activities roughly corresponding to Sections D through V, classified as to when they take place in the evaluation. Some commence primarily during an early (or "pre-") stage; others in what I call a "getting started" stage; some depict the completion of a written evaluation plan; and, finally, some activities involve executing the plan.

The remaining five chapters are of three types. Sections E, W, and X take place *throughout* the evaluation and are the "aids to getting it done properly." In Section Y, I present cost analysis as an evaluation option. And, in Section Z, I discuss with you some potential avenues for further learning. Look the chart over carefully, and then let us proceed.

Overview Chart: Evaluation Essentials

Evaluation activity	Section in which it is discussed	The evaluation plan stages			
		Preplanning stage	Getting started on the plan	Writing the plan down	Executing the plan
1. Identifying Stakeholders	Section D	Primary	✓	✓	✓
2. Gaining Understanding of the Organizational/Social/Political Context	Section F	Primary	✓	✓	✓
3. Describing the Program	Section G	Primary	✓	✓	✓
4. Understanding the Program	Section H		Primary	✓	✓
5. Developing Initial Evaluation Questions	Section I		Primary	✓	✓
6. Considering Possible Instrumentation	Section J Section K Section L Section M		Primary	✓	✓
7. Determining Evaluable Questions	Section N		Primary	✓	✓
8. Finalizing the Evaluation Plan (Design)	Section O Section P			Primary	✓
9. Determining Procedural Aspects of the Plan	Section Q			Primary	✓
10. Analyzing Data	Section R Section S			✓	Primary
11. Answering Evaluation Questions	Section T			✓	Primary
12. Reporting Evaluation Results	Section U			✓	Primary
13. Helping Stakeholders to Use the Results	Section V	✓	✓	✓	Primary
Aids to getting it done properly					
Maintaining Relationships with Stakeholders	Section E	✓	✓	✓	✓
Managing the Evaluation	Section W		✓	Primary	Primary
Abiding by Appropriate Evaluation Standards	Section X	✓	✓	✓	✓
Additional evaluation option					
Conducting a Cost Analysis	Section Y	✓	✓	✓	✓

What Is Evaluation?

Evaluation is taking place everywhere around us. You most certainly have engaged in evaluation within the past day. But what *is* evaluation? The popular definition of evaluation according to the dictionary is "to ascertain the value or amount of" or "to appraise." Indeed, you do this all the time. When you go to the store to make purchases, you determine the value of things. You might ask: Is it worth it? You look at the cost of an item and determine whether, in fact, its value to you exceeds the cost. You make an appraisal.

Perhaps the most common kind of evaluation that you might engage in is *product evaluation.* If you are looking to buy a new flat-screen television, you examine several different products. And when you do, you gather information about their technical specifications, their size, their attractiveness, and the cost. You make an appraisal. Sometimes these appraisals are done at an instinctive level. You might just look at competing products and make a decision, all while processing data in your head, perhaps unknowingly, about what you believe to be differences between the two products.

Sometimes, you or I might be more systematic in our evaluations. I recall that when my wife and I bought our first house, we listed the attributes that we thought were essential. Some items we considered to be necessary and other items were viewed as optional, but preferred. All of these attributes were listed on a piece of paper, and we developed columns for each of the three competing houses and rated each of the characteristics. Then the "evaluation model" became somewhat more sophisticated. We indicated those dimensions that needed to be present in order for the house to be considered (e.g., three bedrooms). This was a "necessary, but not sufficient" list. We then further differentiated between the houses by addressing additional ways of appraising the data. Values or weightings were attached to each of the dimensions. We needed to decide which ones, for example, were more important and then provided a weight for each. We asked: What are the weightings for each—the relative importance? Was having an additional bathroom more important than whether the house was landscaped well? How much more important? If landscaping was weighted at "1," would an extra bathroom be a "2" or a "3"? Thus in a way we were doing an evaluation based on a number of criteria weighted differentially based on our view of their relative importance.

Evaluating products—like a house—is one kind of evaluation. You might also evaluate people—*personnel evaluation*. You could make judgments about whether you would like to develop a friendship with an individual or whether a particular painter or electrician seems trustworthy and dependable. If you are in a position where you supervise personnel who work for you, you are engaged in evaluation. Or you might need to decide which of several applicants should be hired for a position. Personnel evaluations, again, require an appraisal, or an evaluation, including making judgments about relative value. Sometimes these kinds of decisions are made based on impressions—just instinct. Other times, those making such decisions are more systematic in performing these evaluations.

A third kind of evaluation is *policy evaluation*. Policies are general directions for action without necessarily having a particular program or plan in mind. So again, at the everyday level of evaluation, one might be evaluating a potential policy decision of whether to go on a diet. No specific diet plan is necessarily in mind; thus it is a policy being evaluated—not a program. This policy evaluation might consider such questions as, what are the potential benefits from commencing this policy—this course of action? In doing this, you might consider what you know about the relationship between being overweight and in good health. You might ask, "Is following this course of action compatible with my lifestyle, and, if not, is that acceptable? And what are the costs to me either in dollars or in terms of modifications that I would need to make in my lifestyle if I were to pursue that course of action or policy?"

Another kind of evaluation is *program evaluation*. Before discussing program evaluation, it is important that I add a brief side note. In program evaluation, evaluators can gather data about personnel (teachers, caseworkers, students, clients, etc.), but the focus is not to make judgments about these individuals. Products might also be a part of the program that is being evaluated. Thus data might also be gathered about products, but the primary purpose is not evaluating the products. Rather, evaluators are interested in using this information collectively to better understand the program in which participants or products are involved.

Now let us consider the nature of program evaluation. Suppose that you wish to enroll your child in a preschool program and need to make a choice about which one to select. Let me make the example simpler by assuming that you have become convinced of the benefits of the Montessori preschool approach, but there are three schools within easy driving distance that all claim to be "Montessori." In doing this evaluation, you might visit the three schools and observe in the classrooms. You might look at the activities in which children are engaged. You might look at the number of adults per child. You might look at the number and type of manipulatives available. All of these are relevant things to be examined. But if you wish to be systematic, you should select the kinds of things that are typically a part of a Montessori program—that follow the Montessori philosophy. When you have compiled that list of elements or activities, you must consider the possible ways to see whether those things are actually taking place. That is, you want to evaluate whether a Montessori approach is *really* being implemented—whether the program is really operating in a Montessori way. Thus you would want to examine: Does multiage grouping take place? Are there work centers? Are areas of study interlinked? Do children have a 3-hour work period available? Another element to examine is whether the teacher is Montessori-trained.

To the extent possible, you also want to examine what results are being achieved. Are the children happy? Have they increased in maturity? Do they have a love of learning? What have they learned?

To summarize, I have talked about evaluating *products, personnel* (or individuals), *policy,* and *programs.* In this book I focus on *program evaluations.*

PROFESSIONAL PROGRAM EVALUATION

Now let me separate the examples given above, which are everyday evaluations, from what I will call *professional* evaluation. As you have seen, there is great variation in the way that everyday evaluation takes place. These informal, nonprofessional evaluations range from somewhat systematic (perhaps even—or almost—"professional") to almost instinctual. For example, listing criteria and weighting them for relative importance as in the evaluation of various houses discussed above was relatively systematic. At the other extreme of everyday evaluations are those that are almost instinctual—a decision based on "I just had a gut feeling."

To be "professional," evaluation must be conducted in a systematic way. In essence, it is an inquiry involving the gathering and assessment of information in a planned and methodical way. Some authors use the term "disciplined" to describe activities such as professional evaluation and other forms of inquiry that are conducted in a systematic way. In this sense, disciplined inquiry refers to engaging in a procedure that is objective and one in which others are able to easily discern the steps that were taken. Finally, in disciplined inquiry, findings or conclusions have credibility. The manner in which the study was conducted must be so complete that the recipient of the evaluation has little doubt that the results are meaningful. Disciplined inquiries must carefully set in place procedures to consider errors in reasoning, data collection, or analysis of data. Credibility is established by paying heed to these potential sources of error and eliminating them, or, at minimum, exploring what they are and how they might influence the findings.

EVALUATION AND RESEARCH

Both professional evaluation and "research" are forms of disciplined inquiry. How do they differ? Sometimes the two are virtually indistinguishable. This is particularly true when considering evaluations performed by those who consider evaluation as basically a kind of applied research. But many other evaluators take quite a different look and assume pragmatic positions about evaluation, which are closely associated with reflecting users' needs and respecting their input and viewpoints.

The main distinguishing characteristic between research and evaluation is that the former *seeks conclusions* and the latter *leads to decisions*. Research seeks to add to the body of knowledge (typically of or pertaining to a particular academic discipline). Implicit in the concept of "knowledge" is that it is applicable across settings, across geography, and across time. By this I mean that the findings seek to be applicable *to like programs* anywhere, and be as valid in a year (or two or three) as they are now. Evaluations, as I wish to describe them, address the here and now (this program at this time) and attempt to provide insights that might lead to program improvement decisions. Evaluations recognize that there may be differences between programs that even have the same name. These differences are largely attributable to context—that is, the people involved and the particular situation.

Another important distinction between research and evaluation is "who asks the questions." Evaluation seeks to answer questions posed by, and of importance to, a client. Generally, a researcher defines the question he seeks to answer; researchers seek conclusions that add to understandings about the knowledge base.

Let me explore with you how disciplined inquiry is applied to an evaluation situation. In the example given earlier in this chapter, I discussed the evaluation of the Montessori schools. In that situation, the data collected would need to be justified as relevant indicators of the program characteristics by carefully studying the Montessori philosophy and other writings to discern the program elements that must be present to justify a program being categorized as Montessori. The procedures for amassing data would need to be considered nonarbitrary; rather, they must be well defined. What precisely does a particular program characteristic look like? You will need to consider: How will I unambiguously know when I see it? That is, how would I know that multiage grouping is taking place? In essence, what characteristics should be present? Furthermore, the person(s) gathering the data should be considered free of initial bias (or at least those biases should be specified as part of the evaluation). A legitimate professional evaluator should not enter the process with a predisposition to saying one or another program is best. Also, the way in which data are analyzed should be reasonable, easy to follow, and free of error. It should be patently clear how pieces of information (data) were analyzed (i.e., added together, or in some other way compared), or otherwise refined into more meaningful descriptions of results. Finally, the findings should be justified solely by the data. Evaluations may not take a broad leap to conclusions beyond the specific findings of the study.

EVALUATION DEFINITION

For those in need of a formal definition, let me provide one. But I will be brief. Formal definitions, detailed descriptions, and ponderous writing are not in keeping with the focus of this volume. Rather, I prefer to explain by offering examples and by raising rhetorical questions that lead the reader (you) to think about evaluation.

So, here we go. Most simply stated, evaluators state that evaluation is *judging the merit or worth of an entity.* This, in fact, is a statement of the *goal of evaluation.* The goal is to "value" in a systematic way. This valuing consists of two aspects. As you have seen, a part of judging is the determination of the *merit*—the intrinsic value of the entity being studied. The dictionary describes merit as intrinsic rightness or goodness "apart from formalities, emotional considerations, and so forth." Intrinsic goodness! What does *intrinsic* mean when I am talking about a program? If a program does well—that is, what it is supposed to do—it has merit. But is it sufficiently meritorious to satisfy the needs of a particular context? Think of my house-buying example. If a house has a large, ultramodern bathroom, then as a bathroom it might be considered meritorious but not have greater worth to me as a house buyer.

As we see, there are also *extrinsic* aspects to be considered. While the program may be meritorious, we ask what is its *worth* within our context? Is the high merit exhibited valuable within the particular program's context? Thus we seek to value or evaluate by considering both merit and worth.

The above provides a definition of evaluation based on its *goal*. Note, however, that I have stated that evaluation, along with research, is a disciplined inquiry. Thus we need to consider the *process* for reaching the stage of being able to judge merit and worth. This process requires systematic, unbiased context-sensitive behavior. In a sense, then, the various sections that I present in this volume are the *process definition* of evaluation.

A CONFUSION OF TERMS

Now let me deal with some of the confusing terms associated with evaluation. *Assessment* is a term that is often used synonymously with *evaluation,* but it is different. Another term that we often hear is *appraisal.* A very brief clarification is in order. My interpretation is that each of these three involve valuing (judging merit or worth). *Evaluation* is the favored term when we talk of judging a program. *Assessment* is employed when one refers to the clients of a program. This is particularly true in the education field, where we are constantly confronted with things like state assessment tests and national assessment of education. In each of such cases we are assessing students. *Appraisal,* I believe, is more relevant when we talk about program staff. Think of teacher appraisal, for example. Summary: We *evaluate* programs; we *assess* client knowledge; and we *appraise* staff.

Another kind of term is *testing.* I view this as different in nature from the above. *Testing is the process used for giving tests.* Tests are instruments for gathering data. They do not, in and of themselves, include a valuing component. They may subsequently be given value and enable judgments to be made. Thus I consider testing as a means of assessing, appraising, or evaluating.

Enough said.

RECAP—SECTION A
What Is Evaluation?

- Research and Evaluation—"Disciplined" Inquiry
  - Research—conclusion oriented
  - Evaluation—decision oriented
- Professional Evaluation
  - Product evaluation
  - Personnel evaluation
  - Program evaluation
- Evaluation Goal—Judging Merit or Worth
- Evaluation Process—Read This Book
- Other Terms
  - Assessment
  - Appraisal
  - Testing

EVALUATION PURPOSES

Another issue: Evaluation writers tend to distinguish between what they call "formative" evaluation and "summative" evaluation. *Formative evaluation* generally takes place during the early stages of the implementation of a program. It is conducted in order to provide information for program improvement. This generally means that the evaluation information would indicate how things are going. The evaluation information, for example, would highlight problems related to whether program activities were being conducted—and being conducted in a proper manner. Formative evaluation might also provide some early indication about whether program outcomes—the goals of the program—are potentially achievable. Did some early testing of clients show that they were not making sufficient intended progress? Formative evaluation is generally conducted primarily to benefit in-house staff. That is, it is information for those who are conducting the program so that they can make improvements. Such improvements might refer to modifications to ensure that the original program plan is complied with or might suggest changes in the program as conceived. The latter type of formative evaluation is the situation where evaluation results are used beyond fidelity concerns to re-form (form anew) the program. Michael

Patton refers to this latter type of formative evaluation as "developmental evaluation." In his conception, the evaluator's engagement is more proactive than is typical in most formative evaluations.

Summative evaluation is information designed to serve decisions—usually major decisions. This might mean making a decision about whether the program has been successful. Thus the results of a summative evaluation might lead to decisions about whether to continue the program or abandon it. A summative evaluation might also lead to decisions about implementing the program more broadly: "We have tried it out and it works. Let's do it at three other sites." Summative evaluations, thus, are primarily conducted for those who will make decisions about the program. These people might be administrators within the organization that sponsored the program, or they may be individuals within an external funding agency that has supported the program.

Robert Stake, a noted evaluation writer, is reputed as having offered the following pithy distinction:

- When the cook tastes the soup, that's formative.
- When the guest tastes the soup, that's summative.

Let us examine that distinction further. When the cook tastes the soup, he wants to decide whether all the ingredients were there. He thinks, "Did I put enough onion in? Should I have put in more?" If so, then he might change the written recipe. But there is another aspect to formative evaluation, and that is asking the question: "Did it taste good?" The first of these deals with *process*—the characteristics of what is included in the soup (or in an evaluation, this might be the various program activities). The second of these is looking at *interim outcomes*. Were the results positive? (In a program evaluation, this might be the same as looking at whether the short-term outcomes of the program were being accomplished.)

Obviously, then, when the guest tastes the soup, the major question is: "Did he like it? Was it good?" (That is, did it have merit and worth?) On the face of it, this would seem like a summative decision. The cook will consider whether the guest likes the soup in order to determine whether to continue offering the soup as a menu item. But perhaps there is more to it than that. What if the cook meets with the guests—the customers at the restaurant—and asks them how they liked the soup. What if *they* say it needs a bit more salt? Apparently, we have reached some summary stage wherein the cook has determined that it is appropriate to serve to guests. But there still is a formative element to the process. The cook might taste it again and decide that maybe it does need more salt.

And so I now propose an ever-so-slightly different description of evaluation purposes. I personally believe that a great deal of formative evaluation takes place in practice and only very occasionally do we conduct summative evaluations. More frequently, however, we engage in evaluation exercises that I would call "summary formative evaluation." That is, there is a formative period that has taken place, but at some point it is summarized or concluded. In my example, the cook decided to serve the soup. In a program evaluation, we frequently have an end-of-year evaluation report. It may be sent to program sponsors (given to the guests), but it nonetheless will provide information for modifying or improving the program (the cook will add more salt than was called for in the original recipe).

Furthermore, each of these evaluation purposes has both process and outcome elements associated with their conduct. A program process occurs—activities take place and interactions happen—and there are outcomes. Sometimes these are short term, like the learning that takes place at the end of a unit. Sometimes these outcomes are longer term, like at the end of the year or the end of the program. Think of these as evaluation "types." Note further that evaluation may have different *purposes*: formative (of two kinds) and summative.

Table A.1 depicts these evaluation purposes and evaluation types. Study the table.

TABLE A.1. Evaluation: Purposes and Types

| Purposes of evaluation | Types and audience | | | |
	Process	Interim outcomes	End-of-evaluation outcomes	Audience
Formative implementation evaluation	×	×		Program staff
Summary formative evaluation	×	×	×	Program staff, stakeholders
Summative evaluation	×		×	External audience, stakeholders

I point out to you now that there is another kind of evaluation question. Evaluators are often asked to work with stakeholders in determining program needs—referred to as *needs assessment*. In carefully examining the program as it currently exists and obtaining the views of those involved, the evaluator seeks to determine whether there are things that are believed to be *necessary* (not simply wanted) for the proper functioning of the program. As a further part of the needs assessment, evaluators might seek to examine the potential relevance of possible changes.

Now let me continue with my cook–soup example. Let us suppose that instead of making a soup, the cook felt that there was a need to add soup to his menu both because it would attract customers and would add a large-profit item. In the needs assessment, the evaluator might: look at menus of other restaurants; survey customers about whether they think soup would be a welcome addition to the menu; consider whether ordering soup might detract from their current ordering of salads; and what kinds of soup might be most appealing. This is a needs assessment.

As we proceed through this book, I highlight the particular aspects related to conducting an evaluation. I address the reasons for doing evaluation. I talk about evaluators and their capabilities. I consider who might be the most critical audiences for the evaluation. I consider how important it is to understand the nature of the program to be evaluated. Finally, I discuss the actual procedures involved in conducting an evaluation. The procedures will primarily be applicable to the two purposes of formative evaluation, but also will be relevant to summative evaluation.

GAINING ADDITIONAL UNDERSTANDING

Further Reading

In this section, and all that follow, I suggest some relevant further reading. I do not simply provide references. Rather, I have attempted to select, where possible, readings that are direct, to the point, and informative. Also provided with each is a brief comment indicating why I believe that the reading might interest you.

Bickman, L. & Reich, S. (2005). Profession of evaluation. In S. Mathison (Ed.), *Encyclopedia of evaluation* (pp. 331–334). Thousand Oaks, CA: Sage.

Bickman and Reich provide an excellent overview of the nature of the evaluation profession.

Mathison, S. (2008). What is the difference between evaluation and research and why do we care? In N. Smith & P. Brandon (Eds.), *Fundamental issues in evaluation* (pp. 183–196). New York: Guilford Press.

Sandra Mathison provides a thoughtful discussion of the differences between research and evaluation.

Patton, M. Q. (2010). *Developmental evaluation*. New York: Guilford Press.

Michael Patton describes developmental evaluation as either a preformative stage and/or one that is especially applicable to evaluation of programs that are dynamic and which keep developing and adapting. See Chapter 1.

Scriven, M. (1996). Types of evaluation and types of evaluator. *Evaluation Practice, 17*(2), 151–161.

Michael Scriven coined the terms "formative" and "summative" evaluation and talks about these terms as well as a host of other topics.

B

Why Do Evaluations?

As shown in the previous section, individuals are constantly placed in positions where they *need to make decisions*. They constantly have to choose. Likewise, administrators are placed in the position where choices need to be made between competing programs or courses of action. Ideally, these choices are based on a determination of which alternative is likely to produce the greatest benefit. And so, for example, in a health program, stakeholders might want to know which program improved the patient's health the most. Or in an education program, the issue might be student learning. Clearly, these are not easy things to measure. There are many facets to good health; one needs to be clear about the dimensions considered when a judgment is to be made on whether good health has been attained. Likewise, student learning has many facets aside from competency in reading, mathematics, and language. Expectations are that students will develop in other ways as well. Is problem-solving ability part of the desired educational outcome? What about attitudes?

While I have discussed decisions related to competing programs or courses of action, not all decisions are comparative. In some instances, program administrators might simply want to gain evaluative information about the status of a single program. This might lead to questions such as: Is the program operating in the way that we had anticipated? Are there any apparent deficiencies? Are participants satisfied?

MAKING DECISIONS

How are these various decisions to be made between competing programs? Typically, as decision makers examine the alternatives, many of them have a hunch about which they think to be best. These hunches or guesses are based on prior experience and practical knowledge. This practical knowledge is some combination of their own personal beliefs, interests, and experiences related to situations, which are in some way comparable to the decision at hand. Researchers refer to this as *working knowledge*. I certainly do not dismiss working knowledge as an important component in making decisions. Relevant and associated experiences certainly are important in understanding potential decision choices. But trust in our own instincts based on working knowledge alone goes only so far. Studies done by social scientists have documented the weaknesses and flaws in relying too extensively on such knowledge.

Another kind of personal knowledge is an understanding of the local situation; that is, those who would make decisions are influenced by the context in which they operate. They know their programs (or believe they do), and this *context knowledge* finds its way into practical knowledge or mindset; they trust their own perceptions of the program setting—its operation, its strengths, and its weaknesses. Of course, their perceptions are likewise not infallible.

Furthermore, programs about which decisions are being made sit within a political context, which influences decisions. These *political contextual concerns* exert influence on how decisions are made.

Clearly, there is also a need for more systematic data (information) to be a part of this decision process. This is especially true these days, given the extent to which the demand for accountability has become so prevalent in our society. People need to be convinced that program decisions, once made, were based on sound data. Enter the need for *professional evaluation*—disciplined inquiry directed toward a particular program and the potential decisions that might be made about it.

ISSUES FOR PROFESSIONAL EVALUATION

What kinds of issues does professional evaluation pursue? In the discussion above, I talked about *making program comparisons*—that is, making a choice between several programs. Sometimes, as in the Montessori example provided earlier, program staff or administrators might seek to make a choice between two or more programs currently in operation—but still, it is a comparison. Choose one. In professional evaluation we seek to eliminate biasing effects—that is, things that would make the comparison unfair. Each program must be considered in a comparable way with comparable conditions. The professional evaluation associated with such decisions is called *comparative evaluation*. Other times, however, a new program is being implemented, and the issue is whether it is worthwhile to consider this new program. That is, is it better than the existing program? The comparison, then, is with a program already in operation. This too involves a comparison. The issue becomes, "Compared to what?"

Some program comparisons focus not only on outcomes, but also on "how" the results were attained. Which particular aspects of the program had the greatest impact in obtaining the particular outcomes? In these cases, one is seeking to answer a causal question. Causality is extremely difficult to determine. Imagine a tobacco cessation program that included taking a particular medication, meeting monthly with a counselor, and meeting weekly with group participants. How does one determine which of these is responsible for attaining the desired results, or alternatively, the relative contribution of each? Typically, evaluation information for these types of decisions requires carefully controlled *experiments*. That is, we must create control groups that are randomly selected (i.e., a participant has an equal chance of being selected for any of the groups), and the intervention that the two groups receive should be the same except for one of the program characteristics. Then we are able to attribute the differences in outcomes or achievements to that single characteristic—there is a causal relationship. These kinds of studies are called randomized controlled trials (RCTs). Frequently, random assignment is not possible or warranted. In those instances, evaluators can attempt to provide indications of causality by conducting *quasi-experimental designs*. One such example is the use of a carefully selected comparison population—individuals or groups intentionally selected to match the control population (i.e., the individuals in the program being evaluated). Quasi-experimental evaluations provide less of a guarantee that causality can be truly established. High-level quantitative methodologists have derived sophisticated statistical models that can approximate causal conditions of RCTs, but we will not discuss those here.

We pause to note that it is extremely difficult to conduct such evaluations (experimental or quasi-experimental) in small programs, local or other. The number of program participants might be too small to attain random selection for the program and its "control" or comparison group. Moreover, the close proximity of program participants and their ability to communicate with each other leads to questions about whether the program and its comparison maintain true differences. These are summative evaluation questions and are not the primary focus of this book. However, this is discussed to some extent in Section N.

Some decisions, however, are not based on comparisons but instead take place within a single program and the basis for a decision might be whether a *particular standard* has been met (e.g., "Have 80% of the clients ceased smoking?" or "Have 75% of the students at the school achieved at the specified level on the federal standards established by the No Child Left Behind Act?"). Professional evaluation is especially relevant for decisions related to the determination of whether a standard has been met. Working knowledge clearly does not suffice in providing an answer to such a question. Hunches about something like having achieved a particular standard lack adequate specificity.

Another kind of standard that is often used is based on the results determined by a "normal" population on standardized tests. This is explained more fully in Section K.

Yet another type of decision might address issues related to the *implementation* of a specific program. This more basic kind of question refers to whether the particular processes envisaged were *in fact* implemented as planned. (In this case, we are dealing with something analogous to the patient compliance issue—did patients actually take the medication twice each week?) Or, as another example, did students in the classroom actually receive the instruction on a particular topic? In this case, the decision might be whether the particular attributes of the program—the activities that went on in the program—were in fact the ones intended. As I noted in the prior section, formative evaluation might also be proactive by not only examining fidelity, but also by working with program staff in modifying programs.

At a somewhat more esoteric level, the evaluation might seek to understand the *logic* of why certain actions take place within the program and their relationship to the desired outcomes of the program. That is, did certain program actions lead to unanticipated results, either positive or negative? (More on the logic of programs in Section H.)

Sometimes we do evaluations not for the decisions that are to be made, nor the decisions that will accrete. The role of evaluation in these instances is subtler—more future-oriented. Some evaluators envisage a broader purpose for evaluation. Their view is akin to the Chinese proverb about the greatest form of charity. To wit, "Give a man a fish and he will eat for a day. Teach a man to fish and he will eat for a lifetime." In the case of evaluation, the meaning is that evaluators seek to provide those associated with the program with a better understanding of their program and an *increased capacity* to understand evaluation, and to the extent possible, incorporate this into their regular activities. To achieve this evaluative purpose, evaluators strongly engage participants in the conduct of the evaluation.

Not all decisions are necessarily made at the conclusion of an evaluation. Sometimes there are *deferred decisions,* or decisions not necessarily intended to be made at a proximal point in time. In such cases, evaluations can add to one's understanding of a program. We know that evaluation is only one input among many that play a role in decision making. Other factors are involved, including costs, political feasibility, stakeholder values, and prior knowledge and decisions. One major evaluation writer, Carol Weiss, uses the lovely term *decision accretion.* Decisions do not just happen from an evaluation; they grow, they develop. Evaluation properly done should be part of that accretion. An evaluation, thus, might not lead to an immediate action, but could contribute to a knowledge base that aids in a later decision about the particular program under study.

Why do evaluation? We do professional evaluation in order to allow better decisions to be made (currently or in the future), to add to an organization's ability to learn about its program, and to further an organization's capacity to continue to benefit from evaluation. We care about improving programs in these many ways because we are incrementalists, and we know that in a small way this will help to improve society.

RECAP—SECTION B
Issues Addressed by Professional Evaluation

- Making Program Comparisons
  - Determining causality
    - Randomized controlled trials
    - Quasi-experimental
- Looking at Outcomes of a Single Program
  - Meeting preset evaluation standards
  - Comparison to test norms
- Looking at Programs Formatively
  - Examining implementation fidelity
  - Helping programs to change (developmental evaluation)
  - Examining the program's logic
  - Building an organization's evaluation capacity
- Providing Information for Deferred Decisions

GAINING ADDITIONAL UNDERSTANDING

er Reading

dy, M. M. (1983). Working knowledge. *Knowledge: Creation, Diffusion, Utilization, 5*(2), 193–211.

I consider this paper to be a "classic." It describes quite completely the role of evaluation and other information in the decision process.

Weiss, C. H. (1980). Knowledge creep and decision accretion. *Knowledge: Creation, Diffusion, Utilization, 1*(3), 381–404.

Evaluation does not answer all questions immediately. Answers to decisions "accrete." This classic article is very informative.

A footnote: I have always liked the Carol Weiss and Mary Kennedy papers. I strongly recommend that you read these articles. I know that decisions accrete and that working knowledge is a part of the decision process. Nonetheless, I believe that there are many instances where evaluation information has a primary immediate impact on decisions.

Owen, J. M. (2005). Change. In S. Mathison (Ed.), *Encyclopedia of evaluation* (pp. 51–53). Thousand Oaks, CA: Sage.

John Owen discusses the role of evaluation in influencing change.

Mark, M. (2009). Evaluation, method choices, and pathways to consequences: Trying to make sense of how evaluation can contribute to sensemaking. In K. Ryan & J. Cousins (Eds.), *Sage international handbook of educational evaluation* (pp. 55–73). Thousand Oaks, CA: Sage.

This chapter by Melvin Mark goes beyond the focus of this section, but it is worthwhile reading. I particularly suggest that you read the section entitled "evaluation as assisted sense making."

Time-Out: The RUPAS Case

At this point, I ask you to take a time-out from your A-to-Z reading. You have learned about what evaluations are and why doing them has value. Before proceeding with the rest of the sections, I ask you to read the following case study. You will have chances to consider this case as you read the remaining sections. While the case is brief and does not offer the detail of an actual evaluation situation, you will have some opportunity to apply what you learn in each section.

The Rural Parents' Support Program (RUPAS)

A Community Well-Being Case Study

NICOLE EISENBERG

THE PROGRAM

Family Matters (FM) was a community agency whose goal was to help disadvantaged families cope with the challenges of raising their children. For a little more than 10 years, FM had developed programs aimed at helping low-income families by providing information and social skills that could help parents support the healthy development of their children.

FM was located in a large city in the Pacific Northwest of the United States. Its headquarters were in an old area of town, in a rather run-down building where many of the other tenants were also non-profit organizations. The interior of the agency's office was well kept but crammed with desks, shelves, conference tables, computers, office supplies, and boxes upon boxes filled with paper.

The agency was run by Amy Wilson, a busy, vibrant and cheerful woman in her late 50s. Amy and two colleagues—who were friends

Nicole Eisenberg, PhD, is a researcher at the Social Development Research Group at the University of Washington in Seattle. She does consulting work for the Centro de Estudios de Desarrollo y Estimulación Psicosocial, a research center in Santiago, Chile.

23

from their college years—had founded FM about a decade ago, and the agency had grown to a staff of 12 people. Aside from sharing a strong commitment to their work, the members of the agency had also built friendships among themselves. Most of them were women who had university degrees in the social sciences (e.g., psychology, education, sociology, anthropology). Some had considerable experience in the field, while others were young and fresh out of college.

FM ran several programs, but their biggest one was the Rural Parents' Support Program (RUPAS). The goal of RUPAS was to provide training for parents living in remote, rural areas so that they could better foster the development of their young children. The program, aimed mostly at mothers, served families who lived in areas with little access to social and health services or early education centers. It basically offered parents training on how to stimulate their young children's development in areas ranging from appropriate nutrition to cognitive and social skills. (RUPAS focused on the younger age group, given that older children—6 years and older—attended elementary school.)

RUPAS was a social program with a strong nonformal education component. It used a parent education curriculum developed by FM that extended over a 2-year period. First, FM identified communities in need—basically, rural communities where there were no early childhood education resources and where enough families with young children resided. In each community, FM staff worked with community leaders (e.g., priests, school teachers or principals, pediatricians or family doctors) to identify mothers who might be willing to become "Parent Leaders." Parent Leaders would essentially become parent educators who worked informally with groups of parents, passing on the information included in the RUPAS curriculum.

The mode of operation for RUPAS was that FM provided training to the Parent Leaders, who in turn offered workshops for other members of their communities. The training of the Parent Leaders took place in weekend-long workshops where all of the Parent Leaders came together. Then each Parent Leader organized a group of parents in her community and held weekly (or biweekly) meetings with them. FM supplied the Parent Leaders with materials that they in turn used in their group meetings. Parent Leaders received: (1) a Parent Leader Booklet; (2) a Parent Booklet for each one of the parents (mothers) in the group; and (3) Child Booklets with activities for the children of the participating families.

The Parent Leader Booklet contained information and suggested activities, with precise instructions for the Parent Leaders. The booklet was divided into chapters and subsections, and at each meeting parents focused on one of the sections. For example, there was a section on nutrition with information about healthy diets for children, nutritional guidelines, suggestions for dealing with overweight (or underweight) children, recipes, and so on. There were also suggested activities for the parents, such as things they could do with their children or in their homes to promote healthy eating.

The Parent Booklets followed the same chapters and sections as the Parent Leader Booklets and included the same information, except that they did not include tips specifically designed for the Parent Leaders, such as how to lead the group, what group exercises could help, or how to approach certain hot topics. The Child Booklets similarly followed the same chapters and sections, but included only activities specifically designed for children (e.g., coloring pictures of fruits and vegetables with crayons). These child-focused booklets included activities for kids in a large age group (ages 0–6), but the parents and Parent Leaders received ideas on how to modify activities to serve children who were at different developmental stages and therefore had a diverse set of skills (e.g., simply read the story to the babies, ask toddlers to identify specific things).

The basic topics covered by the RUPAS program included physical health and nutrition, cognitive development, social development, emotional development, motor development, creativity, discipline and behavioral management, and school readiness and learning. The booklets used a conversational and friendly style, with straightforward language, no technical jargon, and plenty of graphics. The contents were "taught" in a very concrete manner, through numerous examples based on the lives of two fictitious children—Sally and John—whose experiences were common to these families.

FUNDING AND BUDGET

FM was supported in part by state funds, and in part by charitable foundations focusing on social and educational programs. FM first obtained seed money from the state of Washington to launch the RUPAS program. The funds were used for the most part to develop the curriculum, pay for salaries, and to train the staff. FM also secured extra funds from the Children's Trust, a local philanthropic foundation, and this money helped pay for travel costs involved in identifying appropriate sites for the program and for the publication of the educational booklets.

In terms of the program's budget, the first year was clearly the most expensive one, since the curriculum had to be developed and the staff had to be trained. After that, the program ran on a fairly low budget. FM staff trained Parent Leaders and provided ongoing supervision and support as well as the booklets and other inexpensive supplies. There were costs involved with assessing needs in new communities, and the obvious administrative costs, but overall, the program was quite efficient.

EARLY IMPLEMENTATION

For the staff members at FM, RUPAS meant a great deal. They devoted energy and expertise into creating their curriculum, deciding how to run the program, developing the booklets, and thinking about how to best approach their program participants. But despite their good intentions, the program had a rocky start. Like the old saying goes, "It is easier said than done." FM staff selected Rose as a key person to implement the program. Rose was in charge of identifying the communities and finding mothers willing to become Parent Leaders. She traveled to rural locations in Washington state to meet with people and spent many hours talking with community leaders. Rose was an outgoing, friendly, and talkative soul with a natural talent in establishing social relationships. During a short period, she had accumulated a large number of contacts and made important progress, but unfortunately she had a personal family emergency that required her to take a prolonged leave of absence from her job. Given the unexpected nature of her problem, Rose did not have time to explain to her new contacts what had happened and make a smooth transition out of her job. Finding someone to replace Rose and quickly reestablish her contacts proved harder than expected, especially since it was impossible to replicate the personal relationship that Rose had established with the people. This meant a big setback, since some community members felt "let down" by Rose's disappearance.

Eventually, most of the inconveniences were ironed out, and RUPAS began operating at six different sites. The sites were spread all over the state—some located more than 350 miles away from each other—requiring considerable travel for RUPAS staff.

COMMUNITIES AND FAMILIES

The communities where RUPAS operated had many similarities, despite their individual challenges and characteristics. They were all rural communities with a substantial number of families living below the poverty line. Although the communities varied in terms of their actual distance from urban centers, they all shared a lack of services and retail.

The population served by the program was composed mostly of working poor Caucasian families. The families lived in the countryside, either in old houses—some dilapidated and barely standing—or in tiny trailers. Many were two-parent families, but there were also plenty of single mothers. Most of the husbands worked minimum-wage service jobs—they served at restaurants or grocery stores, pumped gas, or did construction and road work—while most of the wives stayed home with the children. Some families worked in farm labor as well. Some parents worked more than one job, because making ends meet for a family was just not possible on a single, minimum-wage income. The women who did work outside of the home had similar jobs, but unless they had family members or neighbors willing to provide child care, it was tricky to find employment given the lack of day care for their children. There were also families on public assistance, especially single mothers caught in the dilemma of needing jobs but not having readily available or affordable child care. In addition, getting to and from work was often a problem. Living in the country meant being far from the jobs, and affording frequent vehicle maintenance in an area of dirt roads was often beyond the families' reach.

Some families had members who suffered substance abuse. Alcoholism was an old problem out in the country, but more recently, people were falling into methamphetamine abuse. Some people had started using drugs just to be able to keep up with demanding work hours and three jobs. In other cases, there were disruptive behaviors and mental health problems that had been undetected and untreated, probably in part because of the isolation and the lack of health and social services in the areas.

Most children in these communities stayed home with their mothers or relatives until they were old enough to go to kindergarten. When they were around 5 or 6 years old, they began to take the bus to school in the nearest town. At the schools, teachers often complained that the children were not "ready to learn" and lacked "basic literacy skills." Parents were glad to send their children to school, but sometimes did not understand the demands that the school required of them. There were few instances where teachers and parents could meet, offering very few opportunities to bridge the gap between them. Moreover, teachers felt they faced so many other problems—aside from unprepared children or distant parents—that they had little time to deal with these issues. The schools were underfunded and had difficulty recruiting qualified teachers, and students' scores on the state's standardized tests were low. Results from recent studies indicated that rural districts generally scored lower than their urban and suburban counterparts in the state. Approximately 30% of third graders met state standards in the rural schools, compared with close to 41% in the urban ones, and 57% in the suburban communities.

*   *   *

One of the areas where RUPAS operated—which in many ways was representative of other sites—was located in the northern part of the state. Although not the largest farming area in the state, this area nonetheless was a top producer of milk and berries (blueberries and red raspberries), and in 2007 its crop production had a market value of over $300 million.

Local people's lives here were paced—to a great extent—according to the seasons. Winter was long and wet, rain fell almost every day, and the sun was seldom out. Snow was less common, but in some years people got snowed in and spent weeks indoors with nowhere to go. It was a beautiful area, with so much green and water and mountains, but the lack of sunlight sometimes had devastating effects on people's moods, and there were few activities for young children when it was constantly cold and wet outside. Fall and spring were intensely beautiful and colorful seasons, and summer was probably the busiest for the farming families. It was also a period of increased tourism, which sometimes carried the benefit of extra cash.

Mary was the RUPAS Parent Leader in this community. She had two boys, who were aged 2 and 4 when she began the program. She was a stay-at-home mother, and her husband, Tim, worked at a big commercial farm. Tim sometimes spent long periods away from home, working extra hours at the farm to increase their income. This meant that Mary was alone with the boys for most of the day and did all of the household chores. They lived in a trailer park a few miles from the farm. Their trailer home was cramped, with only two rooms. In the bedroom, Mary and her husband shared a bed, and the two boys shared another. The other room served as the kitchen, living, and dining room. They had an old dining set (a hand-me-down from Mary's sister when she moved away), a couch from the thrift shop, and a big, modern, expensive-looking TV. There were lots of plastic toys in a couple of bins and all over the floor, where the boys played. When possible, Mary bought some books for the boys, but the youngest one was quite good at tearing them apart—even the board books—so they did not last long in good shape.

Mary felt lucky that her husband had work and that they had a relatively safe place to live. However, they often had difficulty paying bills. Sometimes Tim brought food from the farm where he worked, but especially during the winter, when local fresh fruits and vegetables were not in season, the family's diet consisted heavily of pasta and canned soup. Mary tried to buy these in bulk when she and Tim traveled to the nearby town on weekends, but many times she ended up buying food at the overpriced market that was closest to her house. It bothered Mary that she could not provide for her kids as she would like to, but overall she felt she was better off than many of the other people she knew, especially since so many people had been laid off from their jobs.

Mary decided to become a Parent Leader because she was eager to find activities for herself and the kids. She had always been an active person, but with the boys so young, it was often hard to get out and do things—not that she felt there was much to do around the area. She had been thinking about finding a job, but she really didn't have anyone to care for her boys. Before getting involved with RUPAS, she sometimes got bored just watching them play and doing housework. She loved her kids dearly, but sometimes resented how isolated she felt by being a stay-at-home mom. Her family lived far from her, so she had no one to help her watch her children. Like most parents, she struggled with figuring out how to best bring up her children, and the lack of role models had sometimes left her wondering what to do when faced with the issues of developing children—sleep problems, sibling rivalry, picky eating, tantrums, and so forth. RUPAS seemed like a fun way to learn things that could be useful to her, as well as a great way to connect with other moms. She recruited a diverse group of parents and was a responsible leader.

RUPAS staff members were immediately happy with the decision to recruit Mary as a Parent Leader. They all liked Mary and admired her energy and good humor. However, they soon realized that Mary was unable to reach all of the families that RUPAS needed to serve, such as the families of the new Latino migrant workers who had recently joined the community.

CHALLENGES

Latino families had begun to arrive in the state many years ago, mostly from Mexico and Central America, but the extent of their involvement in farm work was larger now than it had ever been. In many parts of the state, Latinos were still a minority group, but in some towns in the eastern part of the state, they constituted the majority of the population. Some families had been in Washington for years and were legal residents, but other families were recent, illegal immigrants. Many of the people doing seasonal farm work were illegal Latino migrant workers. Some of these laborers were men who left their families behind in their countries of origin, but others came with their families or had children once in the United States. These families differed from other working-class poor families mainly in that they did not have permanent homes or sufficient English language skills.

In designing the program, the staff at FM used a parent-education model that was based on weekly meetings that spread over a 2-year period. This system seemed to work just fine for some families, but certainly not for migrant workers who spent short periods of time in the communities, working the fields during a season, and moving on to find other work when that was done. There was just no way for those mothers to commit to participating in RUPAS for a year or two.

In addition, there was the cultural and language barrier. The program materials were in English, which was useless for many of the migrant workers who spoke Spanish or even dialects from their original communities, and many mothers were afraid to participate in any program at all, given their illegal status. They seemed to feel that the more invisible they stayed, the better it was for their families and their futures. But despite their invisibility, FM could not ignore them. The staff at RUPAS felt an obligation to reach out and serve them as well, but had trouble figuring out how to do it.

At the same time, RUPAS staff members started noticing some new problems in the sites that they felt were implementing the program "successfully." There were many examples of situations that needed intervention.

On one site visit, Zoe—a staff member from FM—met with a parent group in the eastern part of the state. Six mothers had met in a small room adjacent to a church and were working on a chapter in the curriculum that addressed the topic of child discipline. The mothers began to talk about their own experiences as children, about being disciplined by their own parents, and the topic of spanking surfaced. This led to one mother disclosing being abused as a child. Her experience was traumatic and her feelings were raw. There was crying and suffering in the room. The Parent Leader did not know how to handle it. She felt awkward, kept silent, lost direction of the meeting, and was unable to deal with the situation.

On a visit to another community, Zoe noticed that the mothers in the group were sitting around a table cutting animal figures with scissors and coloring the cutouts with crayons. The mothers were doing an activity that was intended for the children. The activity had detailed instructions in the Parent Booklet, but it was not an activity designed for mothers to carry out, it was for their kids. After the meeting, Zoe tactfully debriefed with the Parent Leader and realized that this was not the first time that a situation like this happened in this group. Somehow, the Parent Leader and the mothers had misunderstood which activities were meant for adults, and which for the children.

Carmen, a Parent Leader, complained to Zoe that the mothers in her group spent the entire time chatting and eating cookies, and she didn't know how to get them back on track and keep the focus on following the program curriculum. The mothers had a great time and showed up very faithfully each week, but keeping the focus was really hard. On the other hand, Rebecca, also a Parent Leader, had the problem of nonattendance. The mothers were busy, their children very young, and although they liked the program, their turnout was always very irregular. When they did show up, they had missed so many meetings that they were "out of the loop" because of the content they had skipped. Rebecca had tried changing the schedule and the location of the meetings, but nothing was working. She was about to quit.

THINKING ABOUT THE FUTURE OF THE PROGRAM

Problems were not limited to what happened at the local rural sites where mothers implemented the program. Back at the community agency Amy Wilson, the agency's director, worried about securing additional funding to continue with the program. The state's seed money covered a 4-year project, but would eventually run out, and Amy wanted to secure at least another 2 years' worth of funding for RUPAS. They were now nearing the end of the second year, but she realized that given the time frames posed by the funding agencies, she would need to begin applying for new grants pretty soon. She had confidence in herself and in her colleagues, and she had plenty of anecdotes to show how they were helping parents and children, but somehow these anecdotes did not seem enough to persuade other foundations and sources of funding. She also had questions of her own: "Have we made it clear what our expectations are? Can we expand our focus to include the families of migrant workers? How can we more efficiently manage the increasing costs of traveling to local sites? Can the booklets and materials be improved? Are we meeting our goals?" She also knew she had to find ways of demonstrating what was positive about the program and convincing possible funders that RUPAS was a worthwhile investment.

Amy devoted her time and energy into networking with different foundations. In doing so, she noticed that all of the potential new grants included evaluation requirements. She was surprised that over the years she had had so little exposure to evaluation. Just the word scared her, reminded her of elementary school tests or doctor's physical exams. But it was something that was popping up more and more often in everything she read and in every conversation with potential funding sources. She knew she had to think about evaluation and somehow include it in her work, but really didn't know where to start or how to go about it. She had her hands full just running the agency and program; it seemed beyond her reach to also have to "evaluate" it. But she wondered whether she really had a choice—it just seemed like something that *had* to be done.

DISCLAIMER

This case study is based on several actual programs that I have worked with over the years. However, it is a work of fiction that synthesizes aspects from different agencies, programs, and people—even different countries. Most of the "facts" presented are based on real situations that I have encountered in my work, but things that happened in one place are blended with those that happened in another, so that the result is an "imaginary tale" and not a reflection of any real program.

C

Who Does Evaluations?

Evaluations are done by people called "evaluators," but that's not all. Many people can and do conduct evaluation as long as they are engaged in identifying questions, collecting data, and analyzing in a systematic fashion. Clearly, larger and more formal evaluations are done by those who have the training to be identified as professional evaluators. Typically, this means that they have engaged in an academic program in which they have learned about the various steps involved in conducting an evaluation, have appropriate technical training in data collection and analysis procedures, and have developed sensitivities to dealing with stakeholders in order to appropriately understand the questions to be addressed.

But many other people in program settings engage in evaluation, or could engage in evaluation if they have the appropriate mindset toward systematically acquiring and using data to answer their program-relevant concerns. Evaluations can take place by either trained evaluators or others with some training and appropriate sensitivities to the particular setting.

EVALUATOR SETTINGS

One kind of setting for evaluators is when they are hired as outside consultants to conduct the evaluation. *External evaluators* (typically well-trained professionals) are engaged to examine programs of which they are not a part. Hiring an external evaluator provides the advantage of "distance"; that is, there is no presumed bias because the evaluator is neither a part of the program nor formally involved in the program.

Sometimes, evaluators are *external* to a program, but *internal* to the organization encompassing the program. Thus, for example, evaluators employed within a school district might have the assignment of evaluating a particular program in the school district. They are external to the program in that they do no participate in it, but internal to the organization. In this instance, the questions of distance and bias are quite mixed. On the one hand, these evaluators presumably do not have an interest in protecting the image of the program. On the other hand, depending on the program's status and political potency within the organization and lack of total independence from the program, there is the possibility of evaluator bias. In this instance, as in the prior example of a fully external evaluator, evaluators are usually well-trained professionals.

Sometimes evaluators act in more of an *evaluation advisor* role in helping to facilitate the conduct of an evaluation performed internally by the staff of a program. In this instance, the internal staff may seek the advice of the consultant on some technical matters but would be responsible for much of the conduct of the evaluation.

The above example of a primarily (but not totally) internal evaluation might be taken to the next level, where internal staff either appoint one of their own members as the evaluator for their program or as a group engage in the evaluation. *Internal evaluations* are sometimes viewed as likely to be subject to bias by the self-serving interest of members. In addition, in some cases program funds may be set aside for evaluation so that the program's livelihood may affect the internal evaluator's continued employment. For evaluations that are designed to form judgments about the quality of the program and to make decisions of major consequence about the program, internal evaluations are not recommended because of these potential deficits. However, where the purpose of the evaluation is to gain understanding of the program's processes in order to consider what has not been properly implemented and potential improvements in program activities, internal evaluation can be quite useful. The intimate knowledge of the internal evaluator or evaluation team about the program simply adds to the evaluative understandings.

MULTIPLE ORIENTATIONS TO DOING EVALUATION

Who are evaluators? Do all evaluators go about their work the same way? Do evaluators differ in how they approach their work? Is there only one approach to doing an evaluation? No, there are many views about how to do an evaluation. These views are influenced by different conceptions of the purpose of evaluation. That is, those who write about the topic may have different feelings about why we do evaluation—essentially, they differ on the primary role of evaluation.

At its essence, evaluation is about assessing the merit or worth of an enterprise—a program. Does this program work? The reason for asking the question and how one goes about finding the answer differentiates these approaches to evaluation. In some instances, one might want to determine the answer in order to make judgments about whether the program has complied with requirements and achieved its intended ends. That is, evaluation assists in making decisions about the future of the program. Another view of evaluation addresses a shorter time frame and seeks to gain understandings about the program, its processes, and its short-term accomplishments in order to provide information for program and organizational improvement as well as further development. Some evaluators view their work as having the potential to not only improve decisions about the program in question, but also to provide insights for similar programs in other places (almost akin to research). Some evaluators feel strongly that evaluation has a moral obligation in the way in which it is conducted to improve and foster social justice. More recently, other evaluators have come to view evaluation as an agent for fostering organizational change and learning. That is, evaluation does not just judge merit and worth, but through the engagement of the various participants enables them to better understand the process of acquiring information about their programs.

Now this may sound confusing—what do I mean by "some do this, some do that"? Let me boil this down to three general prototypes of evaluation orientations. I will call these (1) use-oriented approaches, (2) values-oriented approaches, and (3) methods-oriented approaches. A brief description of each may be helpful.

Use-oriented evaluators generally view the primary concern and emphasis of their activities as fostering evaluation use. Evaluation use takes on many forms. Most of the evaluators in this category feel that the process of their evaluation should be oriented in ways that strongly engage participants so that the likelihood of their subsequently using the evaluation results in decision making is enhanced. Use also extends not only to actual decisions, but also to gaining understanding of the program and changing views about it. Many in this general category further recognize that the very act of participating in the evaluation is itself an important activity in terms of evaluation. This participation increases the potential for evaluation use by increasing the evaluation capability of the participants. They view this increased evaluation capacity as potentially leading to organizations being capable of self-learning. The methods that all of these use-oriented evaluators employ seek the active engagement—the participation—of a somewhat limited number of those directing and conducting the program, who are recipients of the program, or who are otherwise influenced by it. We call these people as a group "stakeholders." The focus, then, is to possibly attain either short- or middle-term use of the evaluation findings to improve the program and make changes or longer-term impact by providing program understandings or by improving the organization's evaluation capacities.

Values-oriented evaluators feel that determining values is the essence of good evaluation. Values-oriented evaluators differ in how they place emphasis on this concern. Some ascribe a strong role to the evaluator, personally, in systematically reaching judgments of merit or worth.

Others feel a special obligation to assure that all voices are heard as a part of the evaluation. Many feel that there are members of our society who are not well represented in evaluation efforts, such as certain marginalized and low-income populations. In order to counter the lack of representation of these groups in the evaluation process (and the frequent inability to get them engaged), the values-oriented evaluator feels a special obligation to attempt to define their value positions and to assure that they are part of the evaluation agenda.

Furthermore, some within this group take the constructivist or relativist philosophical position that reality is socially constructed—namely, that a single "truth" does not exist. Facts are only valued as they are interpreted by individuals. Thus these evaluators place a high premium on a process that engages a great variety of participants in an interactive mode in which multiple perspectives are expressed.

What does this latter group of values-oriented evaluators have in common? They generally seek the participation of a *large group of stakeholders*—not just deep participation with a more limited group of stakeholders as use-oriented evaluators might do, but active engagement of many (or all) relevant groups. And this active engagement is designed to involve the stakeholders directly to the process of placing value on the findings ("Is the program good?"). Goodness or value of a program is not determined by the evaluator's analysis of the data, but by the understanding of the multiple perspectives. In the absence of attaining as broad-based a participation as desired, these values-oriented evaluators would seek to personally assure that the views of those not represented are a part of the process.

The *methods-oriented evaluators* strongly believe that only adherence to methodologically sound (i.e., scientific) practice is capable of assuring that those who receive the evaluation can trust it. Moreover, the concern for potential generalization of the findings to other audiences demands such a scientific approach. Methods-oriented evaluators feel that they should do an evaluation that would be broadly accepted as appropriate by the scientific community. Such an approach typically demands the using methods that are experimental in nature. This is clarified in Section P.

Now, let me make it clear; *all* evaluations have concerns about use, values, and methods. But what distinguishes the approaches is which of these three areas reflects their *primary* orientation.

> **My View:** In this book, I emphasize an evaluation use orientation. That is, I view the primary emphasis in evaluation as potentially fostering the use of the evaluation information. However, I seek to do so in ways that value the perspectives of broad stakeholders from diverse communities, but does so without losing the virtues of intense participation by a smaller group of stakeholders. Moreover, I seek to adhere to the highest standards of methodological soundness without losing the focus on the local context and specific program.

Please be assured that all of the steps that I discuss in this book have applicability to the other orientations as well. What may differ is the extent to which sections of the book have more or less salience.

Finally, it is important to note that while I have found it possible to adhere closely to a use-oriented role in most of the evaluations that I have conducted, there are instances where this might not have been possible. The context of the program and the expectations of stakeholders might have led me to the necessity for a more hybrid form of evaluation—for example, in instances where there was a demand for more generalizable findings.

For you, as an evaluator, be clear on what is expected and whether that role conforms with your interests and capabilities.

RECAP—SECTION C
Who Does Evaluations?

- Evaluator Settings
  - External evaluators
  - External to program, internal to organization
  - Evaluation advisor
  - Internal evaluations

- Orientation to Doing Evaluations
  - Use-oriented evaluation
  - Values-oriented evaluation
  - Methods-oriented evaluation
- My View
  - Orientation to use
  - But respect other people's perspectives
  - Adapt as necessary

GAINING ADDITIONAL UNDERSTANDING

Case Study Exercise

My teaching philosophy has never centered on giving lectures. Instead, I seek to foster understanding through discussion and active learning. This book is an extension of that philosophy.

I want you to consider the case study of RUPAS, which you first read (pp. 23–32). Consider who might do an evaluation of that program. Can this be done by an internal evaluator? If so, would that be a member of the FM staff? Would that suit the purposes that Amy Wilson has in mind? Would an external evaluator be more appropriate?

If you are reading this book as part of a class, you may wish to discuss this with other readers.

Further Reading

Alkin, M. C., & Christie, C. A. (2004). An evaluation theory tree. In M. C. Alkin (Ed.), *Evaluation roots: Tracing theorists' views and influences* (pp. 12–65). Thousand Oaks, CA: Sage.

This chapter provides an overview of the various evaluation theoretical perspectives.

Barrington, G. (2005). External evaluation. In S. Mathison (Ed.), *Encyclopedia of evaluation* (pp. 151–152). Thousand Oaks, CA: Sage.

The author provides a brief summary of the distinctions between internal and external evaluation.

Love, A. (2005). Internal evaluation. In S. Mathison (Ed.), *Encyclopedia of evaluation* (pp. 206–207). Thousand Oaks, CA: Sage.

Arnold Love has written books on internal evaluation. This is his brief description of what it is and how it's done.

Stevahn, L., King, J. A., Ghere, G., & Minnema, J. (2005). Establishing essential competencies for program evaluators. *American Journal of Evaluation, 26,* 43–59.

Stevahn and colleagues establish a taxonomy of the essential competencies for program evaluators.

Tyler, M. C. (2005). A fundamental choice: Internal or external evaluation? *Evaluation Journal of Australasia, 4*(1/2), 3–11. Available at *www.aes.asn.au/ publications/Vol4No1_2/fundamental_choice.pdf.*

This article provides a balanced description of the strengths and weaknesses in internal and external evaluation.

— D —

Who Are the Stakeholders for an Evaluation?

In Section A, I noted that evaluation is "decision oriented" as opposed to research that is "conclusion oriented." I further indicated that while there are three general orientations toward thinking about evaluation, I would focus in this book on a "use orientation." That is, I take the viewpoint that evaluations seek to provide information helpful in making decisions or in increasing understanding. Thus when I do evaluations I need to be generally aware of what decisions might be made and who will have a hand in making those decisions. These considerations are important in determining the "audience" for an evaluation.

STAKEHOLDERS, NOT AUDIENCE

Now let us step back for a moment and consider the term *audience*. I have used this term because it is sometimes used in the literature. But the term is imprecise; "audience" generally refers to individuals who will be receiving a message—a television audience, the audience at a play, an audience with the Pope. Evaluators are not looking to address an audience. Evaluators want to *engage people* in the activities of an evaluation so that they will feel part of and committed to the evaluation. Evaluators want to *hear from* the so-called audience, not simply address them. Evaluators want to *participate with* the audience. And so I prefer to use the term "stakeholders"—those who in some way have a stake or an active interest in the program. We have alluded to some of these people in prior sections of this book.

WHO ARE THE STAKEHOLDERS?

Stakeholders are all of those individuals who have an interest in (i.e., are somehow vested in) the program that is to be evaluated. This includes clients of the evaluation, other program staff, program participants, others in the organization or in the community.

There are many people who may claim to be "stakeholders." Think for a moment about all the individuals who might in some way have an interest or a stake in a program. Examine, for example, the multiplicity of individuals who might constitute appropriate stakeholders for a program at an elementary school. There is the program administrator— the evaluation might reflect on how well she is managing the program. There are program staff—the evaluation might influence how they conduct their job. There are the students—is the program benefiting them? There are the parents of students—is this a program in which they want to have their student included? There are special constituencies of parents (e.g., special populations), perhaps underserved groups—is this program appropriate for their children? There are the principal and the school administrators—does the program constitute an appropriate use of school district resources? If the program is externally funded, there are representatives of the state or federal government agency or of a private foundation—should this program be re-funded or, alternatively, reshaped? There is the community at large—are there elements of the program that reflect badly on their community?

FOCUS ON PRIMARY STAKEHOLDERS

By now you most certainly have developed an awareness that many stakeholders can lay claim to being an appropriate individual or group for inclusion in the evaluation process. Indeed, the evaluator can become overwhelmed in trying to satisfy and appropriately include all potential stakeholders.

Stop! First, let me make something clear; evaluators do not deal with stakeholder *groups*. Evaluators work with *individuals* who may represent or be part of different stakeholder groups. I think it is best to work with individuals—specific individuals.

What is an evaluator to do? A key question then becomes: How do we deal with so many stakeholders? Several evaluation writers have suggested that evaluators should recognize that while all stakeholders should be heard, should have input, there is a need to pay special attention to some stakeholders. There are a number of ways in which these priorities can be established.

Which of these stakeholders do we focus on? We can partially answer this by returning to these questions: Who makes decisions? Who influences how decisions are made? Beyond that, who is affected by the evaluation? But mostly, who wants to use evaluation information? These questions, perhaps, provide insight into the potential stakeholders on whom we should focus.

Who Makes Decisions?

Consider first the issue of *who makes or influences decisions*. Perhaps the most simplistic view is to assume that those who have *commissioned the evaluation* (those who hired the evaluator) had a purpose in mind, had a reason for asking for the evaluation, and thus are likely to want evaluation to be an input to their decision making—to be important in their decision making. Perhaps they are the ones who want to know: How is my program doing? In my experience that is sometimes true, but I have seen individuals in various roles who want answers. Those who commissioned, asked for, or contracted for an evaluation certainly may have been included in that group. But they are not the only ones who make or influence decisions; others who are more engaged in the program might be more appropriate as potential stakeholders. They might be the people who have a real interest in the evaluation, because they are "closer to the action" and want to make decisions to improve their program.

Moreover, in many or most situations, decisions are not formally unilateral—that is, they cannot be made solely by one person—but instead require *agreement among several individuals*. Perhaps the head of an organization and the director of the program must reach agreement. Perhaps there are others involved who *officially* make decisions about the program. There are many others who may *unofficially* have a strong influence on decisions. Think, for example, of vocal and active community members who, while not making decisions, certainly influence them. Think of program participants who might make their voices heard. And there are many others. Each must be considered part of the potential stakeholder group for the evaluation.

Frequently in small local programs that are funded by *state or federal contracts* there is an evaluation required. The program director (or someone in the organization whom she reports to) hires an evaluator. Is the focus of the evaluation to be on decisions that the program director is going to make or on decisions to be made by the funding agency? Or both? Is this possible? It is necessary that external evaluation requirements (and their intents) be complied with, but the relative importance of these stakeholders is a function of the organization of the program, its funding, and what decisions might be made.

Who Cares about Use?

Making or having the potential for influencing a decision are important prerequisites in determining on whom we should focus. But that is not enough. My philosophy of evaluation, my use orientation, helps to guide me in how I determine which stakeholders to pay particular attention to. I start with a strong belief that the role of evaluation is to provide information that will lead to important changes and improvement in the program. I am guided by the conviction that it is essential for evaluators to do everything in their power to see that evaluation findings are considered within the process of decision making; I want evaluations to be conducted so that the evaluation will play an important role in program improvement.

Guided by that belief, in this book I focus more directly on those *individuals* within the system who have a strong interest in seeing the evaluation conducted and who might potentially have the power to use, or influence the use, of results. I call these individuals who are likely to be potential users of the evaluation *primary stakeholders*. Then I pay special attention to the information needs designated by these individuals. Why only primary stakeholders? Quite simply, it is impossible to attend appropriately to too vast a group of stakeholders. I want to focus on those who care and who will likely want to use, and be able to use, evaluation findings as a basis for considering potential program improvements.

How do you find primary stakeholders? You as the evaluator need to be attentive to seeking out and gaining access to these primary stakeholders—individuals who might use the evaluation to make program improvements. Some seemingly primary stakeholders may be thrust upon you—you have no choice. For example, you must be attentive to the needs and directives of the program director or other individuals who contracted for the evaluation. But if their interests appear to be only superficial—if they have but scant concern about evaluation information and making decisions—then your attention to them is somewhat lessened.

Frequently, these report commissioners (those who contracted you to do the evaluation) must be viewed as the "gatekeepers." They control access to those on whom you might focus your attention. Try to talk with them about who else might be interested in and potentially use the evaluation information. Indeed, persist in seeking out the names of those potential users. In doing so, you would have implicitly gained their permission to proceed in approaching those who might be, in the truest sense of my definition, real primary stakeholders. These are people on whom I wish to focus the major part of my attention.

Other Interested Stakeholders

A cautionary note, however: It is important to note that I recognize that these primary stakeholders do not constitute the full group that the evaluator must consider. The professional evaluator still must be sensitive to the variety of *other interested stakeholders*. Talking with and understanding the perspectives of stakeholders who may, for example, lack the power to be actively engaged in the evaluation is a major evaluator responsibility. It is important to ensure that the broader stakeholders' interests are somehow brought to the attention of the primary stakeholders, and their *concerns* are *potentially reflected* in the evaluation.

DIFFERENCES IN STAKEHOLDER PARTICIPATION

I have an expanded notion of the involvement of primary stakeholder use. I recognize that there are added benefits when evaluators can more extensively engage specific stakeholders in actively participating in the conduct of the study. Engagement in the evaluation assists in transforming the organization. A further benefit of this expanded participation by stakeholders is an increased knowledge of evaluation and increased appreciation of it. This may lead to future acceptance and receptivity to evaluations and possibly increased capacity to conduct evaluations themselves.

Now consider the kinds of potential relationships that evaluators might have with various stakeholders. In fact, evaluators interact with stakeholders in many different ways. A thoughtful evaluator wants to gain the understanding of stakeholders about what they consider to be the important evaluation issues or questions to be examined.

Sometimes the thoughtful evaluator wants to be assured that stakeholders understand the evaluation design—the set of procedures that the evaluator will employ—so that they will be reasonably confident in and accepting of the accuracy and appropriateness of the evaluation findings. Sometimes the thoughtful evaluator will want stakeholders to participate in instrument development. Stakeholders will usually play a role in data collection and analysis. Many times the evaluator will want stakeholders to assist in examining findings and determining their implications. And on and on.

Evaluation does not get completed all at once. There are many *stages* in an evaluation, and we can conceive of the involvement of appropriate primary stakeholders for an evaluation in relationship to the different stages or steps that an evaluator pursues. Even individual primary stakeholders will differ in the extent to which they participate in the various evaluation activities. Consider for a moment the various activities in which you as the evaluator might engage. One of the first things you must do is to frame the evaluation questions—to reach agreement on what issues are to be addressed, what questions are to be investigated. Furthermore, you need to determine which stakeholders to gather data from, what measures to be used, how data are to be collected, what analyses might be appropriate. Who should be involved in each of these activities? The evaluator also needs to understand how findings are to be reported and how better to use the evaluation information. (Please note that each of these and other activities are discussed in subsequent sections. See all that you have to look forward to!)

Now consider for a moment all of the groups from which primary stakeholders might have been drawn: program directors, organization heads, program staff, program participants, funding agencies, and communities. Not every primary stakeholder can be engaged in each stage of the evaluation. Professional evaluators disagree on which stakeholders can be actively engaged in each of the stages of the evaluation. I say "actively engaged" because, of course, it is possible to get general impressions and viewpoints of others prior to each activity.

I recommend that not only do you consider which stakeholders to include at each stage of the evaluation, but also how deeply these stakeholders are to be involved in the activity. For example, the evaluation design activity, which is more technical, might include a much more limited group of stakeholders and in a much more restricted role. I refer to this as *deep involvement*. There are many other aspects of the evaluation where it is more appropriate to involve many stakeholders (primary and others), but in a less engaged manger. This is *broad involvement*. Think carefully about what is best in your situation.

RECAP—SECTION D

Stakeholders for an Evaluation

- Stakeholders, Not Audience
- Who Are the Stakeholders?
- Focus on Primary Stakeholders
  - Individuals, not groups
  - Who makes decisions?
  - Who cares about use?
  - Input from other stakeholders
- Differences in Stakeholder Participation

GAINING ADDITIONAL UNDERSTANDING

Case Study Exercise

Consider the RUPAS example. For the purposes of the rest of the exercises, assume that there is an external evaluator. Whom do you believe to be the primary stakeholders? What other stakeholders would it be important to get information from? Parent Leaders? Are there others whose views should be included? (Please note, in this example and in all that follow, it might be helpful to refer back to the case study to refresh your memory.)

Further Reading

Alkin, M. C., Hofstetter, C. H., & Ai, X. (1998). Stakeholder concepts in program evaluation. In A. Reynolds & H. Walberg (Eds.), *Advances in educational productivity* (pp. 87–113). Greenwich, CT: JAI Press.

This chapter is especially good at discussing stakeholder selection and how stakeholder involvement differs within different evaluation theoretic positions.

Brandon, P. R. (1998). Stakeholder participation for the purpose of helping ensure evaluation validity: Bridging the gap between collaborative and noncollaborative evaluations. *American Journal of Evaluation, 19*(3), 325–337.

This journal article discusses stakeholder participation and maintains that it can increase the validity of evaluations.

Hood, S. (2005). Culturally responsive evaluation. In S. Mathison (Ed.), *Encyclopedia of evaluation* (pp. 96–100). Thousand Oaks, CA: Sage.

In this section, Stafford Hood describes ways of better including the perspectives of multiple program stakeholders in designing culturally responsive evaluations.

Taut, S. (2008). What have we learned about stakeholder involvement in program evaluation? *Studies in Educational Evaluation, 34*(4), 224–230.

This article summarizes key factors explaining success or failure of stakeholder involvement in evaluation.

Taut, S., & Alkin, M. (2010). The role of stakeholders in educational evaluation. In B. McGraw, P. Peterson, & E. Baker (Eds.), *International encyclopedia of education.* Oxford, UK: Elsevier.

This chapter provides a particularly good description of the distinction between deep involvement of a few stakeholders versus less active involvement of a broad range of stakeholders.

E

How Are Positive Stakeholder Relationships Maintained?

Conducting an evaluation involves far more than just using evaluation methods. Having technical expertise is important, but the ability to deal with people is essential. After all, isn't that ability a necessary part of all that we do? So let me be specific. Evaluation is a human activity involving social interaction. Evaluators do not work in isolation of stakeholders. Although the nature of the evaluation may influence the extent to which there is contact between evaluators and stakeholders, even the most research-like evaluations involve interpersonal relations.

I talk in the next section about the political, social, and organizational context, and implicit within that discussion is the topic of politics—the need for the evaluator to be sensitive to the political context. But I refer here to more than that; the topic is the development and maintenance of ongoing relationships with people, specifically primary stakeholders. Maintaining a positive relationship with stakeholders does not in and of itself make an evaluation successful, nor does failure to do so make an evaluation bad. However, positive stakeholder relationships can have an important impact in either direction.

There is no simple formula for attaining a positive relationship with stakeholders. Indeed, as I reflect on my experiences, I note great differences in the extent to which I was able to engage positively in different situations and considerable variation in the means used to develop those positive relationships. I do, however, note some important components that were present and which helped to frame the relationships. In my view, the essence of good interpersonal relationships is the achievement of *credibility, respect,* and *trust.*

As I have noted in research that I have done on this topic, *credibility* is in part initially perceived and partially acquired. In essence, credibility refers to the extent to which the evaluator is believable and, in turn, to which the evaluation is believable. As an evaluator, you bring to your assignment particular expertise and experience. This expertise and experience—particularly the perception of it—defines initial credibility. And when you as the evaluator have relatively limited experience and expertise, the task of acquiring credibility is greater. The manner in which you conduct yourself can lead to acquiring credibility. As you demonstrate expertise, your perceived credibility is enhanced. Some may think that charisma is an important part of credibility—and it is. But in something as long lived and intense as an evaluation, charisma needs to be backed up by action.

Respect is both a goal and the means of attaining that goal. That is, showing respect is an important factor in gaining respect itself. The definition of respect provided by the dictionary is "worthy of high regard." Remember, you do not have to be liked (although it's helpful if you are) but you should strive to be worthy of respect.

Again, the dictionary refers to *trust* as to "place confidence in." If an evaluator has credibility and is respected, then stakeholders will place confidence in his or her actions and judgments. As you can see, there is a great deal of overlap between the goals of respect, trust, and credibility. Perhaps I should not have considered these three goals as distinct from each other, but instead asked you to consider them as part of a general pattern—respect/trust/credibility (RTC).

GAINING RTC (RESPECT, TRUST, CREDIBILITY)

I discuss below the several means for attaining RTC: evaluator cooperation, communication, personal demeanor, and program/context understanding.

Cooperation

As an evaluator you should be viewed as someone who is interested in *cooperating* and helping to attain the common purpose of improving a program. Cooperation implies a commitment and a willingness to be part of something. An essential part of cooperation and collaboration is the willingness to accept diverse views. Furthermore, no one is perfect—be tolerant of imperfections in those whom you deal with.

In a way, cooperation implies creating a sense of collegiality. You will be working together in a team effort. To the extent possible, you want to display collegiality and to build rapport and not be viewed as a hostile "other." Please note, however, that collegiality is professional in nature. You want to be seen as someone committed to assisting in the improvement of the program—that is your focus. Collegiality does not mean being a "buddy" or a "drinking pal."

Communication

Obviously, communication is an important part of building positive stakeholder relations. How do you interact? You socially interact, you talk, you listen. Good communication is essential to building trust. It relies on careful listening, clear messages, and timeliness of response.

A good communicator is a good *listener*. You will want stakeholders to feel that their views are being heard. You must display a desire to understand what stakeholders have to say in words or what they communicate in their gestures and expressions. Careful observing is also a part of the listening process.

Your own communications should display *clear messages*. Simple language that is understood and appropriate for stakeholders will add to your credibility. Important ideas can be communicated without massive technical verbiage or pedantic language. I hope the style of this book has convinced you of that.

Immediate feedback or *timeliness of response* is important. Your credibility is enhanced by your responsiveness. You gain credibility as someone who cares and wants to be responsive by being timely. Furthermore, unresolved issues should not be allowed to fester—lack of a timely response allows it do so.

Finally, let me add a caveat. It's fun to have fun, but *use humor with care*. One person's humor may be construed as another person's insult. Humor may offend people's ethical, religious, or ethnic sensitivities. Humor may be taken personally. So in using humor, remember to have respect for others.

Personal Demeanor

Maintain an appropriate personal demeanor. The way that you act influences how you will be perceived and, subsequently, the RTC that you engender. Here are a few helpful guidelines. There are many others as well.

The way in which you *conduct yourself* in personal interactions is important. Be civil. (We could use some of that in our legislatures as well.) Remember that you are usually dealing with other professionals, and it is appropriate that you show respect for their expertise and personal experience. Try to maintain patience. Listen to what stakeholders have to say and "keep your cool" whether you agree or disagree. Above all, don't become hostile or display anger or annoyance.

Remember also that your job is *not* providing "*personal opinion.*" Rather, it is finding and presenting systematically derived "fact"—data that can be interpreted by different individuals (including stakeholders) as fact. If asked for a personal opinion, provide it, but make clear that it is your opinion and not evaluative data.

How you dress affects how you are perceived. Maintain a manner of dress consistent with the context. Don't come in dressed in a way that says, "Look at me and my fancy (expensive) clothes." Nor should you arrive on the scene in clothes too casual or shabby. The advice that I give to my evaluation students is: "When in doubt, dress Macy's."

Understanding Program Context

A major part of building positive stakeholder relationships is not saying something stupid, not seeming to be ill informed. Make sure that you understand the program and its issues. Moreover, reflect on the particular positions and *points of view* of individual stakeholders with whom you are dealing. Where are they coming from? How do they view the program? These understandings will ensure that better communication takes place and that professional collegiality is not damaged.

RECAP—SECTION E
Positive Stakeholder Relationship

- Goal
  - Acquire respect
  - Acquire credibility
  - Acquire trust
- Means
  - Evaluation cooperation
  - Communication
    - Good listener
    - Clear messages
    - Time lines
    - Humor with care

■ Personal demeanor
■ Understanding program context

CONCLUDING NOTE

Maintaining positive stakeholder relationships is an important topic, but as you can see from the above discussion, it is a difficult one to grapple with in terms of any kind of precise description of what is required. For that reason, the topic is barely dealt with, if at all, in most evaluation textbooks. I believe that many of the important components have been touched upon in this section. I urge you to consider these things when you conduct an evaluation.

GAINING ADDITIONAL UNDERSTANDING

Case Study Exercise

• Consider that you are the external evaluator of the RUPAS program. What aspects of *your* résumé are potentially beneficial in helping to gain credibility?

• What personal experiences have you had that enable you to better relate to the context and to the various stakeholders?

• Examine the communication skills listed in the section recap and reflect on your personal strengths and areas for further improvement.

Further Reading

Chavis, D. (2004). Looking the enemy in the eye: Gazing into the mirror of evaluation practice. *Evaluation Exchange, 9,* 8–9.

This is a quirky little piece about "all things evaluation," but in a way it sheds light on maintaining relationships with stakeholders.

Rodriguez-Campos, L. (2005). *Collaborative evaluations: A step-by-step model for the evaluator.* Tamarac, FL: Llumina Press.

This book provides numerous guidelines for engaging collaboratively with stakeholders. In particular, suggestions that can help create positive interactions are found on pp. 112–128, 137–140, and 187–189.

F

What Is the Organizational, Social, and Political Context?

Programs do not exist in a vacuum. Programs are not containerized. There is a broad milieu—a broad context—that surrounds them. This context consists of the larger community, comprising various people who have opinions and can influence the program. And there are various diverse communities, some of whose views are inadequately represented. There is a political context, which influences the programs and, indeed, the evaluators. Who likes the program? Who dislikes the program? Are there some individuals who would gain from positive or negative findings in an evaluation? Are there some issues that are "electric," too hot to touch? Why? What about the organization itself? What about the program and the governing entity surrounding the program? What are the various agendas? What are the expectations? In this section, I consider some of these organizational, social, and political factors.

ORGANIZATIONAL CONTEXT

Programs have a *history*. This history reflects decisions and involves those currently or previously within the program. It also involves individuals within the larger organization encompassing the program and the encouragement or constraints that they provided. Try to understand the program's history. Who was instrumental in starting the program? Whose idea was it? What were the motivations for establishing the program?

If the program is to be *newly established*, many of the same questions may also be asked. Who advocated for the creation of the new program? Who preferred the old program and maintained that a new program need not be established? Within the organization, there may be program stakeholders who desire an evaluation and others who would be threatened by one. You need to consider what *motivated* the conduct of an evaluation? Who asked for it? Who wants it? Does the request come from the larger organization? Do they have an agenda? Are they open to real evaluation? Is there political pressure within the organization to satisfy the demands of a funding agency?

Upon deciding that you will pursue an evaluation, it is important that you familiarize yourselves with historical and political issues that may have led to the program's existence, hindered its expansion, or contributed to its being implemented in an unintended manner. Sources that might prove to be helpful in ascertaining this kind of information include existing organizational literature, newspapers, other types of media, government registries, governing board records, and archived materials.

SOCIAL CONTEXT

Consider now the social context. By this I am referring to the community. Every neighborhood, every community, has within it people. What are the economic characteristics of this community? Are there primary occupations that can be identified? What kind of housing exists? Is there a large welfare population? One can quickly gain a sense of what a certain community is like by using Google Maps. The "street view" feature of this Web-based resource allows you to "walk" down a street in most neighborhoods. Thus, without leaving your office, you can see where parks, libraries, or liquor stores are located within different communities. However, this does not preclude your physically getting into the community.

Various individuals might be affected by the program in one way or another. For some, the continuance of the program might be viewed as beneficial. For others, the discontinuance of the program might be applauded. Particular aspects of the program might be viewed as intrusive or controversial. People in the community might think (or say): Do I want these people (clients) in my neighborhood? How will this affect the traffic on the streets that I drive? Do I want my son, daughter, wife, or friend participating in such a program? Does this program offend my ethics? Are vulnerable constituencies having their voices heard? Are there race or religion issues that I object to? Clearly, not all community views can be taken into consideration. You as the evaluator should at least attempt to gain some understanding of these sentiments.

My message for evaluators: Go into the community and get a feel for the social context. What are their social moods? Do they know about the program? Do they have strong feelings about it? Do they have any feelings (or knowledge) about it? Looking at the community, you can also begin to understand whether there might be bicultural or language issues. If so, the program needs to be sensitive to these. And if the program in its conduct does not display these sensitivities, you at least need to comment on this to those who direct the program.

Aside from sharing this information, you, the evaluator, personally need to be attentive to these issues in conducting the evaluation. You must be sensitive about how you get information from various stakeholder groups because there will also be implications for data collection. Most certainly, how you report evaluation findings, both in format and potentially in multiple languages, is of concern.

There is another aspect of the social context that warrants mention. Communities have value systems, ways of operating, views on acceptable behavior. This sets a tone not only for the program, but also for clients in the program. Participants come to the program with value systems embraced by their own family, friends, and social group. These varying views affect the way that they will experience the program and what they will consider to be acceptable.

Indeed, although there are commonly accepted community value systems, there are also sets of beliefs among segments of a community that are less widespread. This is particularly true for traditionally underrepresented groups. Make an effort to meet with diverse groups and hear them out.

POLITICAL CONTEXT

Noted evaluation writers have said that all evaluations are political. Evaluation is inherently political. Within evaluation there exists politics. There are interests to be served, views and preferences of individuals, and there are various relationships. These all create a political force. And as much as we might like to think that we are engaged in an apolitical research-like endeavor, that is wrong. Evaluation is essentially a political activity. Let's talk about it.

First, let me make this clear: Politics as such is *not all negative*. Programs themselves are created through a political process. There are political mechanisms that helped create the program and continue to foster it. At the start, some people had a view about a way to achieve particular goals. Others needed to be convinced of the propriety of the proposed set of actions. Some might have disagreed. There was a give and take. Finally, a political consensus was attained. Programs reflect a political consensus—a compromise—and an accommodation of multiple views.

Because programs were conceived politically, the results of evaluations might potentially disrupt this politically derived program. Evaluations could disrupt the power balance that created the program, and there are many aspects to this politically accommodated balance. Clearly, the program being evaluated was created within the organization sponsoring the evaluation. However, there may also have been strong community views expressed during the program's creation.

So we now look at community from a political perspective. These community voices (both proponents and opponents) have views about the evaluation being conducted and should be considered a political factor. Program opponents, while possibly wanting an evaluation, will certainly have views about what they would consider to be desired results. Strong community advocates of the program might be hesitant about an evaluation because they don't want to see the program changed. Alternatively, they might want an evaluation in order to validate their position.

What to do? Consider the community influentials who might have thoughts about the program, its evaluation, or its outcomes. Ask as broadly as possible about whom you should talk with in the community in order to get a better understanding of the diversity of views about the program.

Aside from the evaluation purpose being political, the *evaluation process* is political as well. Consider for a moment what evaluations do. In an evaluation, the viability of a program's goals is examined. In formative evaluation, for example, we might question whether the logic behind program activities is sound—whether these particular program activities are capable of attaining the desired goals.

A further indication of the political impact of the evaluation process is found in what we evaluators do in an evaluation. We assist in determining which stakeholders will participate and in what way. We jointly decide who are the primary stakeholders. We obtain input from the larger stakeholder audience, but we are constrained by how attentive we can be to each stakeholder. Who gets selected and participates in the process is a measure of power. It is political. Evaluators cannot respond to all stakeholder points of view and represent them equally. Thus evaluators risk politically antagonizing some groups.

Evaluators collect data; evaluators interview people; evaluators analyze data. All of these process activities have political consequences. Stakeholders participate in the process. In doing so, they learn about the program—perhaps reinforcing their own biases. Knowledge is power (or so they say).

> *My Advice:* Recognize the political reality of evaluation. It exists and reflects various partisan views, but personally conduct the evaluation in an unbiased fashion. Always be sensitive to the political context surrounding your endeavor.

RECAP—SECTION F
Organizational, Social, and Political Context

- Organizational Context
  - Program history
  - Reasons for establishing new program
- Social Context
  - Get to know the community
  - Groups affected differently
  - Be aware of diverse segments of community
- Political Context
  - All evaluation is political
  - Political is not all negative
  - Identify political focal points
  - The evaluation process is political—be careful
  - Be sensitive to the political context

> *Thinking Ahead:* In Sections O, P, and Q, I discuss the development of the evaluation plan. I urge you to now be aware of potential political and organizational issues that might need to be addressed in the plan. By this, I mean begin to consider the manner in which sensitive issues might be dealt with. Consider whether the views of stakeholders in the community or the organization might interfere with the conduct of

the evaluation. For example, will access be limited or hindered by those antagonistic to the program's continuance?

Being "in the know" about community, political, and organizational issues and points of view adds to your ability as an evaluator to relate to the various individuals who are connected to the program, including stakeholders, program staff, and those whom the program serves. This helps you to make sense of what you perceive and of the information you gather. Contextual knowledge will assist in understanding the nuanced occurrences unique to this particular program.

━━━━ GAINING ADDITIONAL UNDERSTANDING ━━━━

Case Study Exercise

In thinking about the organizational, social, and political context for the RUPAS case, consider the aspects of the FM organization that might affect the evaluation. What factors immediately stand out? What are the characteristics of the communities that might affect the success of the RUPAS program? What other organizational, social, or political aspects of the context might be relevant?

Resources

Google Maps—*www.maps.google.com.*

As I mentioned, the "street view" feature here is quite useful and can be activated by going to the website above, entering the address of interest in the search bar, double-clicking on the flag that marks the point of interest, and clicking on the "street view" link.

Further Reading

Moll, L. (1992). Bilingual classroom studies and community analysis: Some recent trends. *Educational Researcher, 21*(2), 20–24.

While this example is one that is specific to education, the discussion about understanding the sociocultural context of communities is undoubtedly applicable when evaluating all kinds of programs. Pay particular heed to the "funds of knowledge" perspective.

Weiss, C. (1973). Where politics and evaluation research meet. *Evaluation, 1,* 37–45.

Carol Weiss opened the door on thinking about politics in evaluation. This paper, originally published in 1973, is a classic.

Weiss, C. (1993). Politics and evaluation: A reprise with mellower overtones. *Evaluation Practice, 14*(1), 107–109.

This is a "response" to the earlier paper with a more positive tone about how evaluation use can be obtained despite politics.

Rosenberg, H., Stratham A., Wang G., & Letven, E. (2006). The politics of local control and program evaluation in community context. *Journal of MultiDisciplinary Evaluation, 3*(4), 58–80. Available at *evaluation.wmich.edu/ jmde.*

This paper provides a case study of an enormously complex set of political and organizational constraints to the conduct of an evaluation. As you read it you might consider the role of the evaluator and what else they might have done.

SECTION
G

How Do You Describe
the Program?

One of the first steps in performing an evaluation is gaining a clear description of what constitutes the program. But first, let me talk about what I mean by "program." The dictionary defines a program as a complex of people, materials, and organizational structures having a particular objective. These are the program components.

PROGRAM COMPONENTS

Think for a moment about the definition I presented. It involves *people*, but the focus is not on evaluating the people—that would be personnel evaluation. It involves *materials*, but the focus is not on evaluating the materials—that would be product evaluation. These people and materials are structured in a way that they interact. That is, there is an *organizational structure* governing how people and materials jointly interact in trying to do something for program recipients. People do things with materials. There are sets of prescribed activities involving the people and the materials that indicate what is to take place. In a program, we prescribe what materials will be used, often in conjunction with people, and when this will take place.

Programs also have identifiable *audiences*—clients of the program. These organized, structured activities are conducted with a specific group of individuals in mind. That is, there are people who are the object of using materials or of the actions of program staff. There is also a contemplated improvement, or a betterment, of a particular group that constitutes the goal of the program. The program should have a *purpose*. We are doing this set of activities involving people and materials to improve, or better, particular services that are to be provided to some individuals. We want to improve, for example, our own local welfare-to-work program, and by doing so, benefit program participants.

PROGRAM SIZE AND ORGANIZATIONAL LOCATION

Programs may be freestanding—that is, created to serve a single purpose. Usually, however, programs are encompassed within a governing agency, a larger organization. Sometimes the governing agency and the program are nearly synonymous. Other times, the governing agency may consist of a number of different programs. Thus programs may occur at different levels of an agency. Programs may also differ in size.

Think for a moment about the great variety of entities that might be considered to be a program. In an elementary school, there might be a special program to enhance mathematics learning by engaging children in doing art projects that involve mathematical concepts. Or the whole third-grade mathematics teaching activity at a school might be considered a program. One might also evaluate the entire third-grade curriculum of a school or school district, including the various subject areas and multiple outcomes. Or a state government might conduct a statewide evaluation of third-grade mathematics. Programs come in different sizes and are typically components of larger organizations that themselves might be considered programs.

PROGRAM DIFFERENCES

Programs that are to be evaluated, clearly, take on many forms. It seems that we typically think of "new" programs as those that need to have their worth determined. For example, picture an alcohol abuse program that has been operating for some time and people are generally happy with it—or perhaps not happy with it. A new concept appears in the literature that seems to promise a more effective way of achieving the same goal. A new program is then established—to be tested, to be evaluated. What is asked: Does this approach that we read about in the literature, and are now implementing, really work? Or, more precisely, does it really work better for us than what we were doing now—for us, in our situation, in our location?

However, programs to be evaluated need not be new. One could simply say, "We've been doing this program for some time. It is our regular activity. We believe that we are satisfied, but perhaps we ought to verify that it is working as well as we think." We simply would like to know, "How are we doing?" Unfortunately, that occurs all too infrequently. We more often accept what exists and seek only to evaluate what is "new."

Programs to be evaluated might not differ in their components but might involve differences in organizational structure. For example, within a county social service agency, a program might involve a reshuffling of responsibilities to different constituent agencies. That is, in an attempt to challenge the traditionally segmented provision of social services, a social service agency might centralize all services under one roof. Or a program might involve a change in reporting within the organization that administrators believe will increase efficiency. Or staff responsibilities might be modified with different staff members taking on added responsibilities (or different responsibilities altogether).

WHAT SHOULD WE KNOW ABOUT PROGRAMS

And so, now, let us consider what we need to know about a program before beginning to evaluate it. At its simplest, we want to know (1) what the program intends to accomplish, (2) who it serves, (3) what are the services provided and their sequence for potentially achieving those accomplishments, and (4) what people and materials are required for providing these services. We also want to know what is *not* included in the program.

What Does It Intend to Accomplish?

What does this program hope to accomplish? Why does it exist? Clearly, a third-grade mathematics program exists to teach children mathematics—that mathematics which is generally acknowledged to be "third-grade level." However, there are differences in what are believed to be appropriate outcomes for teaching mathematics in the third grade. Perhaps the goals of the program are tied to achievement on standardized tests. These goals help shape the program. Perhaps, also, success on standardized tests is only a part of the goals of the program and other outcomes are also considered to be important. What other goals are there? Perhaps the community and the school district have other considerations that they consider important—facilitating everyday understandings of mathematics, or liking and feeling comfortable with math.

What specific concepts are intended to be learned? It is relatively easy in general terms to talk about why the program exists—what it hopes to accomplish (e.g., teaching mathematics). But, as the old saying goes, "The devil is in the details." What specific behaviors are to be modified? What specific attitudes are to be changed? If there are multiple objectives (i.e., multiple important desired outcomes), it is important to know whether they are of equal worth. Do certain areas play a greater role in informing an overall judgment about the program? The evaluator may gain some insights into the goals and objectives deemed to be important by examining performance measures currently in use (if there are any). One cannot assume, however, that the measures in place necessarily match the intended objectives.

Who Is to Be Served?

Another element in understanding the program involves the determination of *who* is to be served by the program. In the third-grade mathematics example, the initial answer might be "third graders." However, that is simplistic. Are there unique characteristics of the third graders that should be understood in developing an evaluation? Which third graders? Do we want to know about how different subgroups of students are performing? How were students selected to participate in this program? Were some third graders at this school included, or were all of them? If some third graders were selected, which ones participated and how did they differ from the full complement of third graders? Alternatively, perhaps some students were selected from a variety of third-grade classes to participate in an after-school activity. Again, it is important to know how students were selected and how they differed in systematic ways from nonparticipants. Identifying who is served by the program and accurately describing them is an essential part of understanding the program. It is not as easy as it might seem.

What Services Are to Be Provided?

Programs are further defined by the general approach they take in working with clients (i.e., those served) to achieve desired goals. This general approach consists of services and structured activities. An important part of understanding the program is defining the unique set of activities and procedures that the program *purports* to provide. What is the schedule of activities? Do activities vary from day to day? Is there a plan that defines the activities specifically?

For example, my project team conducted an evaluation of an arts project that teaches mathematics concepts. We found the following program aspects: Third-grade students receive additional classroom instruction in math and literacy using an art-based curriculum. Specifically, they participate in 1 hour of journal-writing activities connected to art for 12 weeks followed by 1 hour of math activities related to basket weaving for another 12 weeks. During the math component of the program, students are taught measurement skills and use geometry concepts to create their baskets.

What People and Materials Are Required?

There are stipulations in the program plan about the physical materials that are needed for activating the plan (e.g., textbooks, workbooks, and art supplies). Moreover, there are particular intentions with respect to personnel—the program providers. We need to consider whether the number of personnel and the amount of time available for providing the program services matches plan requirements. Also, were there special skills, aptitudes, or training requirements that were to be present in these program providers? Are they present?

What Is *Not* in the Program?

I noted earlier that it is important to also clarify what is *not in the program*. The program to be evaluated could be part of a larger entity that has multiple programs. In that instance, it is important to identify which aspects are uniquely a part of the program being evaluated and not of adjoining or encompassing programs. It is important to identify which personnel are part of the program being evaluated. For staff who are part of multiple programs within the same organization, it is necessary to identify the portion of their time and the nature of activities that are not a part of the program to be evaluated. The same goes for materials, equipment, procedures, and all other aspects of that which constitutes a program.

Sometimes a program activity is part of a larger program. It could be a "designed supplement" to an ongoing program. The program to be evaluated might occur simultaneous to the larger program or it might, for example, be a follow-on entity. Thus it is essential to understand which features are part of the regular program and which are uniquely a part of the "add-on."

LEARNING ABOUT THE PROGRAM

Now that we have talked about "what is *a* program," let us consider how you as the evaluator can begin the quest to understand *the* program to be evaluated. Remember, no matter how technically skilled (or not skilled) you are as an evaluator, *you must first be a learner*. You should try to learn about the program from both examining written documents and interviewing individuals who can help to provide insights. These are not necessarily sequential activities but do, in fact, involve continuous interplay. You might learn from documents; you could get clarification in doing interviews; you might consult documents again to further elaborate your understandings; and, finally, perhaps talk some more. Let us together consider each of these in turn, remembering that there is a back-and-forth between them.

Documents to Review

The first step in learning about the program is examining the various program documents. At this point, you will not be seeking to understand the success of the program, but, rather, the *intent* of the program—what the program developers say it is and what they say it does. There are five main types of documents that might be examined: the *written program proposal materials, guidelines of the funding agency, program materials, management documents,* and *past evaluation reports* (if any).

Most important is the *program proposal*. In many instances, a written proposal has been prepared either to obtain funding for the program or to authorize its establishment with existing resources. A proposal certainly is the case when the program has been externally funded. In instances where the program has received funds from an external source, proposals might have been sent to a state government, to a federal government, or to a charitable foundation, among others. In those cases, the program designers were required to specify goals of the program and what it hoped to achieve, the resources that would be employed, and how the program would operate. If the program was established within the organization, and with new internal funding or a reallocation of funding, there most likely would have been a plan or description of what the program was to be. In this instance, staff and other individuals within the organization considered the need for doing something new—modifying their existing procedure—and wrote documents indicating what they hoped to accomplish with this newly reformed program and how they intended to do it.

What information can you obtain from the program proposal? Clearly, you will want to know what were presumed to be the *goals of the program* (e.g., reducing obesity) and the specific *objectives* that are presumed to lead to that goal (e.g., learning about different food values and calories).

You will also want to know the names given to particular activities that will be engaged in for acquiring such skills (a particular curriculum). As you dig deeper, it is necessary to obtain further specific understanding about *program activities*. Simply knowing the name of an activity is not enough. Names have many meanings, and establishing the particular meaning attached to the activity's name is essential. Next, you need to know when exactly each activity will occur, for how long, and with what time line: Are there specific program materials that will be used (computer programs, handouts, status assessment sheets, etc.)? Are there particular engagement strategies that program staff will employ (lectures, peer interaction, counseling, empathy, companionship, etc.)?

Furthermore, you want to discern the *intent* of those who developed the proposal. Developers might have had various working meetings or enlisted work groups to consider various issues. If documents from such meetings were available, they would be a helpful resource. You want to know what people were thinking when they developed the proposal. This is comparable to trying to know the legislative intent behind particular bills passed by Congress.

It is important to sound a certain cautionary note here. Goals, activities, and intents as specified in the program proposal do not always ring true. Primary stakeholders may not have fully agreed with the program proposal. Moreover, in the natural course of events the program may have undergone change. Looking at the program proposal provides a historical context. Subsequent examination of materials and interviews will refocus your program understandings.

Furthermore, if an externally funded program is part of an existing set of programs that are funded in many places, then there is a need for that program to conform to the particular *guidelines of the broader programs* (typically, funding agencies). In that instance, it would be important to obtain the overall program guidelines of the funding agency to be sure that the specific program proposal did in fact conform to those guidelines and to provide further insight into the meaning of what is included within the proposal. For example, if the program were supported through state funds to decrease cigarette smoking, you would want to become aware of the overall guidelines of that state program. In fact, these overall guidelines should be acknowledged or implicit within the program proposal, but if possible, it is best to examine original funding source guidelines.

Another source of important documents in understanding a program are the written *program announcement materials* that may have been sent to various constituencies describing the new program. A new program having been established, the program developers wanted to "announce" its arrival. Staff had to be informed that the program had been approved along with being provided a reminder about the program characteristics. The written documentation might include an e-mail or flyers. There was also a need to inform clients (or potential clients) of the program. Thus brochures or other materials advertising the program might have been prepared. Finally, the community at large could have been informed of the program through a variety of the above information sources, but might also have been informed through a newspaper article. All of these are avenues for learning about the program.

A second kind of document to be examined in seeking to understand the program are the various *program operational materials*. You can obtain enhanced understanding of how the program operates through examining the various materials that are used as a part of the program. The program may have handouts that were distributed to clients, including instruction sheets or worksheets. In some cases, these may simply provide descriptions of intended activities or expectations. In other instances, these materials are the documents that are used as a part of the particular program activities. Also, it is important to examine the forms used to record program participation.

Program materials include various *management documents*. For example, you might gain greater understanding of the program by examining a listing of the staff and their program responsibilities. Also, management documents might provide information on the minimum competencies required of staff. Is there a specific language competency necessary? Is there a need for specialized training related to the nature of the project? Is a particular academic background required? What kind of cultural competencies are needed? What kind of prior experience are newly appointed staff expected to have?

Along with the listing of staff, it is important to obtain an organizational chart, if one is available. Who is in charge of the program? What are the formal staff reporting responsibilities? Do some staff have direct reporting responsibilities? Are there staff who report to someone outside the organization? But note: formal reporting charts do not always depict what really transpires.

Finally, an important program management document is the *budget*. This provides insight into the costs associated with various personnel and program materials. Essential, also, is an understanding of the various other program expenses. The amount allocated for evaluation is also an important item. You bet!

The fourth major kind of program material is *prior evaluation reports*. If the program had previously been evaluated, then obtaining past evaluation reports will provide insights about the program that will aid in subsequently fashioning an evaluation. What you primarily want to know from previous evaluation reports are comments about program implementation. Had the program been implemented as it was described in the program plan? What might the reports tell you about the operation of the program? Are you in fact looking at a program that varies in substantial (or minor) ways from what it purports to be? Examining the evaluation reports helps you to understand what the program was when it was last evaluated. It may be different today, but it is helpful to obtain the written picture provided by the prior evaluation report. Viewing past achievements is of less concern because you will be concerned about the current accomplishments of the program. However, viewing past achievements may well offer clues to areas that require the evaluator's attention.

Interviewing Stakeholders

Aside from documents, interviews are a key part of the process of understanding the program. A substantial amount of informal interviewing takes place at the very early stages of reaching agreement about the evaluator's hiring or participation in the evaluation. You might think of this as the "getting to know you" stage. This in itself is very important because building a relationship with critical individuals in the program is the first step in building evaluator credibility. But it is also the start of getting to know the program. It is important to identify the individuals who are most likely to be able to respond to important questions that you still have about the nature of the program. In trying to gain understanding, you will need to talk with those who are most knowledgeable about the program, whoever they may be. Generally, this would include a meeting with the project director. Also, key staff might be the foci of your interviews. Administrative personnel within the larger organizational context can often shed light on the program and its goals and intentions vis-à-vis the larger organization. Frequently, it is appropriate to include people who are not currently part of the program, but who had previously been instrumental in developing it.

I would not include clients or community at this stage of the evaluation when your concern is gaining program clarification. You as the evaluator want to know what the program is supposed to be—that is, how program leaders think the program is supposed to operate, rather than how the program is functioning, or how some would like it to operate. These involvements occur at a later stage of conducting the evaluation.

Much can be learned from initial interviews with staff and from subsequently examining program documentation as I have previously described. However, many questions remain after the documents are thoroughly examined. Additional interviews may be necessary and appropriate to clarify understandings about the program. Documentation and interviewing are complementary activities; the evaluator may go back and forth in seeking clarification.

One cannot evaluate a program without fully understanding what the "it" is. Getting clarity on "it"—the program—is an essential part of the evaluation process.

RECAP—SECTION G
Describing the Program

- What We Need to Know about Programs
  - Intended accomplishments
  - Who is served
  - Services provided
  - People and materials required
  - What is *not* in program
- Learning about the Program
  - Documents
    - Written program proposal
      - Goals
      - Activities
      - Developer's intent
    - Guidelines of funding agency
    - Program materials
    - Management documents
    - Prior evaluation reports
  - Stakeholder Interviews

─────GAINING ADDITIONAL UNDERSTANDING─────

Case Study Exercise

What do you know about the RUPAS program? What does it intend to accomplish? Who is to be served? What services are provided? What people and materials are required? What is not in the program? What else do you need to know, and how would you go about getting that information?

Use the headings in the first part of the recap, where appropriate, to summarize what you know about the RUPAS program.

Further Reading

King, J. A., Morris L. L., & Fitz-Gibbon, C. T. (1987). *How to assess program implementation*. Newbury Park, CA: Sage.

This booklet in the CSE Evaluation Kit discusses program implementation, and in doing so describes the various components a program that an evaluator should be aware of.

Kushner, S. (2005). Program evaluation. In S. Mathison (Ed.), *Encyclopedia of evaluation* (pp. 334–338). Thousand Oaks, CA: Sage.

Saville Kushner has produced a broad description of program evaluation. As related to this section, look particularly at his discussion on the nature of social programs.

SECTION

——— H ———

How Do You "Understand" the Program?

What am I talking about in this section? "Understand the program"? Quite simply speaking, we want to know whether the things the program says it wants to do are logical—do they make sense? I want you to consider whether the activities intended to be engaged in can be conducted in a credible manner and that accomplishes the program's goals. Is there reason to believe that if the program does a particular activity that it will be better able to conduct a follow-on activity? Furthermore, is it correct to anticipate that the result of this sequence of activities can logically be expected to lead to program success?

THEORY OF ACTION

Evaluators refer to these kinds of understanding as the program's *theory of action*. In essence, what do those who run the program believe will result from the various actions (or activities) conducted? You may wonder whether coming up with a program's theory of action is the evaluator's job. Not really! Ideally, programs will be so well constructed that activities have been carefully delineated and have an appropriate rationale for the sequence of activities. In those instances, it may not be necessary to engage in a theory building exercise. But having such a rationale is frequently not the case. The program theory might be

71

implicit in the heads of program staff. They might believe that they have sensibly and systematically developed activities to fit certain purposes that would ultimately lead to the desired goals. However, unless made explicit, it is difficult to examine and determine the legitimacy of the program's rationale.

LOGIC MODELS

One way to display the program's theory is through what evaluators call *logic models*. This simply means a depiction or diagrammatic representation of the various activities, which are shown in a way that indicates their progression and their linkages.

Often, evaluators need to help program personnel develop and make explicit the logic model for their program. A warning is in order, however. I believe it is important that evaluators not engage in the construction of a logic model based on *their* own perceptions of this kind of program. It is inappropriate to develop a logic model solely on the basis of what research tends to say about programs of the type under consideration. Evaluation, as I have noted innumerable times, should focus on the particular program in question and the unique context that encompasses that program. Thus the question really is: What did program developers intend to do and what was the logic behind that sequence of activities? Your job is to assist program developers, program staff, and others in making that rationale explicit. You might provide information from the research literature that seems relevant, but that should only be input to be considered by stakeholders and must not supplant the program staff's own rationale.

WHY IS THIS IMPORTANT?

There are several reasons why developing a program theory and depicting it in a logic model is important. Obviously, the process of considering a program's theory at an early stage can lead to better understandings of the intended program. Sometimes different staff members have different ideas about how a program should be run. Engaging in the process of examining program theory helps the staff to create a shared vision or understanding of the program.

Furthermore, when program staff examine the logic behind the relationships between activities, they may well decide to make important changes in the program. Too often, program developers simply list a set of activities that they presume will be important in attaining ultimate outcomes without reflecting on the reasons for those decisions. This might occur through having visited another program, seeing activities that were conducted at that site, and thinking, "That would be a good thing to do."

Developing packages of activities, considered as a program, without attempting to understand why the results or consequences of implementing an activity might be important for the accomplishment of subsequent activities is foolhardy program development. Ideally, the evaluator's insistence on pointing out these inconsistencies can lead to substantial program improvement at an early stage.

Failure to begin the evaluation without having a logical program is also not a good use of the evaluator's time. What would be accomplished by doing an evaluation of a logically inconsistent program? As a result of such an evaluation the evaluator, indeed, might conclude that the program didn't work—meaning that the theory behind the program was faulty. What a waste of time! Up-front work on improving a program theory would save valuable evaluation resources (and program resources).

Another benefit to the evaluator is that the logic model depiction of the program theory would provide a guide for examining specific program activities and their proper implementation. You, the evaluator, would know what to look for in observing the program. Furthermore, having the logic model enables you to consider the particular consequences that might be associated with each activity and, thus, it might aid you in more precisely selecting appropriate outcomes and relevant measurement instruments.

WHAT DOES A LOGIC MODEL LOOK LIKE?

Now let us examine what a logic model might look like. A logic model is a picture showing the inputs, activities, outputs, and outcomes of the program. Moreover, the logic model shows the specific linkages between those components. Let me first define each of these terms.

The four key terms to remember in considering logic models are (1) inputs, (2) activities, (3) outputs, and (4) outcomes.

1. *Inputs* refer to the resources dedicated to conducting the program. This includes such things as money, facilities, and staff and volunteer time.

2. *Activities* refer to what the program does with the inputs to fulfill its mission. What things are supposed to take place within

this program? What processes will be carried out in order to fulfill the purposes of the program? This includes things such as conducting a workshop, providing financial incentives, and having counseling or mentoring sessions.

3. *Outputs* refer to the results or short-term consequences of conducting an activity. Have people acquired new skills? Have individuals changed their attitudes in an appropriate way?

4. *Outcomes* refer to the benefits derived from having conducted this program. Typically, we think of benefits to the participants of the program. The program had a goal, a purpose, a reason for existing. Was this goal accomplished?

Figure H.1 depicts the relationships between inputs, activities, outputs, and outcomes. Please note that in this model I have indicated two separate activities, each having its own outputs, and these outputs in turn lead to the accomplishment of the program's outcome and ultimate impact. This is a fairly simple logic model diagram.

A PARTIAL LOGIC MODEL

Now I would like to try something out on you that is substantially more complex. In doing so, I want you to consider that this volume, *Evaluation Essentials*, is a *program*. It is a learning program designed to lead to understandings about evaluation. The activities in this program consist of the various sections within this volume. "Who are the stakeholders for the evaluation?" is an activity in which I, as the implementer of this program (this teaching program), engage you. I am exposing you, in each of the sections, to various learning activities. In some cases, the activities are sequential. For example, you must learn about the program before you are able to engage stakeholders in developing a logic model. In other instances, activities are parallel—meaning that they are not interdependent and may be conducted simultaneously.

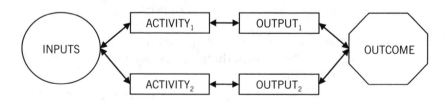

FIGURE H.1. Simplified logic model diagram.

I, as the author, had in mind a program theory that governed the selection of sections for this book and guided their sequence. Based on my experience, I thought that the activities and sequence were logical. Figure H.2 depicts the first part of that theory of action. The logic model in that figure covers only a portion of my program theory. It goes as far as the activity related to the development of the evaluation plan (Sections O, P, Q). As you read through this volume, I invite you not only to modify this preliminary logic model based on your reading, but also to continue to extend the model to its ultimate outcome—*becoming an informed evaluator.*

Why not spend a few minutes now looking carefully at Figure H.2? Doing so will serve, in part, as a review of topics we have covered in previous sections. It also provides a preview of coming attractions. (Sorry, no popcorn provided.)

GETTING STARTED

How do you get started? The notion of logic models, or of program theory, is not usually well understood by potential stakeholders. A good starting point is meeting with stakeholders to explain what a logic model is and why it is important (much as we have discussed earlier in this section). It is important for you to point out that while the exercise will benefit you as the evaluator in being better able to measure processes and outcomes; it also is of great value to them and the program. Furthermore, the process of developing the logic model will help stakeholders develop a common language to describe what they are doing and will facilitate greater understanding of their program.

At UCLA, I currently have an evaluation capacity-building project funded by the university. It focuses on the dozen or so university programs designed to provide outreach to high schools with large numbers of underrepresented students. My doctoral students and I work with staff members from these projects to initially develop logic models to describe the program activities in which they are engaged. Mark Hansen, who heads the project, typically starts with a several-hour workshop, basically describing logic models and what they look like. The next step is to have participants bring written material about the program for their use as a resource when constructing their own logic models. Initial logic models, if they have one (rarely), are also brought to the meeting. Participants are asked to answer three questions: (1) What are the ultimate goals that you hope your program will accomplish? (outcomes); (2) What program changes must take place in order to accomplish these ultimate goals? (outputs); (3) What activities are part of this program? (activities). This discussion is stimulated by a

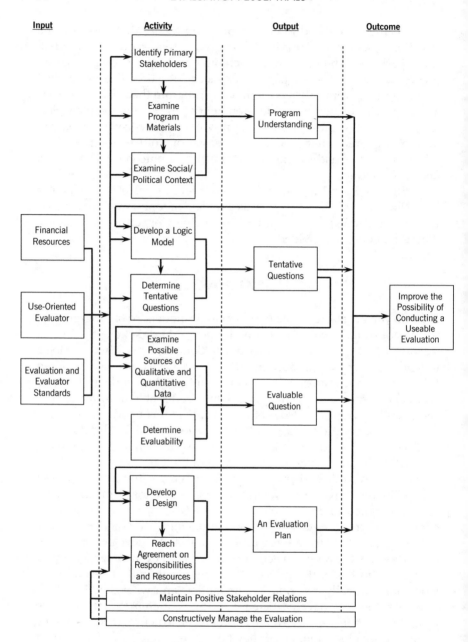

FIGURE H.2. Evaluation fundamentals: Partial logic model.

consideration of subquestions that asks what the program consists of, what the program does, and what sorts of services are provided.

You will notice that the first of these questions relates to outcomes, as I have described them earlier; the second relates to outputs; and the third describes the activities that are intended to take place. Missing from this question list are the inputs (or resources) that are to be provided. I tend to put this on hold temporarily until much of the rest of the model is worked out.

Participants produce a long list of items for each of the three categories. Mark works with them to examine the list to identify closely related items that might be grouped or combined. He also tries to reduce the lists by combining repeated themes or ideas.

The next step involves listing the activities' outputs and outcomes in separate columns and discussing how items in each column relate to the next. For example, what specific outputs are expected through engaging in a specified activity? Moreover, how might that output along with other outputs contribute to the potential outcome?

Mark does this by transferring items in the lists onto Post-it notes with different colors for activities, outputs, and outcomes. This makes it easier to arrange items into sequences, chains, or pathways. He draws arrows to show these relationships and to indicate a probable direction of influence. He points out that sometimes activities are sequentially related to each other. For example, program staff recruitment precedes and enables staff training, while training enables the implementation of an activity. Thus arrows can be drawn between these stacked activity items in order to show these relationships.

In the working session, we provide four pieces of advice: (1) arrows should show the relationships between individual items in the logic model, (2) every activity should have at least one arrow leaving it, (3) every output should have at least one arrow entering and at least one leaving it, and (4) every outcome should have at least one arrow entering it.

A dilemma that evaluators sometimes face is where to start. Does one start with the ultimate goals or outcomes and indicate what kind of outputs or short-term outcomes would be necessary for their accomplishment and what activities lead to those outputs? Or does one logically proceed from activity to output to outcome? That is, if programs plan to do particular activities, what potential outputs do they anticipate from each, and how does that lead to desired outcomes? As you can see, from the description of the workshop that we conduct, the process is allowed to work in both directions simultaneously.

With respect to inputs, a topic that I avoided earlier, it is important at some point to specify the nature of those resources or inputs that are being made available. Assuming that one was evaluating a continuing program, then the inputs generally were thought to be sufficient for providing the activities, which were specified. Consideration of the inputs reaches greater importance if discrepancies in relationships arise in the discussion of the logic model—for example, if an activity does not logically lead to a needed output. This might suggest the need for a modification of activities. In that instance, the available inputs provide the resource boundaries for what activities might be added or modified.

And so, engaging in the process of constructing a logic model provides a depiction of the program theory—the logic behind what the program intends to do. This depiction is a representation of the program at one point in time—but only one point. Logic models are "living documents" that can and will change over time and should be revisited with stakeholders.

RECAP—SECTION H
Understanding the Program's Logic

- Theory of Action
- Logic Models
  - The program developers' intent—not the evaluators'
  - Program staff can benefit
  - Evaluator's job made more explicit
- Elements of a Logic Model
  - Inputs
  - Activities
  - Outputs
  - Outcomes
- A Partial Logic Model (example)
- Getting Started
  - Explaining concepts to participants
  - Bringing in relevant materials
  - Identifying goals, outputs, activities
  - Developing and sharing relationships
  - Are the inputs sufficient for accomplishment?

resources

——— GAINING ADDITIONAL UNDERSTANDING ———

Case Study Exercise

Here are some activities that take place in the RUPAS program: create booklets, identify Parent Leaders, organize parents in a community, organize community meetings, supervision by RUPAS staff. Are these all of the activities? What else would you add? What do you believe to be the short-term outcomes related to activities or groupings of activities? What is the goal or expected long-term outcome of the program?

Note: This would be a particularly interesting group or classroom activity with participants playing the roles of Parent Leaders, Amy Wilson, or Zoe, and a helpful evaluator—you?

Further Reading

Bickman, L. (1987). The functions of program theory. In L. Bickman (Ed.), *Using program theory in evaluation* (New Directions for Evaluation, No. 33, pp. 5–18). San Francisco: Jossey-Bass.

This article by Bickman is the foundation for much of the subsequent discussion of the topic; it describes the importance of program theory in evaluation.

Frechtling, J. A. (2007). *Logic modeling methods in program evaluation.* San Francisco: Jossey-Bass.

This is an introductory text on logic modeling complete with many practical suggestions and examples.

Kellogg Foundation. (2001). *Logic model development: Logic models to bring together planning, evaluation and action.* Battle Creek, MI: Kellogg Foundation. Available at *www.wkkf.org/Pubs/Tools/Evaluation/Pub3669.pdf.*

This development guide describes logic models in easy-to-understand language; it is widely used and cited.

McLaughlin, J. A., & Jordan, G. B. (1999). Logic models: A tool for telling your program's performance story. *Evaluation and Program Planning, 22,* 65–72.

As the authors note in the abstract to this paper: "This paper describes a logic model process in enough detail that managers can use it to develop and tell the performance story for their program."

— **I** —

What Are the Questions/Issues to Be Addressed?

The evaluation questions form the basis for an evaluator knowing what to do in the evaluation. They are an essential part of subsequently developing an evaluation plan. But how do we get to that stage? Developing an understanding of the program is a necessary first step for the evaluator. Next, examining or helping to develop the program logic model (as we have discussed) is often helpful in developing evaluation questions—or, more broadly, the issues to be examined. But there are many aspects to a program and many potential questions that might get raised. It is simply not possible to look at everything that key stakeholders might state as questions of interest. There are limits. So what might you do?

KINDS OF EVALUATION QUESTIONS

A program may have many goals, or outcomes, as I have referred to them in the logic model. Which ones are we to look at? All of them? No, not likely. And, as alluded to in the prior section, stakeholders might simply ask: How are we doing? This is such a seemingly simple question, yet so complex. We need to know what "how are we doing" means. Doing with respect to what? Does this mean that what is asked for is whether the goals—usually long range—have been attained?

The program may not have been operating long enough for such an expectation to be reasonable. Lofty goals (e.g., curing an addiction to smoking, developing more responsible citizens) often cannot be accurately determined in the short periods of time typically allotted to an evaluation. The program may very well have to continue for a longer period before such outcomes can be seen. Perhaps there are questions about some of the program's outputs that are presumed to lead to the goals or outcomes? Yes, these are more likely to be examined in short to moderate periods of time. For example, abstinence from using tobacco for 3 months or successfully completing a citizenship course might be considered to be measurable outputs.

Another set of important questions could be related to the implementation of the program—to the getting started and getting off the ground. One issue is whether the stipulated program activities are being implemented or put into action in the manner expected. Various questions of this type might be generated. Or, in the early implementation of the program, the concern might relate to how various activities are interacting with each other. Are there unneeded redundancies? Was the logic that led to the creation of these activities faulty? Program developers might have made judgments about how participants would engage in the activities and their reaction to them. Did these judgments bear out? Some other issues might be about participant satisfaction or interest.

Stakeholders might have particular concerns about certain of the specified activities that constitute the program. For example, the logic model might specify or anticipate a particular outcome of an activity (e.g., students feel more comfortable with mathematics). Thus the focus (or one of the foci) of the evaluation might be to examine a simple relationship within the logic model.   Check back !

GETTING STARTED ON DEFINING QUESTIONS

Clearly, there is a world of possible questions that might get examined. What should you as the evaluator consider in eliciting the questions or issues that key stakeholders consider to be important? Let me suggest some factors that might guide your evaluation efforts:

1. Communicating the evaluator's role.
2. Identifying stakeholders to be involved.
3. Emphasizing the desire to pursue meaningful and useful questions.

4. Finding questions that need answers.
5. Understanding the legal or funding agency obligations.

Evaluator's Role

First, a cautionary note: It is important that you recognize that the decision about evaluation questions is not yours to make. You, as the evaluator, want key stakeholders to own the evaluation. It is important that they come to recognize that the evaluation is being conducted to suit their program's needs. You might be aware of issues raised in the literature related to programs of the type being evaluated. However, as I noted in the prior section, the primary focus of questions or issues to be addressed should not be dominated by the literature. Programs cited in those writings may very well be different from the one you are evaluating—and the context most certainly differs. Relevance for local needs should be the first priority. Your interest in hearing and focusing on their questions should be strongly affirmed at the outset. Make clear that the questions to be examined will be their questions, based on their concerns. These questions may be subject to later revision.

Stakeholders to Be Involved

One of the first tasks in determining the questions or issues to be addressed is identifying the stakeholders who are to be involved in this process. I have already considered this question generally in Section D, but it is so important that a very brief review is in order. I have noted that there is a broad group of individuals who might be considered stakeholders in a program. Furthermore, it is my view that the evaluator cannot attempt to deal fully with all of these groups on major decisions. Deciding on the evaluation questions is that kind of major decision. This issue is very important, because the evaluation questions chosen will shape the evaluation. There is a group—a manageable group—of involved stakeholders whom I have referred to as primary stakeholders. You, as evaluator, want to know what questions are of specific interest—maybe even urgent interest—to these involved stakeholders.

While these primary stakeholders are the individuals who will be proposing potential evaluation questions, you understand that for the evaluation to be of value it is necessary to understand other points of view. To put it simply: Theirs is not the only view in town. The views of the broader stakeholder group should be heard. But let's not get confused, it is not possible to satisfy everyone's desire for the evaluation. As the Bible says, "No man can serve two masters." However, it is helpful for you to "hear out" what those alternate views might be. You might be working with a program director and some key staff, but you as evaluator should meet with others. Put your ear to the ground, so to speak. What concerns do participants in the program have? What about program staff? What about others in the community who might be affected by the program? What are the views of marginalized groups that may not have opportunity to actively participate?

Your obligation as the evaluator is to alert the primary stakeholders, who are your major decision-making constituency, about the other views and issues that might be relevant. Your task is not to impose these questions from other groups or to imply that they should be included. You simply want to alert those who will be selecting questions of evaluation concern about the additional possibilities.

Pursuing Meaningful and Useful Questions

Unlike research studies where the investigator often frames the questions, evaluations are owned by stakeholders. You want to be able to answer questions that are important to them. Thus I would like to discuss the process of working with primary stakeholders to develop the evaluation questions.

First, do these stakeholders have concerns? Do they want to know something about the program? What are they unsure about? Initially, you might set no limits on this inquiry. Any question goes. Participant stakeholders should be made to feel free to say whatever they think is important. Encourage them to say whatever comes to mind—no restrictions. You as evaluator should encourage this openness to the presentation of a broad spectrum of possible questions. There will be ample opportunity to sort through, reflect, and modify these questions later.

If participants have difficulty getting started, the evaluator might offer some general assistance. For example: Do you want to know something about the program's outcomes? If so, which ones? Are there some aspects of the program and its operation that concern you? Also, what kind of decisions might the evaluation help you to make? Do you want to judge the program as an entity? Do you want to see where to make changes? These kinds of questions should spark some kind of response. It is important to remember that general guidelines, as above, should remain general. Do not suggest specific questions, and do not let your disciplinary inclinations "lead" the evaluation.

At some point there should be a narrowing of the best questions. Now you and primary stakeholders need to examine these "sorta" questions and refine and consider them. You as evaluator should seek to assist stakeholders in clarifying the specific tentative questions raised. You might ask for clarification: "I'm having trouble understanding what that means, can you restate it in a simpler form?" This is a first step in clarifying questions. The question should be perfectly clear to you, or it is not possible to proceed. If you don't understand it you can't evaluate it.

Furthermore, you need to determine whether the questions are specific enough and definable. For example, the question, "Is the program doing well?" is not answerable in that form. What does "doing well" mean? You need to get to specific questions that clearly delineate what is considered good, so that "doing well" will have meaning.

Finding Questions That Need Answering

Another step in the specification of meaningful questions is determining whether the questions are ones that really demand an answer. "Really demand an answer"—what do I mean by that? You want the evaluation to help answer a question. The issue, then, is whether the question is real. You want to know whether the answer is already known. If stakeholders already know the answer, why ask the question? Is it relevant? You want to be assured that the question is not so trivial that it's not worth pursuing that issue.

Questions might be brilliantly stated, but if people don't want answers, then they have no value. You need to know, for example, whether a course of action has already been decided and this evaluation question is just window dressing. Have they already decided what they believe is the answer and the action that will be taken? Is there no, or little, likelihood that the answers to the evaluation question will lead to program changes or even to changes in attitudes, understanding, behavior, and the like?

In my work, I like to apply a litmus test of a sort. I might take the question that they have stated and propose some realistic potential evaluation findings. I develop some "what ifs." Then I would ask what that finding would mean for their program. I might ask whether there were changes they might make in the program based partly on these findings. The issue of whether the proposed questions are those that primary stakeholders really want is further pushed by varying the findings and asking yet again what future actions might be implied. For example, I might present very positive findings and ask the questions of possible use. What difference would it make? What would you do differently? Would it change your current opinions? Then again, I might provide potential negative findings and ask about the implications. In instances where some kind of participant response would appear to be warranted but no action or change of attitudes is elicited, I would inquire further. I might ask why they feel that no action is warranted. I might say: "If we do the evaluation, and the outcomes are positive/negative and you then see no action that would be taken or views changed, why do you want to ask this question?" Typical responses might be that the evaluation findings were not on target with what they had in mind for the evaluation question. This either leads to a further refinement of the question or to a better understanding on my part about appropriate measures for the question.

Sometimes the response to my question about potential use elicits a different kind of statement that is also quite fruitful in focusing on the proper evaluation questions. This is a kind of contingency response— "Yes, but . . . " Let me explain this by providing an illustration. I might ask them to imagine, in evaluating a school mathematics program, that there were positive findings on the mathematics test used to measure the program achievement. And so I might ask, "Would you plan to extend the program or to continue the program?" You might receive a response, "It depends." "Depends on what," I might ask. "Well," the involved stakeholders might say, "on whether students enjoyed or didn't come to dislike mathematics, and on whether teachers were positive about the program." Thus in this line of questioning you have potentially introduced additional questions important to stakeholders that might have real relevance. The mathematics achievement by itself is not sufficiently important to lead to potential action. But use of the evaluation results also depends on student and teacher views. These issues may very well merit having evaluation questions. This too should be discussed.

You want to do a meaningful and useful evaluation. Let's face it, life is too short to be engaging in evaluations that don't have meaning to stakeholders and are not likely to be used. And focusing on important, needed, and wanted questions is a first step to use. The bottom line: Engage stakeholders during the process of suggesting questions in a manner that helps to determine whether they really want answers. Are they potentially amenable to inspiration and the possibility of change? Does someone intend to use the evaluation?

Fulfilling Legal or Agency Obligations

Many programs are externally funded—sometimes from larger governmental agencies. For example, a local welfare program might receive funds from a state agency for a particular local program. In these instances, the funding agency may have specific reporting requirements. These requirements may simply focus on a verification of the activities implemented and the services provided. These kinds of process measures thus need to be a part of the evaluation agenda. Or the agency might demand that certain outcome data be presented. This must be complied with.

A program might also be funded and approved by its own agency, but at a higher organizational level. Thus, for example, a school district might approve a reorganization of a particular program at the school level. The staff at the school had heard about the new approach to teaching mathematics and asked to modify an existing program. In this instance, the district may have provided additional resources for this "new" program. Even if no new resources had been provided, the act of authorizing the conduct of the program carries with it specific obligations. What does the school superintendent expect will happen as a result of this program modification? What does he or she want to see? What are the implicit (or explicit) questions that emanate from that level? Further investigation might be necessary.

RECAP—SECTION I

Getting Started on Defining Questions

- Evaluator's Role—Working toward Stakeholder Ownership
- Identifying Stakeholders to Be Involved
- Pursuing Meaningful and Useful Questions
- Finding Questions That Need Answering
  - Apply the "litmus test" of potential use
- Understanding Legal or Agency Obligations

➤ *Some Next Steps:* Getting started in identifying *tentative* questions or issues is really just a first step. Before finalizing the evaluation questions, I will ask you to consider several other things. In Section J, we (you and I) examine sources from which data are acquired for answering questions. In Sections K, L, and M, I present a description of methods used for acquiring quantitative and qualitative data. Finally, in Section N we will reexamine whether the questions are answerable. In doing so, I ask you to consider some additional insights: Are the evaluation resources sufficient to answer the question? Are the questions stated in a way that information could be attained? Are there potentially appropriate instruments available? And so, *read on.*

⎯⎯⎯ GAINING ADDITIONAL UNDERSTANDING ⎯⎯⎯

Case Study Exercise

Consider the RUPAS case description:

- Whom did you previously identify as the primary stakeholders?
- What kinds of questions might be considered desirable for program improvement purposes?
- What kinds of questions might primary stakeholders want to ask in order to strengthen their case for further funding?

If you are reading this book in a classroom (or other group) context, engaging in some role playing might provide added insights about the question development process. In the role play, some evaluation learners might take on the part of previously identified primary stakeholders; others might constitute an evaluation team. Conduct an interview and attempt to determine what you think might be the questions to be addressed in this evaluation.

Further Reading

Friedman, V. J. (2006). The power of why: Engaging the goal paradox in program evaluation. *American Journal of Evaluation, 27*(2), 201–218.

    This author indicates a procedure for examining how to evaluate which goals are most important. This might be helpful in thinking about the issues of focusing on important questions in the evaluation.

W. K. Kellogg Foundation. Evaluation Questions. *Evaluation tool kit.* Available at *www.wkkf.org/Default.aspx?tabid=90&CID=281&ItemID=2810012&LanguageID=0, www.wkkf.org/Default.aspx?tabid=90&CID=281&ItemID=2810013&LanguageID=0,* and *www.wkkf.org/Default.aspx?tabid=90&CID=281&ItemID=2810014&LanguageID=0.*

    This guide from the Kellogg Foundation tool kit provides a concise discussion of how to develop questions.

— J —

Who Provides Data?

What are "data"? (Note: The seemingly peculiar use of a plural "are" verb with the word *data*. In fact, data is the plural of datum. Thus, as awkward as it may sound, we use the plural.) Now, to continue, data are information. They are information that have been collected by the evaluator in a systematic fashion or acquired data, which have been collected systematically. So where do these data come from? How does the evaluator know which data are most relevant?

First, I ask you to consider the notion that evaluators are surrounded by data. Indeed, almost anything could be considered data. Think of a substance abuse program. What kinds of data might be required in an evaluation? Do people cease using drugs permanently or for some specified period of time? Do people attend required sessions? What are their attitudes toward drugs? Do they physically feel better? Do those who know them feel that improvement has taken place? What are their feelings about the content of the program? Are program participants interacting positively with each other? Is the program really a viable one? Are the program activities those that were intended? Are the staff performing adequately? There are more questions that might be asked which suggest data. The world of a program is filled with data and with questions. One issue is *which data are relevant*?

AGAIN, BE CLEAR ON THE QUESTIONS

In order to know which types of data are relevant, evaluators must be clear on the questions that they are being asked to answer and why individuals with a vested interest in the program, stakeholders, are asking those questions. Therefore, not only are purposes for evaluating and evaluation questions highly interdependent, but evaluators are responsible and obligated to assist stakeholders in articulating, specifying, and prioritizing the questions the evaluation should answer. (I know that I have been harping a lot about "questions"—but it's really important.)

Evaluation issues to be addressed, as seen from the list of questions noted above, can be quite diverse. The important thing in defining data requirements is to identify the focus of the data to be acquired. What are the questions being asked and what are the data sources related to such questions?

FOCUS OF THE DATA

So how should you approach this? First, it is important to consider the potential focus of the data. Who or what does the question ask about? I want to examine with you the various possibilities. The issue: *Who or what is the focus of the question?*

Questions of concern, for example, might focus on the program participants. Let us consider a school situation. We might want to know about the students. Did they perform well academically? We might wonder, also, whether the program is having an impact on program staff—teachers, for example. What about the impact on other people in or out of the program? Parents or the community at large may fall into this category. Finally, the focus of the evaluation and the area in which data are to be acquired might be the program itself or even discrete activities within the program. Are these activities functioning and are they having the desired impact?

Data might be acquired *directly* or *indirectly* about each "who" or "what." Now, what do I mean by this? Directly refers to obtaining the data from those who are the focus of data acquisition. That is, if the focus is students, then direct acquisition implies that you as the evaluator might obtain the data from the students themselves. I have shown each of the data focus possibilities in Table J.1. As we examine and discuss each of the cells in this table, consider which cells involve direct collection and which involve indirect collection.

TABLE J.1. Who Provides Data?

	From whom or where are data acquired?				
Focus of data	Participants	Staff	Other stakeholders	Documents	Observation
Program participants	A	B	C	D	E
Staff	F	G	H	I	J
Other stakeholders	K	L	M	N	O
The program itself	P	Q	R	S	T

Now, let us examine the data that may be gathered about program participants directly from them. Direct contact (cell A) occurs in a variety of fashions. You, as the evaluator, could *interview* students (if you will permit me to continue with the same example). Or you might collect information directly from these student participants through the use of *questionnaires*. Let me stop here for a moment and remind you that the focus of this section is from whom or where data are collected. I mention instruments only for illustrative purposes without providing detail since data collection instruments are discussed more fully in the next several sections.

Still in cell A, data might be acquired directly from participants by *self-report*. In this instance, the evaluator is not dealing specifically with asking questions of the "evaluatee" (another one of those funny evaluation terms that simply means the person being evaluated). Examples of this might be logs or diaries that students maintain in which they reflect on their experiences.

The third form of data acquisition from participants themselves is *performance data*. This is the one with which we are most familiar. The classic example of this data form is tests given at the end of a program to determine the extent of specific skills acquisition. Think, in a school example, of reading test results.

The other first-row cells in Table J.1 represent data collected indirectly about program participants (students, in the example we have been using). Thus we must ask those who have ample opportunity to observe them about the extent to which they are performing appropriately and well. In the school example, we might contact staff directly and interview them about the students. We might ask teachers to respond to a questionnaire about the students. We might examine teacher notes or comments about students. All of these fall within cell B. But it is not only teachers and other program staff who are in a position to provide data about students. Think also about other stakeholders, including administrators, parents, and community members. For broader data considerations, about the program itself and its operation, program funders and others might be thought of as additional stakeholders and be a valuable source of information about program participants (cell C).

Documents are another valuable source of evaluation data (cell D) about the participants. Some preexisting documents that are available were created for a prior particular purpose. Such data that are extracted from archived documents are information that is revisited to determine whether they are relevant for current purposes. Examples of these types of data typically consist of the various administrative records, other information stored in databases such as attendance records, or prior-year standardized test scores. Documents might also include collections of photographs, recordings of program events, and so forth. Unlike preexisting documents, some documents were created for current purposes, such as materials produced by participants, and currently available.

Another source of data about participants (also indirect) is *observation of those being evaluated.* In this instance, we would not ask the evaluatees to comment about themselves, but, rather, gain knowledge through passive observation. The evaluator is observing behavior in order to determine whether, for example, knowledge has been acquired, attitudes changed, or interpersonal relationships modified (cell E).

I will not go through a discussion of all of the cells in Table J.1, but will briefly comment on a few of them. Let us look at the second row, where "staff" is the focus of the data. Program staff could, of course, provide data directly about themselves (cell G). This could be provided through an interview. One topic might be the staff competencies that were presumed to be developed during the course of the program. Data on staff might also be acquired indirectly. Participants might be asked to rate staff performance (cell F), or program documents in the form of various administrative records might be examined (cell I). Perhaps you as the evaluator might want to gain information by observing the staff in action, as they perform their duties (cell J).

I do not want to unduly prolong the discussion related to Table J.1; however, given the nature of the category "the program itself," a brief comment might be appropriate. Let me illustrate what I mean by that category and how data related to it might be acquired. The question might be whether the *program* seems to be working—that is, functioning well. To obtain such data, we might seek the impressions of participants (cell P), or staff (cell Q), or other stakeholders (cell R). Program documents might provide insights into this question (cell S). Such documents could include reports on the program's receipt of materials and implementation of programs or progress of participants generally. Finally, we might systematically observe the operation of the program (cell T).

SELECTING INDIVIDUALS

I have discussed with you the sources from which data might be acquired. However, when one of the sources is *individuals* (e.g., participants, staff, or other stakeholders) another question arises. Do we collect information from *all* participants? Is it possible, for example, to interview all stakeholders? How do we select which individuals will constitute the source of data? Clearly, when only a subsample of a total population (meaning, for example, all of the staff) are to be interviewed, there is a possibility that the data collected might not represent all members of the group. Information might be biased in one direction or another. What can we do?

Sometimes potentially quantifiable data, such as data from tests or questionnaires, will be collected. In these kinds of instances, a wide range of categories of sampling techniques have been described by researchers. One such technique is referred to as *random sampling*. This means that everyone in the total population has an equal chance of being included in the sample. In essence, the technique requires that the people to receive the questionnaire should be chosen in some random fashion. This might involve numbering all participants and then using what is called a random number table. Statisticians have developed procedures for determining the minimum number of people to be sampled in order to affirm that the data collected from the random sample truly represents the total sample.

We conduct sampling to enable us to answer evaluation questions. Thus the nature of the question should help to determine the kind of sampling that will be done. If, for example, you were concerned with seeing the differences that the program makes on men versus women, you might want to use a *stratified random sampling* approach to assure that an equal number of men and women are selected. That is, first develop a list of men in the program and women in the program, and then randomly sample each.

In another situation, suppose that you wanted to know, specifically, how low-income students were doing in a school program. In that case, the sampling should adhere to that focus—low-income students. Then the data to be collected might be *purposive*, and you would choose to sample from that particular population.

A potential confounding effect related to your gathering of what I call quantitative data is the reality of who actually participates. Were those selected to be sampled, in fact, representative of whom the data were collected from? Thus if a survey or an achievement test was administered within a program, were all respondents, or all intended respondents, present? Was there a systematic reason for those who were not present? Were, for example, participants who tended to do poorly not present? If a questionnaire had been sent to a prescribed population, it is important to know the percentage of people who return the survey. Researchers and evaluators refer to this as the *response rate.* It is important that there be a sufficient response such that we can have confidence that the data elicited are really representative. Statisticians differ about what is considered an adequate response rate, but certainly one should expect at the very minimum 50%—but preferably more on the order of 60–70% as the minimum. Again, statistics books can be consulted for more detail on an appropriate response rate for different instances.

Sampling related to the collection of data by nonquantitative methods is more difficult to describe. Types of sampling have been variously described by Michael Patton (see Further Reading): deviant case sampling, maximum variation sampling, homogenous samples, typical case sampling, critical case sampling, snowball sampling, and so on. It really all boils down to "what is the question." A concern for examining major successes or major failures may lead to using *deviant case sampling*—picking individuals at the extreme of the population. The desire for a great deal of heterogeneity in order to capture major themes may lead to choosing a very diverse group—*maximum variation sampling*. A concern for understanding a particular subgroup in depth may direct us to a selection of *homogenous samples*. When the most commonly found (or typical) individuals or group is selected, that is *typical sampling*. Sometimes because of the political situation, there is a need to select a particular case of greatest interest—*critical case sampling*.

Finally, in interviewing, you might want to use a technique of gaining referrals from interviewees of those whom they believe would have the most information and be most helpful. This is referred to as *snowball sampling*. And so, in considering data to be acquired from interviews, observations, or focus groups one needs to be guided by the question under consideration and, thus, there are many ways in which samples might be selected.

RECAP—SECTION J
Who Provides Data?

- Be Clear on the Questions
- Questions Suggest Data Needs
- Focus of the Data
  - Who or what is the focus?
    - Program participants
    - Staff
    - Other stakeholders
    - The program
  - From where are the data acquired?
  - Gathered directly or indirectly?
- Gathering Data from Individuals
  - Types of sampling

GAINING ADDITIONAL UNDERSTANDING

Case Study Exercise

Examine Table J.1 (p. 90). Who are the program participants in the RUPAS case? In considering the questions you posed about the case study in Section I: Are they Parent Leaders or program participants, staff, or both? Identify those individuals or entities that would be designated in each of the vertical columns. From whom or where might data be acquired for each?

You might want to have a group discussion about this.

Further Reading

Patton, M. (1987). *How to use qualitative methods in evaluation.* Thousand Oaks, CA: Sage.

Michael Patton provides an excellent discussion of how to choose a sample—what I have referred to as "selecting individuals."

K

What Are Instruments for Collecting Quantitative Data?

In this section, I discuss the instruments frequently used to collect quantitative data. Any procedure or instrument that provides information that can be quantified—meaning numbers can be attached to the information—is a quantitative method. Quantitative methods show the degree or extent to which certain characteristics are present. Consider a written instrument that asks for an indication of "yes/no" or one that provides for the selection of multiple choices. These can be quantified. But such instruments also might have open-ended questions asking for brief comments. These open-ended questions are generally considered qualitative data because the evaluator must consider these verbal comments and develop a theme from them. On the other hand, the evaluator might develop a coding system for analyzing anecdotal commentary and assigning numbers to them. The point is that various methods can yield either quantitative or qualitative data. And so in this section, I talk with you about the instruments (means of collecting data) that *most typically* yield *quantitative* data.

Why might you want to collect quantitative data? Quantitative data are in many ways easier for people to understand and grasp. Numbers seem to be concrete. When one sees a number, there is the concept of value, of size, and of degree. Furthermore, comparability to other numbers is more easily grasped. For example, if you examine a student's score on a math test, you can see how well they understood the material based on the score received. You might do that by looking at the accomplishment of the student related to a group or to others. If you look at the test scores for all of the students in the class, you can identify common areas of deficiency. If the teacher has expectations about the expected progress of students, then the test score can provide an indication of whether sufficient progress has been made.

INSTRUMENTS FOR ATTAINING QUANTITATIVE DATA

Several types of instruments or measures that individuals respond to can be used to obtain quantitative data. The quantitative data obtained may be related to skill attainment, knowledge acquired, attitudes, values, or ability. Consider the last of these, for example. The Graduate Record Examination (GRE) is an *ability* test used for determining competitiveness for graduate school admittance. This is a measure that presumably measures ability or aptitude. In evaluation, we very infrequently are concerned with ability as an outcome measure. Programs are not designed to improve ability, but to measure what results came out of the program—things like learning attainment or changes in attitudes. Ability tests, however, might be a part of an evaluation in instances where we want to examine the comparability of the program participants and of a comparison group. An ability measure also might be administered at the beginning of a program for the purposes of participant selection. In such instances, a key question might relate to the impact of the program on groups of students at different ability levels.

More frequently, the quantitative measures used in an evaluation are concerned with *achievement* or skill attainment. That is, did students learn seventh-grade mathematics or achieve at a seventh-grade level in mathematics? Did participants learn the steps required to assemble a complex set of machinery? Did they learn the causes of a disease? I will refer to measures designed to assess achievement or attainment as *tests*. They are instruments designed to determine whether knowledge was acquired or a skill attained.

Another instrument that yields quantitative data is a *survey*. Surveys employ procedures in which people are asked a series of questions. The answers to these questions typically yield quantitative data. Surveys can be conducted by telephone. (Think of the calls that you have received—typically at the dinner hour—requesting your response to a survey.) Surveys may also be conducted verbally, perhaps by someone waiting outside a grocery store to ask you a few questions.

I like to consider a *questionnaire* as a particular type of survey—but one that is administered in written form. We are most familiar with paper-and-pencil questionnaires. Undoubtedly, you have filled out many questionnaires asking about your attitudes toward something, or satisfaction about a program, or your evaluation of an instructor. These days, modern technology has allowed the administration of questionnaires through an online computer response. I am referring to this innovation also as a questionnaire because responders are, in fact, themselves reading the question and providing a written response.

Quantitative data may also be acquired using other instruments. One such example is through observation. Normally, observational data are qualitative; I talk more about that in the next section. However, observational systems can be devised that provide quantitative indications of what is occurring within a program setting. These are called observational protocols.

Data that are *self-reported* on an ongoing basis, such as in a log or a diary, can be constructed in a manner that yields quantitative data. I view this as a kind of questionnaire, though as a special case. In essence, there might be specific questions on which respondents are asked to keep records and provide information. This daily log might ask individuals to supply quantitative data on various activities in which they engage, for example, how much time was spent on each activity. Often quantitative data that might be self-reported on a log include such things as: the number of cigarettes smoked for a substance abuse program; the time spent on homework or watching television; or, perhaps, the quantity of various foods eaten.

The bottom line, it seems to me, is that quantitative data can be found anywhere. It is quantitative if one contrives a way of quantifying the information.

ACQUISITION OF DATA

Data may be acquired in a variety of ways. Quantitative data, or information that can be turned into quantitative form, are present and might be obtained before you begin the evaluation or begin to collect new data. These *existing data* may be found both either within the program and external to the program. Think, for example, of prior-year test scores. More frequently, you will need to collect new data because relevant existing data are not available or sufficient. New data might be acquired by administering an *existing instrument*. By this I mean instruments that you can access and use—perhaps, for example, existing published tests. Furthermore, if existing instruments are not available that meet your needs, you may need to create a *new instrument*. I have displayed this in Table K.1.

TABLE K.1. Sources of Data

	Existing data	Existing instruments	New instruments
Achievement measurement	✓	✓	✓
Questionnaire	✓	✓	✓
Observational protocols	✓	✓	✓
Other (e.g., documents, artifacts)	✓		

EXISTING DATA

Within the program there are certainly available things such as records of attendance, absences, health records, or referrals to other agencies or programs. There may be test data that have been previously collected. External to the program, but also existing, you might find valuable data in the various governmental records—possibly census data, crime statistics for the community, or economic indicators. Again, as I have stated numerous times, you, the evaluator, must be guided by the questions being asked in determining the relevance of existing data. It is tempting, of course, to think that a portion of your data collection job can be fulfilled with the ease of using existing data. However, *select only what is needed and what is relevant to the questions being asked.*

FINDING EXISTING INSTRUMENTS

How do you find existing instruments? The evaluation question that you are attempting to answer might have specified certain kinds of attainment on a particular instrument or test as its objective. Thus there is no problem. The choice of instrument is clear.

If that is not the case, how might you go about finding appropriate instruments? One possibility is that tests or other instruments were a part of the program instructional materials. Are these valuable for your question? The answer to that depends on the nature of the question. If the question is solely related to the prescribed curriculum of the program, the test may suffice. If on the other hand, the question goes beyond that, then other instruments are necessary.

There are books that summarize tests that are available. One such series of books are entitled *The Mental Measurements Yearbooks*, which are updated every 2 years. You could look at the *Psychological Abstracts* based on a topic of interest to see what tests or instruments were used in different studies that might satisfy your unique question. Major test publishers also have catalogues listing their test instruments. For example, the Educational Testing Service has a *Test Collection Catalogue.* You might inquire about these at the reference desk of major libraries. Finally, thanks to modern technology, try going on Google or a comparable search engine and indicate your topic (e.g., measuring social adjustment). You will be very surprised at how much you are able to find.

It is sometimes easiest to use an existing measure—particularly when the question is related to measuring achievement. There are many such tests available that have been standardized. By *standardized*, I mean the test has been developed, administered, and scored in a consistent manner. In essence, this means that there was care taken in selecting test items, the conditions for administering the instrument have been well specified, and the way in which interpretations are made has also been indicated. All of this has been documented by the test publisher. Perhaps the most important aspect of a standardized test is that it has been *normed*. That is, the test had been administered to a large group of test takers, and the results of this procedure provided the basis for potential comparisons. The test takers constituting the norming group, in essence, are a comparison group. Scores that those being evaluated achieve can then be compared to this norm. In essence, the test taker's relative position can be determined. Not surprisingly, tests of this type are called norm-referenced tests.

There is a caution to be sounded at this point. You must examine who was included in the norming population to determine whether they were truly comparable to the program participants whom you plan to test. If they were not comparable to your population, then comparisons might be meaningless.

One aspect of the standardization that occurs in norm-referenced tests is examining the reliability and validity of the instrument. *Reliability?* Think about it. What does reliable mean? If something is reliable, you know that you can depend on it. It is consistent. Reliability is measuring consistency. If you give the test multiple times to the same person, it will yield consistent results. Assuming that the conditions of administration were the same, the score will not fluctuate—or, if so, not by much. Standardized norm-referenced tests will report reliability coefficients. This would be helpful information in determining whether you want to use the test.

A test might be reliable, but that does not mean that it is necessarily valid. The dictionary describes the word *valid* as relevant, meaningful, appropriate to the end in view. In essence, *validity refers* to the degree to which the test, and data from it, appropriately capture the concept that the test purports to measure. For example, does the mathematics test really capture the essence of mathematics for the grade levels in which it is to be used?

There are various ways in which validity is determined. That is, researchers have examined various *aspects of validity*. For example, some aspects of validity examine the extent to which a test represents the construct (an area to be measured) whose name appears in its title. Do the items in the test match its intent? Another aspect of validity is used when a construct is quite complex. In that case, a number of different attributes or categories might be represented. All of these attributes are not necessarily of equal importance. Thus the validity concern refers to the representativeness of the sample of questions included in the instrument. Were more important categories represented in a proportional way that indicates their significance to the concept?

Standardized tests are also available for measuring attitudes, values, preferences, beliefs, and so forth—although there are, perhaps, far fewer of such measures. Typically, these tests are in a questionnaire format. They also have norms, and show reliability and validity coefficients.

And now, the cautionary note. It is important to determine whether the test or questionnaire items in the existing measure adequately and appropriately cover the concept intended by your evaluation question. The instrument may purport to have high validity but might still not be *valid for your program*. You need to look carefully at the questions in the standardized test or questionnaire. Do they adequately deal with the evaluation question for your program? You might want to have primary stakeholders sit with you to make that determination.

If only a partial coverage of the intended question is provided, perhaps the instrument could be supplemented by another measure. If, on the other hand, the instrument includes items that go beyond the question, and this is the best available measure, some evaluators suggest extracting information on just the test items available for the question. In essence, this is creating a new measure. If the measure had been standardized and reliability and validity calculated for the whole test, they would not be applicable to your revised measure. This may not be of great concern if generalizing your findings to other places is not an issue, which it frequently is not. Moreover, it is not ethically appropriate to use existing measures that are for sale and to modify them. However, instruments that were used in research studies are typically available with the permission of the author.

DEVELOPING NEW INSTRUMENTS

Let us now talk about the process for developing new instruments that yield quantitative data. I focus on the development of questionnaires and achievement tests and only briefly touch on the construction of other, less frequently used measures.

Questionnaires

Let us now consider the development of *questionnaires*. I've commented earlier on the nature of a questionnaire. In essence, it is an instrument consisting of a series of questions and other prompts designed to obtain responses typically related to attitudes, behaviors, or points of view. There are a variety of formats used in questionnaires. I will highlight four of the most frequently considered format types: the *two-option format*, the *forced-choice single-option format*, the *multiple-option format*, and *rating scales*.

The *two-option format* is basically the one that requires a "yes" or a "no." Or a "true" or a "false"—perhaps even "agree" or "disagree." You are familiar, of course, with true/false tests. This option is appropriate when the question requires a dichotomous response. It may be appropriate in this option to also include a "don't know" or "not sure" choice possibility.

Another format, the forced choice single option, provides an opportunity for the responder to select a single answer from a number of possibilities. This is often referred to as a *multiple-choice format*. That is, one makes a choice from multiple possibilities, for example, "Which of the following is the person whom you most frequently would turn to for health advice?" Options in this situation might be physicians, nurses, friends, parents, counselors. This forced-choice single-option format is best for collecting information about actions, behaviors, or other characteristics. When you develop the instrument, you should be sure to write the choices carefully so that they do not overlap. You do not want a respondent's choice to fit within two categories. Frequently, an "other" is provided as a possible response.

The third kind of questionnaire format provides *multiple options*, and the respondent can indicate all that apply: "Which of the following individuals have been helpful to you in this program? Check all that apply." In essence, this option is equivalent to allowing respondents the choice of saying "yes" or "no" to a number of questions in the format of a single item. All items checked meant "yes" or "agree" (or perhaps "no" or "disagree," depending on the wording of the question).

The fourth data collection format to be discussed are _rating scales_. Unlike yes/no or option formats, rating scales provide the possibility of gaining understanding about degree or extent of an attitude or belief. It is not simply a question of do you agree or disagree, no or not no, believe or not believe. Rating scales introduce the notion of gradations. Typically, these scales are represented by 5 or 7 points. For example, in what is referred to as a _Likert scale_, respondents might be asked to indicate the amount of agreement or disagreement from "strongly agree" to "strongly disagree." Intermediate points would be "somewhat agree," "uncertain," and "somewhat disagree." This kind of questionnaire format might be efficiently presented as the rating option for multiple questions. Thus the questions might be stated to one side of the page with a 5-point scale, which would be applied to all of the questions listed.

There are a variety of other scaling techniques that carry with them different statistical analysis possibilities. Of these, the most familiar is the _semantic differential scale_. This scale is typically used for measuring attitudes or feelings. It consists of descriptive adjectives and their antonym at each end of the scale and seven "attitude positions" between them. Thus one might have "good" at one end of the scale and "bad" at the other. Or one might list "fair" and "unfair" at each end with seven short lines between them that might be checked. Thus in using this you would measure degree of "goodness."

There are also comparative scaling techniques that provide the opportunity for items to be directly compared with each other. One such scale is called the _Guttman scale_. This and others of that ilk are more complex. However, you can look at some of these other possibilities if you wish. I would suggest, for now, that if you are using a rating scale that the Likert format would usually suffice.

QUESTIONNAIRE CONSTRUCTION

Defining the question well is important. The evaluation question and what it means must be thoroughly defined in order to develop a questionnaire. We considered this issue in discussing the selection of existing instruments and their relevance to your evaluation. The same points must be made in discussing the development of a questionnaire. There are a number of guidelines that I might suggest in questionnaire construction. First, _know your potential respondents_ and their frame of reference. Where are they coming from? How are they likely to react to the question? Be sensitive to their feelings and how they might react to a question or be offended by it.

The question should have a *clear meaning*. Ambiguous questions will yield meaningless data. Double negatives are confusing; avoid them. One serious mistake that many questionnaire developers make is inadvertently including more than one issue in a question. For example, "Did you like the teachers and counselors in the program?" Does a "yes" response mean both were liked? Does a "no" response mean that neither was liked? What is the answer if you liked the teacher and hated the counselor?

The *writing style* and *presentation format* is also important. Don't get too academic. Is the wording simple enough to be understandable, or are there too many technical words? The writing style should be conversational. Furthermore, the way questions are formatted on the paper should be appealing and not confusing. Don't cram questions on the page. Doing so creates a format that looks confusing or threatening. Leave white space on the page.

Question sequence is also important. Generally, think of questions as proceeding from more general to more specific, from most factual to most attitudinal and opinion related. Demographic and personal data are more sensitive; place these questions at the end of the questionnaire.

In order for questionnaires to be reliable, they must be *administered* in a comparable way to all respondents. Clear, detailed instructions for administration are a part of the questionnaire—an important part.

MEASURING ACHIEVEMENT

Perhaps you will find yourself in the position of finding that no achievement test exactly fits the need of your question. You may be forced to construct an *achievement test*. Such an instrument is a test of knowledge and developed skill. We typically think of achievement tests as related to information acquisition, the gaining of knowledge, the understanding of facts or principles. Skill attainment more typically refers to abilities or proficiencies gained from training—such as the skill related to riding a bike, or knitting, or learning a computer program.

First, let me note that a number of things that I talked about in discussing questionnaires are helpful in constructing achievement tests. In many ways, questionnaires may be thought of as the generic type for collecting quantitative information. Achievement tests usually follow a questionnaire kind of format. Participants are asked to respond to a question, to which they provide an answer related to the content knowledge about the program being evaluated. The format of those questions is similar to those that I talked about in commenting on questionnaires.

That is, we can determine whether the content knowledge has been acquired by those taking the test by asking them true/false questions. We can ask test takers to make a forced choice between two or more options that are presented in order to determine whether they have understood a particular concept, for example. Or we can use a multiple-option format in which respondents select all of the options that apply to the situation. Thus, for example, we might ask those taking the test to indicate which of the choices presentedv are considered by health experts to be appropriate preventive procedures for a specific disease.

It is a difficult activity to personally develop an achievement test. When you attempt to develop a new measure of achievement, you forgo many of the advantages of a standardized, norm-referenced test. Clearly, you lose the ability to compare the results obtained by project participants with those attained by a norm group. This may be an important part of the way that standards for valuing are established—particularly in summative evaluations.

As I previously noted, one of the major problems that you as an evaluator always face is whether the measure to be used fits the question. Are the objectives being measured those that you really want? Thus there may be instances where you simply have no choice but to develop an achievement instrument for use in your evaluation of a specific program because no existing instrument fits your need. While you will not be able to expend the effort to standardize it to the extent of developing norms, you will be better able to specify the specific attainments and the specific criteria that you wish to measure. The measure will better fit your program needs.

ACHIEVEMENT TEST CONSTRUCTION

In starting to develop an achievement measure, you will want to very carefully describe each of the objectives to be measured. These should be so well specified that there is little room for ambiguity. In doing so, you will be able to develop specific test items that exactly conform to the objectives of your program. In contrast to norm-referenced tests, tests such as these are referred to by evaluators as *objectives-based tests*. Since objectives-based tests exactly measure the objectives of *your* program, standards for judging may be tied to success on that measure. Thus, for example, one might establish as a standard that a stipulated percentage of participants had satisfactorily completed a specified percentage of questions correctly (e.g., at least 80% of participants achieved 80% or better on the test).

The development process of an objectives-based test begins with an understanding of the content standards. That is, what is the intent of the question related to achievement of learning within the program? What specific learning is implied within the question? This entails a great deal of understanding about what individuals are to learn or understand. You will recall that earlier in developing the questions, I urged you to work with primary stakeholders in fleshing out the meaning of the question. If you did, you would have probed: "What constitutes an adequate answer? What are the components within the question?" Now if you are developing a new measure to answer the question, these prior inquiries, while helpful, are probably not sufficient. A great deal of specificity needs to be acquired in writing the *clearly stated outcomes*.

But understanding the desired outcome is more complicated than that. Outcome indicators can be measured at different levels of attainment. One might gain understanding of a concept at a very peripheral level—say, familiarity or general understanding—but what might be expected and required, and implied in the question, is a far greater depth. Try to gain focus on the *level of performance* implied within the question. How deep an understanding is required?

As you seek to develop a listing of the subobjectives that constitute the question, you will soon become submerged in more questions than you are able to handle. I suggest that you work cooperatively with primary stakeholders in considering *priorities* and weightings within those priorities. Then focus on those subobjectives of greatest importance and relevance. Precise statements of the individual subobjectives of the program must be developed and, from that, test items would be constructed that measure the important skills and knowledge. To the extent to which there are skills that are of greater importance, they should be represented proportionately by a greater number of test items. Typically, some achievement attributes are more easily attained by program participants. These should appear earlier in the test, especially when they are attributes required in order to be able to satisfy items that appear later in the test.

> ➤ *A Word of Caution:* I must repeat a previous admonition. You may not have available the time and resources to make a custom test. Typically, such a task is beyond the resources available for many small- or medium-size evaluations. However, if this is the only appropriate choice, proceed with care and with caution.

OBSERVATION PROTOCOLS

Observations can be conducted in ways that yield rich, in-depth, descriptive data. This is discussed in the section that follows, on qualitative measures. Observations can also be structured in a manner that yields data that are easily convertible to quantitative form. This requires the use of an *observation protocol*—a procedure for recording data in a prescribed manner.

In using such a protocol a specific behavior, or multiple behaviors, must be well described. Observers should be given detailed instructions for identifying the behavior(s). Preferably, a training session should occur to verify that the observer(s) can properly identify what is to be looked for. All observations should occur at well-specified times and for the same durations. In an instructional program, for example, the amount of time the participants are attentive to the classroom task can be recorded on an observation protocol. If there are multiple activities to be observed within a program, an observer might have a list of those particular aspects to be observed and can record either the occurrence of the event or the amount of time spent on each. Even quality of participation of those in the program might be rated on a protocol—perhaps on a scale of 1 to 5.

RECAP—SECTION K
Quantitative Data Instruments

- Existing Data
- Data from an Existing Instrument
  - Finding existing instruments
  - Tests and questionnaires
  - Standardized norm referenced
    - Reliability
    - Validity
- Data from a New Instrument
- Questionnaires
  - Developing a questionnaire
  - Response options
    - Two option (e.g., true/false)
    - Multiple choice

- Multiple options
- Rating scales
- Questionnaire Construction
  - Know your respondents
  - Questions have clear meaning
  - Writing style/presentation format
  - Question sequence
  - Administered comparably
- Tests (Measuring Achievement)
- Test Construction (Criterion-Referenced Tests)
  - Clear specification of outcomes
  - Level of performance
  - Priorities and weighing
- Observation Protocols

GAINING ADDITIONAL UNDERSTANDING

Case Study Exercise

Review the various quantitative measures discussed in this section and keep them in mind for potential use later in developing the evaluation design for the RUPAS evaluation. What instruments could you use? For example, what are some of the questions that you previously developed? Which of them might employ a survey? An observation protocol? Would achievement testing be possible with the children in the RUPAS program? If you specified parent outcomes, how might they be measured?

Resources

Geisinger, F., Spies, R. A., Carlson, J., & Plake, B. S. (Eds.). (2007). *Mental Measurements Yearbook Series* (MMY). Available at *www.unl.edu/buros*.

This yearbook series compiled biannually describes and reviews more than 200 published tests.

Further Reading

Christie, C. A., & Alkin, M. C. (2000). Objectives-based evaluations. In S. Mathison (Ed.), *Encyclopedia of evaluation* (pp. 281–285). Thousand Oaks, CA: Sage.

A concise discussion of objectives-based evaluation is presented in this reading.

Henry, G. T. (2000). Surveys. In S. Mathison (Ed.), *Encyclopedia of evaluation* (pp. 402–404). Thousand Oaks, CA: Sage.

Questionnaires are one form of survey. Gary Henry reviews among other things: survey design, developing, and organizing questions, and administering such instruments.

Metfessel, N. S., & Michael, W. B. (1967). A paradigm involving multiple criterion measures for the evaluation of the effectiveness of school programs. *Educational and Psychological Measurement, 27,* 931–943.

This is an old article and focused on educational situations, but it literally identifies all potential sources of data.

Salant, P. A., & Dillman, D. A. (1994). *How to conduct your own survey.* New York: Wiley.

This is a basic, easy-to-read book about surveys and questionnaires. See Chapter 6 for a good discussion about writing questions for a survey.

L

What Are Instruments for Collecting Qualitative Data?

In the previous section, I talked about instruments that are typically used to collect data that can be quantified. Now let us consider the ways that *qualitative data* are collected.

First, what do I mean by the word *qualitative*? You learned (or already knew) that the term *quantitative* indicates quantity (or numbers). So do we therefore intuit that "quality" is some kind of boastful statement that implies that such data are of higher quality? Some qualitative researchers may think so, but that is not what the term means. Quality is meant to reference the attributes or nature of an entity. What are the qualities or *characteristics* of the entity? Qualitative researchers use their data to provide in-depth understanding of human behavior (individually or in programs), not necessarily describing what results were found or when, but rather, *why* and *how* it happened. Qualitative researchers believe that capturing stakeholders' experiences and perceptions leads to deep understanding of a program. Qualitative data help provide insights into a program by "carrying" potential readers into the program setting. A number of evaluator options typically yield qualitative data. I review a number of these below.

Before talking about specific instruments for collecting qualitative data, let me first talk about *data sources*. In an earlier section, I talked about the different sources from which data could be acquired. Remember? I talked about the three choices of either acquiring existing data, using existing instruments, or developing new instruments. That theme is somewhat less relevant in this section. First, *existing instruments* is not a major topic when it relates to qualitative data. Surely, there are some instruments available such as questionnaires that might have open-ended questions, but these are primarily instruments that are used to gather quantitative data. As noted above, the strength of qualitative information is the opportunity to be responsive to the particular context and obtain the perspectives of those within it. Thus in this section I will not comment further on this category of data source.

Another category previously mentioned is *existing data,* and there are many types of existing data that might yield qualitative understandings. We discussed the various documents that might be available at the program site, or in the community, that yield quantitative data. Likewise, existing documents and other artifacts might yield further qualitative understandings of the program; I refer to these as *qualitative-oriented documents.* Think, for example, of the minutes of meetings, of photographs, or of work samples produced by program participants. Existing qualitative-oriented data might also include e-mails, notes or letters from program participants, or program brochures. Perhaps, also, there are newspaper articles describing the program.

What might you learn from some of these existing materials? How can such data be used? First, with "a grain of salt," so to speak. You did not originally collect these data and, therefore, cannot attest to their accuracy or the context in which they were developed. Treat existing data, especially qualitative existing data, with care. These data provide possibilities for further examination and thoughts about issues that might warrant further examination. Stop now. Before proceeding further, reflect on the kinds of documents, materials, or other artifacts that might be found in a program with which you are familiar.

DEVELOPING NEW INSTRUMENTS

For the most part, the primary data source for gathering qualitative data are new instruments. I talk here about the major types of instruments for gathering qualitative data: *observations* and *interviews,* including group (or so-called "focus group") interviews. Each of these has specified procedures and guidelines for their accomplishment. However, there are options and variations in how the procedures might be implemented; this too will be discussed. Let me further suggest that, to a large extent, the "instrument" is really the evaluator. Qualitative data involve your perceptions, your observations, your interpretations, and these must be carefully bounded. Appropriate training is essential for gathering qualitative data. This section provides a start in that training. *Only a start.*

OBSERVATIONS

Observations, also referred to as naturalistic observations, naturalistic inquiry, or participant observation, are methods used for getting more fine-grained information about a program, activities, participants, or other stakeholders. In terms of observations, does this really mean just watching other people? Well, yes, but it's more than that. Watching is a large part of what doing observation is about. The central idea of observations is to systematically engage in this careful watching until such time that you notice continuing patterns or trends. You want to understand what is happening in as much detail as possible—as you are seeing it take place—as you are seeing it, hearing it, or maybe even smelling it.

I believe that much of what you do and how you do it is structured by your role. The nature of the *observer's role* may vary from external (uninvolved) observer to participant-observer. If you, as the participant-observer evaluator, are involved in the program you might have been enlisted (or volunteered) to engage in the evaluation. In this role, you would be attempting to balance your participation by simultaneously observing and taking notes. Alternatively, evaluators might also be fully external, having no role in the program and being present at activities only as an observer. Many evaluation roles take place in the vast middle ground between the two extremes. The role that evaluators play has implications for the detail of notes they might take, for their understanding of the context, their impartiality (or bias), or their better understanding of the implications of actions or events. The message for you: Be aware of your role and the implications of that role.

I believe that the extent to which you as the evaluator can fully be a participant-observer varies according to the situation. That is, there will be times when you should, ideally, sit back and take in what is going on in the program. An example includes the beginning phases of the evaluation when, if you are an outsider, you are still trying to establish credibility, negotiate access, and learn about the program. However, as you gain familiarity with the program, the possibility and ease with which you can immerse yourself in programmatic activities becomes greater.

Observations vary in terms of *protocol style* and, accordingly, the quality and nature of the information that can be collected. Protocols, then, are the rules guiding how you will go about your work. These protocols guide evaluators in terms of the kinds of information that they need to document. They run the full gamut of looking like checklists to being mostly blank. Checklist-like observation protocols are used when evaluators are interested in documenting whether a prescribed activity was carried out or if they wish to tally how frequently a particular behavior was exhibited. The extreme case of this was discussed in the previous section, where we considered observation protocols designed to yield quantitative data. At the opposite extreme, observations may also take place in an unstructured fashion. This would allow you as the evaluator to capture what is striking to you at any given moment. This unstructured protocol provides opportunities to gain experiential data unfettered by preconceived categories. I personally prefer some middle position on this structure continuum.

Now let's talk about what you might record when you are observing. There are various approaches to *taking notes* while conducting observations. As noted above, you might use protocols or templates describing how you will take notes. These protocols can be very structured and might look like a checklist. Or they can be very open for you to write down whatever you think is important. On the one hand, you might be inclined to use the "write like mad" approach—firmly planted in one area of the room where you would be observing and documenting as much and as quickly as you can. Alternatively, you may wish to exercise a more subtle way of taking notes, which would involve jotting down key words or sketching images in a notepad that you might later use as *triggers* to write up fuller notes. This alternative approach, as you may expect, would allow you to be more flexible in terms of your movement and level of engagement in the activities taking place around you.

So how might you use these "triggers" to develop observation notes? Think about each of the key words or images and try to remember the context. What happened? How did it happen? Who was involved? Can you remember, more specifically, some of the words that were used?

Regardless of the note-taking method used, you must also be aware of several sources of bias that accompany observations. They include seeing only what you choose to see and seeing only what is expected. These kinds of biases can cripple the quality of data being collected, but there are means of accounting for them. For instance, you might document your biases and your opinions of the activities as they are taking place by inserting your *observer comments* into your notes, or journaling about your experiences at the site, or write memos about what might be causing bias. Explaining and accounting for issues that may color your perspective improves the quality and adds to the validity of the data that you collect.

Thus you would have two documents: on the one hand, the detailed notes that you recorded; on the other, a separate set of observer comments. When these are put together, the whole set of documents is called *field notes*, and they become the source of information that you will use for further examination. Keep in mind, however, that you should not try to look for patterns as you are taking notes, because you don't know what you are seeing yet. Just take notes. If you try to look for patterns right away, you will end up missing a large part of what's actually happening.

It's not that easy. The development of *observer skills* requires training and preparation. Good observers should understand the nature of human interaction in order to understand what is transpiring. The ability to concentrate fully on the activity being observed without distraction is vital. Also, good observers should have the ability to separate detail from trivia and describe vividly what is seen.

As with all data collection tools, there are advantages and disadvantages to engaging in observations. Observation data are a source of incredibly rich information that has the potential to more fully describe a context and the direct experiences of individuals, and to better explain their perspectives. On the other hand, this approach could be extremely time consuming and costly. Moreover, it would require that you develop your observation skills. This takes practice. Thus it is often helpful to complement data gathered using observations with data collected using other methods. Otherwise, it may quickly use up the majority of the evaluation budget.

INTERVIEWS AND FOCUS GROUPS

One of the ways that you as the evaluator might gain a deeper grasp of happenings within the program is to collect data by conducting interviews. Generally speaking, the goal of interview techniques is to capture the voices of different respondent groups. I previously have discussed observations and the skills required for using that instrument. These same skills are necessary in interviewing. The interviewer must be a good observer. When we talk to people, there are nonverbal cues. Are some responses given with greater vehemence? Do some questions cause unease? What does that mean? Careful observation is an important part of interviewing.

Interviews can take place in a format ranging from fully structured to unstructured. In a fully *structured interview*, a preestablished protocol consisting of key questions is used. It guides the course of the conversation with little room for probing and adaptation. Structured interviews are designed so that they do not vary from one person to the next (or vary as little as possible). In many ways this is like an orally administered survey, but less efficient. Structured interviews may be appropriate when there is a need for responses to the same questions from each interviewee. Situations that might require structured interviews are when there are many interviewees and there is a concern about the possibility of variability of response and unequal representation of issues addressed.

Semistructured interviews are also guided by a preestablished set of questions. However, questions do not need to be asked in a specified order. Rather, interviewers are free to probe and shuffle questions as needed. This allows the process to be more conversational. If the interviewee said anything that was unclear, the interviewer can ask for clarification and choose to go as deep into the question as necessary.

What are the desired characteristics of questions to be asked in the semistructured interview? First, questions should be specific enough to focus on a single topic yet be open ended enough to allow for multiple response possibilities. Questions should be written in nontechnical, neutral, and natural (conversational) language. It is best to field-test— try out—the questions before going to interview sites.

Appropriate sequencing is important. Recall that in the previous section I cautioned about not asking personal or sensitive questions at the beginning of the questionnaire. This is generally applicable in interviews, but is open to some variability because you want questions to flow naturally, and sequence is partially determined by how natural lead-ins are provided by particular responses. It is important that you be aware of the potential questions to be asked and not have to continually refer to your notes. In that regard, you should have thought beforehand about possible appropriate follow-ups to questions. Namely, the "why," "how," and "when" types of things.

Finally, we have *unstructured interviews*, or informal interviews. While there aren't any predetermined questions, the potential agenda is set by the interviewer. However, in this approach, respondents are allowed to say as much or as little as they wish. They are also encouraged to express themselves at their own pace and in their own terms. In that situation, you as the evaluator would sit down with someone—a potential source of information—and talk with them. But this "talking" can take a number of different forms. The interviewee may bring up topics so that there's an element of "discovery" and letting things emerge in this kind of interviewing. In the more unstructured, open-ended type of interview, think of the psychiatrist who asks a simple question and then mostly says, "I see," or "What do you mean by that?"

Focus groups may be considered as a special member of the interview family. The structure of focus group interviews may also vary as described above. However, focus groups do not occur in a one-on-one setting. Rather, they usually involve a group of between four to 10 respondents. Similar to interviews, a focus group moderator, possibly you, tends to have a set of questions that you might want to ask the group, and the idea is that members of the focus group will have something to contribute or say in response to the question being asked. Once you feel that you have gotten a good amount of feedback or responses from the group, you might attempt to move the conversation on to the next question. But really, there isn't any particular order in which questions are asked because when you have a bunch of people sitting around talking; they'll initiate discussion on many of the issues that you had intended to address. You might even raise those that are not mentioned. As a whole, focus groups provide the benefit of enhanced understandings as a consequence of the interaction among participants. One person's comment provides the gist for another's and extends the idea.

However, disadvantages to this approach include uneven participation by those within the group; a phenomenon called "groupthink," whereby members of the group falsely come to share a common opinion regarding the issue at hand; and lack of control over the direction of the conversation. Taken together, all of these setbacks can translate into valuable time lost to irrelevant discussion. Thus, while focus groups can produce incredibly powerful data, you will need to be a skilled facilitator to balance participation while limiting the degree to which conversations may head into uncharted waters. Furthermore, given the task of trying to control a group discussion, it is wise to conduct the group with two people—one person who facilitates the group while the other person takes notes.

SURVEYS AND QUESTIONNAIRES

We talked about *surveys and questionnaires* in the last section. They are usually thought of as tools designed to collect quantitatively oriented information. However, they also can be used to collect qualitative data. Features, such as *open-ended items*, can be built into these instruments that would be useful for qualitative data collection purposes. Open-ended items tend to be questions that respondents can answer in a word, a phrase, or one to two sentences. Questions that may require lengthier answers are best suited for interviews and focus groups. When included on a survey or questionnaire, open-ended items serve several purposes. First, they enable respondents to provide feedback that is not bounded by numerical rating scales—they don't simply give a number, a ranking, or a rating. Second, by allowing respondents to comment on issues that they view to be important, they go beyond what is normally revealed in a quantitatively oriented survey.

As with all data collection methods, including open-ended items on instruments such as surveys and questionnaires also has its drawbacks. For example, respondents may not answer the question as phrased and use the space for different purposes altogether. They might provide added insights or voice their own gripes. But that, too, is useful. Answers provided in this space may be revealing and provide further understanding and clarification. Responses may suggest trends that were not previously apparent and could lead to further investigation. Similarly, comments may support findings obtained from other sources of data. Typically, surveys and questionnaires are not used as the sole methods of collecting qualitative data. However, certain situations might force you as the evaluator to depend on them for qualitative data. Consider extreme budgetary or time constraints, for example. It simply is less costly to obtain a substantial amount of valuable qualitative information in this way. So whenever possible, I suggest that tools be used in conjunction with other, complementary approaches.

RECAP—SECTION L
Qualitative Instruments

- Observations
  - Observer's role
  - Protocol style
  - Taking notes
  - Observer comments
  - Compiled field notes
  - Observer skills
- Interviews
  - Structured
  - Semistructured
  - Unstructured
  - Focus groups
- Surveys and Questionnaires
  - Open-ended items

GAINING ADDITIONAL UNDERSTANDING

Case Study Exercise

Consider the three major headings in the section recap. Based on the questions that you previously formulated, which of these might be most appropriate methods for gathering the necessary data? What are the pros and cons of each method?

Further Reading

Krueger, R. (2005). Focus group. In S. Mathison (Ed.), *Encyclopedia of evaluation* (pp. 158–160). Thousand Oaks, CA: Sage.

In this encyclopedia entry, Richard Krueger one of the leading scholars on focus groups presents a concise description of that method.

Mabry, L. (2003). In living color: Qualitative methods in educational evaluation. In T. Kellaghan & D. Stufflebeam (Eds.), *International handbook of educational evaluation* (pp. 167–185). Norwell, MA: Kluwer.

This is an excellent, easy-to-read discussion of the qualitative data collection and analysis process.

Patton, M. Q. (1987). *How to use qualitative methods in evaluation*. Newbury Park, CA: Sage.

This is a very complete small book, which is a part of the Center for the Study of Evaluation's *Program Evaluation Kit*.

Patton M. Q. (2003). Qualitative evaluation checklist. *Evaluation Checklists Program*. Available at *www.wmich.edu/evalctr/checklists/qec.pdf*.

This is an excellent checklist of things to think about in qualitative evaluation.

Salant, P. A., & Dillman, D. A. (1994). *How to conduct your own survey*. New York: Wiley.

This is a basic, easy-to-read book about surveys and questionnaires. See pp. 170–174 for a good discussion about interviewing. For a full scholarly discussion of survey, see Dillman's 2007 book.

M

What Are the Logistics of Data Collection?

Many issues can arise in the process of data collection. How do you get started? What arrangements need to be made? In particular, you need to be attentive, first, to the actions necessary in order to gain access to data. Furthermore, you need to give a great deal of forethought to the process of collecting data. Also, you may need to consider steps to take if there are problems with data quality. Finally, and above all, it is important to try to understand the organization's (and stakeholders') viewpoint. Doing so puts you in a position to avoid conflict and to adapt to the situation.

You want to be sure that there will not be hang-ups—actually, there always are, so you want to minimize them. Consider for a moment the potential problems. What if you have difficulty gaining access to those from whom you need data—be it interviews or administering a questionnaire? What if there are scheduling problems? How do you work through problems around poor-quality data? How can you satisfy the organization's concerns about protecting the privacy of participants? Questions, questions, questions. Let's talk about it.

GAINING DATA ACCESS

Gaining access to data is, unfortunately, a common problem for many evaluators. It is probably most often found in large bureaucratic organizations or institutions. In these types of settings, it may seem to evaluators that they are constantly working through red tape and negotiating, negotiating, negotiating. Indeed, data access is one of the more frustrating aspects of evaluation, even with careful attention to prior discussion (and assumed agreement) about issues of access and rules for negotiating disputes.

So how might you as the evaluator go about negotiating access in a practical way? What are the access steps—specifically? What might be the potential barriers related to each step? The first step involves speaking to primary users and making both sides' *expectations* around data access *explicit*. This should be done in the early phases of the evaluation. However, you might receive "push-back" from primary users because the importance of certain kinds of data in answering questions may not yet be apparent to them. Nonetheless, the ground rules for access should be addressed and agreed to orally. It may also help to consider writing them into the evaluation contract, as we discuss in Section Q.

The second step involves *establishing and maintaining relationships* with those in the organization who are considered information *gatekeepers*. You may accomplish this by assessing gatekeepers' potential roles and interests in the program and the evaluation. Then maintaining open lines of communication is important. Doing so helps to ensure gatekeepers' understanding of the purpose and scope of the evaluation. Fostering collaborative, mutually respectful relationships is also important. In this way, you and they are more likely to be on the same page, the same side, and "speak the same language." Sometimes it may be challenging to communicate with gatekeepers. Perhaps they are pressed for time and view you as a further distraction. They simply may not want to work with you or may possibly view you as a threat. Try using different modes of contact. E-mails are used widely now, but picking up the phone is just as easy. Don't overburden the relationship; unnecessary communication can turn off busy people. Or, if necessary, consider gently tapping the organizational hierarchy and raising your concern in a "non-finger-pointing" way. However, remember that you will need to be judicious when doing this because you run the risk of jeopardizing potential future relationships with gatekeepers and other program staff.

COLLECTING DATA

Let us talk first about the things that you will have to do in order to collect data in the field. To collect both quantitative and qualitative data, you will need instruments. We talked about the different kinds of instruments in Sections K and L. But consider for a moment the *administrative preparations* needed to collect data. In the case of questionnaires, for example, consider whether you will have to administer them yourself or whether program staff will be assisting you. If you will be receiving help, who will be helping you? When and where will the questionnaires be administered? Whom do you need to coordinate with to make these arrangements?

As for observations, it again goes back to the issue of negotiation. This applies to all kinds of sites, from the typical classroom to offices to other places of business (even public places such as parks!). From whom should you seek administrative permission? Is there one "right" person to ask? The important thing here is to realize that when in the field, the "right" people who can grant you access may not be obvious and that there may be different levels of access. For instance, if you are doing observations in a school cafeteria, while you certainly should clear this with the program manager, might it not be appropriate to also ask the cafeteria manager for permission to observe? After all, as an evaluator, you are entering someone else's workplace and should demonstrate respect towards those who live out a part of their lives at the site.

What does seeking *permission* directly *from participants* involve? Well, you should tell participants who you are, what you are trying to accomplish, how you intend to go about your activities, and ask if they would be willing to help you through the process. All the while, be mindful of the language that you use and how you interact with participants. As in reporting, avoid jargon and overly technical language— not only because participants might not understand, but because you don't want to be misunderstood as being condescending. At the end of the day, realize that some participants may not allow you access. While that is disappointing, it will be more appropriate to respect their wishes and exclude them from your data collection efforts. Just remember that when you are working with people, one of your primary obligations is to do no harm.

In interviews—particularly focus groups—there are *space considerations*. Think about where the focus groups will be held. How many rooms will you need? Whom do you reserve the space with? How will participants know where to go? Do you need signs? Will you be coordinating directly with participants or, again, will program staff be assisting you in any way? These are the kinds of logistical issues that need to be considered when arrangements are being made in preparation for data collection.

Much can go wrong in attempting to collect data. Despite all your attempts at careful planning, things happen. A number of things could affect scheduling: weather, attendance, an unusual program disruption. Evaluation work may need to be rescheduled. Try to *anticipate possible impediments* and consider ahead of time how you might respond if the "what ifs" happen.

QUALITY OF DATA

All right, now, let's suppose you have been able to collect the necessary data. But what are you to do when you realize that the response rate for the last questionnaire administered was only 20%? On the other hand, what if you were able to collect all of the questionnaires only to notice that there was a lot of missing data because participants did not answer most of the questions? Here we have the same problem in that you have data that can't be analyzed and, typically, if you can't analyze the information you collected, then you can't use it. Game over.

Again, you can potentially avoid many of these problems if you *anticipate possible impediments* and possible areas for improvement before you go out to the field. Consider, for example, the instrument that you use, participants' characteristics, and the timing of your data collection. In terms of the instruments, assess their content, language, and length. Were the items tapping into relevant issues? Was the language used free of jargon and accessible to your audiences? If you are using context-specific language, are you doing so in a manner that is aligned with participants' use? Is the instrument of reasonable length for the participants? Remember, the more complicated and lengthier the instrument, the more time it'll take participants to complete. Respect their intelligence and their time.

Next, determine the characteristics and *needs of participants*. Specifically, think about whether your instrument needs to be translated. Do your instruments ask about topics that are taboo in other cultures? Are the items highly controversial? Do the questions unduly lead respondents to a particular response? Pay heed to the degree of clarity, cultural sensitivity, and possibility of biased responses in your questions.

Finally, consider the *timing* of your data collection. When working with schools, for example, think about whether data collection activities are unreasonably disruptive. Are they taking instructional time away from students and teachers? Be aware of the school's regular schedule and of any special events that might affect data collection. How can you incorporate data collection into the day-to-day routines of the classroom so that it is woven in seamlessly? In places of business with atypical hours of operation or nontraditional organizational structures, consider adapting your activities to the organization's schedule and priorities.

UNDERSTANDING THE ORGANIZATION'S VIEWPOINTS

Sometimes, evaluators' expectations do not coincide with the organization's perceptions of what is best. Organizations feel that they are obligated to *protect the privacy* and *confidentiality* of the people whom they serve. So even though evaluators' services are sought out, it is misleading to think that evaluators are necessarily entitled to full, open access to sensitive information. At the same time, the program you are evaluating is obligated to not make it unreasonably challenging for evaluators. Rather, evaluators and organizations should have measures in place that outline the circumstances under which access can be granted and what the data's explicit uses can be. That's one reason why organizations interested in regulating research and data use create offices or procedures for evaluating the acceptability of research and evaluation; these are typically called *Institutional Review Boards* (IRBs).

An IRB is a committee that consists of a diverse group of researchers and community members. The committee is responsible for reviewing, approving, and monitoring proposed research studies that require involvement of human participants. Specifically, such a board is interested in protecting the rights and well-being of human participants. Most studies submitted for IRB review are from the medical, biobehavioral, or social science fields. While evaluation studies differ from research studies, they may still be subject to IRB review, given the often extensive role that program participants play during the evaluation process.

In addition to protecting the rights and confidentiality of participants, those in charge may have *program interests* that run counter to your possible needs as an evaluator. Organizations are focused on what they can do for program participants. Evaluation is often viewed as an unwelcome intrusion. In their view, time spent on evaluation is time that could be used for program activities. Also, program staff may misinterpret evaluation of the program as an evaluation of their performance. Or they may think the evaluation is being conducted to make decisions about funding or for reorganizing the program structurally.

In all cases, evaluation may seem threatening, and it is the evaluator's job to assuage misunderstandings and reduce threat. This can be done by appropriately engaging participants in the evaluation process and by explaining to participants the purpose and scope of the evaluation and the role of evaluation activities in which they are engaged.

Finally, always try to *balance* your *needs and interests* with those of the organization's and program stakeholders'. Try to minimize the potential burden that the activities you want to carry out will be for participants. Remember that even though your job is to evaluate the program, you do not want to cause harm or disruption.

> ➢ **My Advice:** Try to anticipate all that might go wrong and be obsessive in attending to the details of data collection. (You probably have already guessed that I am pretty obsessive, by nature.) Some further rules of thumb: build a close, respectful relationship with primary stakeholders; be prepared for changed circumstances; and negotiate best possible solutions.

RECAP—SECTION M
Logistics of Data Collection

- Gaining Data Access
  - Make expectations explicit
  - Establish relationship with gatekeepers
- Collecting Data
  - Make administrative preparations
  - Seek permissions from participants
  - Consider space issues
  - Anticipate possible impediments
- Improving Quality of Data
  - Anticipate impediments
  - Be aware of needs of participants
  - Consider appropriate timing of collection
- Understanding the Organization's Viewpoints
  - Protecting privacy and confidentiality
  - Submit to Institutional Review Board
  - Recognize the priority of the program's interests
  - Reduce threat
  - Balance needs and interests

GAINING ADDITIONAL UNDERSTANDING

Case Study Exercise

At this point it may be a little difficult to detail specific logistics of the RUPAS evaluation data collection. However, think about some potential difficulties that you might face (e.g., distance between the different program sites). Other possible problems could include language, cultural differences, travel, and expenses. Reflect on these issues relative to what is listed in the section recap.

Further Reading

Donaldson, S. L., Gooler, L. E., & Scriven, M. (2002). Strategies for managing evaluation anxiety: Toward a psychology of program evaluation. *American Journal of Evaluation, 23*(3), 261–273.

This journal article provides a discussion of the impact of stakeholders' evaluation anxiety and presents some strategies that help to overcome this anxiety. Clearly, this is related to less traumatic data collection.

Fitzpatrick, J. L. (2005). Human subjects protection. In S. Mathison (Ed.), *Encyclopedia of evaluation* (pp. 188–190). Thousand Oaks, CA: Sage.

Jody Fitzpatrick does an excellent job of describing the extent to which evaluators need to act in ways that respect the rights of participants.

Fitzpatrick, J. L. (2005). Informed consent. In S. Mathison (Ed.), *Encyclopedia of evaluation* (pp. 199-200). Thousand Oaks, CA: Sage.

We have discussed the ethical issues related to informed consent in this section. Here is a bit more discussion on the topic.

Sidani, S., & Streiner, D. L. (2010). Final thoughts: A healthy dose of realism. In S. L. Streiner & S. Sidani (Eds.), *When research goes off the rails.* New York: Guilford Press.

This book has 42 short vignettes describing research or evaluation projects gone awry. This final chapter presents a brief summary of "lessons learned."

Taut, S., & Alkin, M. (2003). Program staff perceptions of barriers to evaluation implementation. *American Journal of Evaluation, 24*(2), 213–226.

This article seeks to provide understanding of the logistical difficulties of data collection—and evaluation implementation generally—by examining program staff perceptions.

N

Are the Questions Evaluable (Able to Be Evaluated)?

The issue here is whether the questions are "evaluable." Are they *relevant*? Further, *can they be answered*—and *should they be answered*? Let me review where we are at this point.

First, you have gained a better understanding of the program and its logic. Then some potential evaluation questions were specified. In doing so, you did an initial consideration of the questions that stakeholders really wanted answered. Furthermore, you examined potential data sources, both quantitative and qualitative, that might be appropriate for answering the stipulated questions. And, I hope, you now have some knowledge of the political, social, and organizational context surrounding the program. This will be helpful in determining whether the evaluation questions are answerable. You as the evaluator have several tasks in determining whether the potential evaluation questions are, in fact, answerable. Now let us turn to these issues.

There are a number of reasons why the evaluation questions may not be evaluable (able to be evaluated, or able to be included as questions in the evaluation). Let me deal with this in seven categories: (1) *the nature and stage of the program*, (2) *resources available*, (3) *the nature and relevance of the question*, (4) *establishing standards*, (5) *technical issues*, (6) *ethical concerns*, and (7) *political feasibility*.

STAGE OF THE PROGRAM

The nature and stage of the program offer insights into potential evaluability. Is it premature to ask this particular question? We need to be sure that the program is at a sufficient stage of development that the answer to the question can be ascertained. If, for example, the program is intended to last 3 years with particular outcomes expected at the end of that period, then it would be inappropriate (or should I say foolhardy?) to attempt to measure final outcomes. There must be sufficient time for the program to have operated so that the effects can be accurately assessed.

RESOURCES

The next issue to be considered is resources. What are the available resources? This question will need to be answered in greater detail in developing the evaluation plan, but some initial estimates are certainly called for at this stage. Resources are of two types: fiscal and "in-kind." As in much of life, aspirations frequently exceed resources. We want more than we are able to afford. So check carefully about the number of dollars available for the evaluation. Consider what costs you will need to incur in conducting the evaluation—staff, materials, travel, and so forth. Can an evaluation based on these evaluation questions be done? Especially, can it be completed in a way that you would consider to be acceptable?

Resources not only include the dollars available for funding the evaluation, but also "in-kind" resources, such as program staff time available for certain kinds of assistance (e.g., data collection or clerical help). There is also the matter of equipment or other services to be provided by the client's organization (e.g., printing, computer access, workspace). Determine the extent to which the evaluation will receive needed cooperation and assistance from the client and other stakeholders. How will they cooperate? What program resources will be made available?

Answering some evaluation questions will require a great deal of resources. Consider the trade-offs between different questions. Some questions may consume a substantial part of the budget to the detriment of being able to respond to other questions. Is it worth it?

NATURE OF THE QUESTION

First, there is the evaluation question itself. We have dealt with this in an earlier section. Ideally, at this stage, the question had been sufficiently refined so that it is a real question, rendering the two concerns I state below irrelevant. First, review again the evaluation questions and issues and make sure that you have a firm understanding of what they are. If you do not clearly understand the question, take the necessary steps to gain that understanding.

The first concern is whether the *question* that is to be potentially investigated is of insufficient worth. On the one hand, it might be so trivial that an evaluation based on that question is hardly worth the effort. Alternatively, the answer might already be known. Or, if known, is the answer so simply acquired that it need not be a focus of the evaluation.

Second, we again need to ask ourselves (and stakeholders), "Is this question useful?" Is it a question that someone *really wants* an answer to? Indeed, the issue is more than casually "wanting." Wanting something and using something are different. Is it wanted because someone wants to use the information for program improvement, or to make a judgment about the program? Is this question worth your time as an evaluator, or is it irrelevant?

ESTABLISHING STANDARDS

I like to consider the possibility of establishing standards as a part of the process of considering evaluability. Recall that in Section I, I first discussed the process of working with stakeholders to determine questions of real interest. In part, this is done by creating scenarios describing possible results for each question and asking stakeholders about the extent to which those hypothesized findings would be useful. Description of further gradations of those possible findings served to determine the "value" of potential evaluation results. In essence this process, when followed through, helps to provide standards for judging the outcomes of the evaluation. Authors of one of the further readings to this section refer to this as "front-end-loaded standard setting."

You will note in Section T that there are other ways that data can be ultimately valued, but I like the idea of stakeholders participating in this manner to test the importance of evaluation questions.

TECHNICAL ISSUES

Of course, what readily comes to mind in considering whether a potential evaluation question is appropriate for inclusion in the study are the various technical issues. The evaluator needs to consider whether the question is *measurable*. Is it stated in such a way that an instrument is available, or could be constructed, that would capture the essence of the question? I have discussed earlier the various sources of data that might be used in an evaluation. You as an evaluator should consider these and determine whether it is possible to obtain an appropriate instrument.

How might the data be collected? What kind of *data collection schedule* would be required, and under what conditions should data be collected? Is there sufficient time for data to be collected? Is access to the data resources possible? At this point, you may be quite flexible and expansive and allow for multiple possibilities of data acquisition. Of course, if even in your most imaginative mode there are no ways of gathering the needed data, clearly modifications must be made.

Think further—if the potential evaluation question requires a *comparison* between this program and an alternative, you must consider whether alternative programs are present or possible. Does the evaluation require a design (more on this later) that necessitates random assignment of clients to one of two treatments (alternative programs)? If not, is there another program that could be used for comparison purposes? Could we gain the participation of those in the program not of primary interest?

A related technical issue to be considered is the potential receptivity to the evaluation within the organization. Does a potential data collection plan depend on a greater level of *cooperation and assistance* from staff than is likely to be extended? Will the required cooperation and access be available?

Time available is a technical issue; evaluations are conducted within specified time periods. The evaluator needs to develop a time line for what things will occur and in what order. I have already talked about the time-related issue of a question being too premature in terms of the stage of development of the evaluation. A question might be appropriate in terms of the stage of development, but still could require too much time for its evaluation; it may not be answerable within the period allotted (e.g., the contract year).

ETHICAL ISSUES

There are ethical issues associated with the selection of questions as well. In Section X, I provide some discussion of the various standards for program evaluation. Included in these standards are various ethical concerns related to the propriety involved in conducting an evaluation. These include the manner in which we deal with clients and other staff members. Evaluation must be conducted in a manner that does not intrude into the personal *rights of individuals and organizations*. Participants need to be informed and agree to participate in the evaluation. Individuals' confidentiality must be assured. If the evaluation needs to be conducted in a manner that requires the disclosure of the participants' identities or nature of their response, then this intrusion is inappropriate. So consider carefully what will be required of those who participate in the evaluation. What can happen that is bad or harmful? To the extent possible, seriously consider whether data collection might pose risks and harms to participants. Could the evaluation cause serious disruption to the program or to the well-being of individuals?

Another ethical issue relates to you, the evaluator. As the evaluator, you should not consider the inclusion of a question that might include some *conflict of interest* on your part. A conflict of interest may occur in the evaluation if you have a vested interest, for example, in a particular part of the program to be evaluated. Granted, as I have noted, all evaluations are political, but be alert to questions that it would be imprudent for you to address.

Finally, examine whether, in considering particular questions, the nature of the data are likely to lead to *misleading evaluative information* or conclusions. Attempt to clarify these issues at the outset in order to avoid future problems. Be wary of the kinds of questions whose findings are particularly amenable to potential misuse. (This topic is discussed in Section V.)

POLITICAL FEASIBILITY

In Section F, I discussed with you the need to examine the organizational, social, and political context. I noted that evaluation is political in nature. Evaluation questions inspire a variety of strong views within the political context—views running in many different directions. Consider carefully the *political feasibility* of examining the questions. Will answering these questions (or seeking answers to these questions) be so politically disruptive as to not make finding the answer possible? This does not mean that politically charged questions are beyond examination. Rather, you should contemplate the extent to which the political environment allows the asking of the question.

> **My Advice:** Many potential evaluation questions are not readily evaluable. And many more questions may have been posed than can possibly be addressed. Make a realistic appraisal of the feasibility of proceeding with the evaluation questions as projected by the sponsor and consider where appropriate a possible reduction in scope. Which evaluation questions, and how many, are accomplishable? Consider reducing the projected data collection to what is both doable and most important. It is important that the evaluator makes clear to stakeholders what it is possible to do successfully.

RECAP—SECTION N
Are the Questions Evaluable?

- What Is the Nature and Stage of the Program?
- Are Appropriate Resources Available?
- What Is the Nature of the Question?
  - Question of little worth?
  - Answer really wanted?
- Can Standards Be Established?
- What Are the Technical Issues?
  - Potentially measurable?
  - Data collection possible?
  - Comparison available, if required?
  - Cooperation appropriate?
  - Sufficient time?
- Are There Ethical Concerns?
  - Rights of individuals?
  - Evaluator conflict of interest?
  - Potential for misleading information?
- What Is the Political Feasibility?

GAINING ADDITIONAL UNDERSTANDING

Case Study Exercise

Review again the questions that you asked in Section I. Address each question in terms of the items listed in the Recap for this section.

Further Reading

Cousins, J. B., & Shulha, L. (2008). Complexities in setting program standards in collaborative evaluation. In N. Smith & P. Brandon (Eds.), *Fundamental issues in evaluation* (pp. 139–158). New York: Guilford Press.

Cousins and Shulha do an excellent job of describing the role of stakeholders in establishing a basis for valuing evaluation results. They demonstrate the way that standard setting must precede data collection.

Kirkhart, K. E. (1994). Seeking multicultural validity: A postcard from the road. *Evaluation Practice, 16*(1), 1–12.

This journal article by Karen Kirkhart helped to initiate the discussion in the evaluation field about the need to engage in culturally responsive evaluation.

SECTION

O

What Is the Evaluation Plan (Process Measures)?

Here we are. We have been working toward this—finalizing the evaluation plan. Evaluation plan? What exactly is an evaluation plan? It is a description of how we will conduct the evaluation. And indeed, we have already considered a number of factors that need to be considered in developing a plan: the stakeholders and their values (Section D); the program and its logic (Sections G and H); the organizational, social, and political context (Section F); and the possible questions to be answered (Section I). In Sections K, L, and M we looked at what instrumentation might be used to answer the possible questions. That is, we considered what data could be collected—what information we might obtain to answer the proposed questions. Finally, in Section N, we assessed all of these factors to determine whether answering these questions as the major evaluation focus was a realistic and doable undertaking.

However, you are still missing a few pieces. You need to know how you will collect data. Or, more precisely, in what form and from whom. Furthermore, you need to specify how the data you collect will be analyzed. You will also want to consider how you will use the data to answer your questions. Finally, you will need to think about how you will communicate findings.

THE EVALUATION DESIGN

Now you need to finalize the process by putting a plan together and reaching agreement with stakeholders. But first, let me make a distinction—perhaps an arbitrary distinction—between evaluation design and the evaluation plan. Typically, evaluators consider *design* as those issues related to: what comparisons will be made; how success will be determined; who gets picked to participate in the program and how; what instruments or measures will be used; and when will measurement take place. The evaluation plan includes the design as well as all of the procedural aspects that will make it possible—much of this detail is found in Section Q.

The design consists of both process measures and outcome measures. In this section we talk about the *process measures*. Before doing so, however, it is appropriate to review what I mean by process measures.

PROCESS MEASURES

As you recall from Section A, after talking about the cook and his soup, I presented a description of purposes of evaluation and showed the role of process measures in each of these types. However, you now know, after reading the discussion about theories of action in Section H, that the process is more complex. There are different kinds of processes. On the one hand, there are program activities—the things that are supposed to happen within the program. I call these the *program elements*. When you start collecting the data in the evaluation, you will want to examine whether these various program attributes or elements are, in fact, present.

There is another kind of more complex process to be examined as well. Based on the program's theory of action (as depicted in the logic model), there is a belief that some kinds of mechanisms are *operative*. I refer here to a process that connects an activity with a specified outcome. When, for example, one teaches a unit in a mathematics course, why does one expect that certain outcomes will be achieved? What goes on, or is supposed to go on, in a student's head in order for that understanding to occur? I refer to this aspect of process as *program mechanisms*.

As you might intuit, these various kinds of processes have different applicability to the purposes of evaluation. I have shown this in Table O.1. As you can see, formative implementation evaluation is primarily concerned with program elements. Summative evaluation

TABLE O.1. Purposes and Types of Evaluation

Purposes of evaluation	Process		Outcomes		Primary audience
	Program elements	Program mechanisms	Interim outcomes	End-of-evaluation outcomes	
Formative implementation evaluation	×		×		Program staff
Summary formative evaluation	×	×	×	×	Program staff, stakeholders
Summative evaluation		×		×	External audience, stakeholders

is primarily concerned with program mechanisms. In a summative evaluation, it is assumed that the program has undergone extensive formative evaluation and the program elements are now in place. Thus in a summative evaluation, which generally seeks an understanding of causality, the evaluator wants to understand the program mechanisms that are producing the evaluation outcomes. Summary formative evaluation may include both program element measures as well as program mechanisms. In that instance, the program elements are examined so that lack of implementation of the program can be modified. Program mechanisms are examined not so much for issues of causality, but for determining areas where program improvement might take place.

Now that we have reexamined the types of evaluation and clarified the two kinds of process variables, let me discuss with you how they might be considered in the evaluation plan. As noted, there are program elements and program mechanisms. Let us consider each of these in turn.

PROGRAM ELEMENTS

I discussed the various program elements in Section G, when we talked about "What is a program?" In that section, I mentioned as program elements: people (personnel), materials, clients, and organizational structure. Your job in the evaluation plan is to consider how you will determine whether the program elements have been put in place. You will try to specify these potential steps, in general terms, in the evaluation plan.

Many of the more specific details of gathering these data will not be included in the plan, but will be determined when you subsequently examine the implementation of the program. However, in this section of the book, I provide an indication of some things that you will need to look for.

Consider the following as *general guidelines* for examining process variables (both program elements and program mechanisms). These guidelines should be actively employed when you will subsequently be engaged in examining program implementation. For now, reflect on them, and where appropriate, *incorporate discussion into the program plan.* That will provide a preview for your subsequent collection of data that describe the process information.

Personnel

Now let us jointly think about personnel—primarily, the program staff. Here are some questions: Have the right *number of staff* in the right categories been hired? Have there been personnel turnovers or understaffing due to a failure to hire? Does the staff present at the site have the *appropriate qualifications*? It may well be that for the program to be effective, staff need particular training or unique skills. It may be that the staff need certain cultural understandings or sensitivities. You will want to consider whether the staff is capable of taking the actions required of them in conducting the program.

Furthermore, you will want to know whether the personnel have an *understanding of the program*, an understanding of the program's goals, and facility in implementing the required program actions. *Attitudes of staff* also are important because this might constitute one of the reasons for the program elements' not being put in place. You will want to consider whether the staff is working together in an effective manner. Staff might not be willing to make changes for a variety of reasons: they might hold on to old ideas; there might be conflicts with other staff or administration; or, perhaps, they might be frustrated by trivial obstacles that occur in almost any new program.

Many of the kinds of questions about personnel appropriateness can be answered by examining the program's personnel files. Who are the staff? Are there sufficient staff? You will need to look for information on their academic training and experience. However, some personnel attributes are simply not found on paper and will require different procedures. Interviews and observations are important tools for gathering data related to personnel—and relevant to other components of the program as well. An important area to be covered in interviews is the perceptions of program staff (and the perceptions of others). Do they have appropriate feelings about participating in the program? Are they able to relate well to program clients?

Materials

Programs typically do not consist of personnel alone. Personnel employ methods that include a variety of materials. Materials include such things as computers, books, handbooks, and manuals. You will need to consider whether they are all there. Did they *arrive on time*? Note, however, that "on time" is a relative notion. Ideally, materials will arrive prior to the start of the program, so that staff can become acquainted with them and be ready for full operation when the program starts. Sometimes all materials are not needed at the start of the program, so it will be necessary to compare the time line of the program to when the materials are scheduled to be employed. You as the evaluator will need to determine the extent to which late implementation of the materials affects the program, and the extent to which the conditions are subsequently remedied.

Furthermore, it will be important to examine whether the *materials are being used*. There was a purpose for considering these as a part of the program. Program materials, like evaluations, are best when used. Nonuse means that the program is, in fact, different from what was envisaged.

Program Clients

Programs have clients—individuals who are believed to be the beneficiaries of those programs. The program was conceived with particular clients in mind. That is, when thinking about what kinds of activities, what kind of staff, what kind of materials, and how activities should be structured, these elements were designed to benefit specific program recipients. Thus it is imperative that you examine whether the "who" that the program is addressing is the "who" that had been anticipated. Are they *the right clients*—the ones that had been anticipated? Looking at the makeup of the client population is important in knowing whether the program has been implemented as intended.

What is it about the clients of the program that is important? First, you will need to determine whether their number corresponds to what is anticipated, as specified in the program plan. If there are too many clients, for example, that might be a cause for reduced effectiveness. In addition to number of clients, certain presupposed clients with particular needs, particular characteristics, or particular prior training or educational level had been anticipated. You will need to determine whether these kinds of clients were actually served. Consider, for example, an after-school enrichment program for high-performing students that was intended to improve student outcomes. However, there was an open sign-up that offered the opportunity to any student who wished to enroll. Because of this modification of the anticipated client group, it would be anticipated that the program would perform below expectations.

But beyond the question of appropriate clients, I want you to consider another issue. Are these *clients being retained*? Are clients completing the segments of the program on an appropriate schedule? Are they dropping out of the program en route? All of these are important client-related process issues that you will need to examine.

Organizational Structure

Programs have an organizational structure. Not only are there personnel, materials, and clients, there is also an activity plan that describes how they are to be coordinated and employed. Looking at the program plan, you will need to examine the *intended activities* and the *sequence* in which they occur. Questions you will need to answer include: Did these get implemented in the appropriate order? Did these get implemented in accordance with the program's time line?

Another part of the organizational structure is the program's *administration*. There are a number of issues here including whether appropriate reporting channels are being used. Do those in charge of the program know what was happening? One issue for you to consider is whether there is an active, ongoing record-keeping system. Without an active information flow, program administrators will be unable to note schedule deficiencies and seek to correct them.

What about *facilities*? Are they as anticipated? The program, to operate properly, expected a certain availability of space, and it is important to determine whether that space or comparable space was provided. For example, you might notice that the program is buried in a trailer too small in which to function. The program might not be able to operate properly if there is insufficient room to conduct the program activities as anticipated. Furthermore, while the space may be appropriate in square footage, there might have been special requirements related to configuration. You will want to note whether the space meets the needs of the anticipated program activities.

Many deficiencies in implementation of program elements may be related to a lack of appropriate *budget*. It may well be that the budget contemplated in the plan was insufficient for meeting the needs as stated. This is a plan deficiency that will need to be attended to. The more important question is whether the dollar allocation actually provided and used corresponds with what was envisaged in the program plan. In either case, this information will need to be examined so that program staff can deal with the issue. These budget issues are likely to be already known by program staff—but not necessarily by all primary stakeholders.

PROGRAM MECHANISMS

The previous discussion referred to an examination of program elements. But, as previously noted, process is more complex than that. It also refers to whether program elements (even if seemingly implemented properly) are achieving the desired results—the relevant short-term outcomes. This is the most difficult aspect of process variables.

Well, how will you do it? You will need to reexamine the program theory to see what kinds of activity–outcome relationships are anticipated. As you engage in the evaluation, you will need to consider the program theory that you described or the logic model that you might have constructed with clients (see Section H). That logic model helped to define the rationale for why different activities were taking place. Discrete activities were employed, or put in place, to achieve particular short-term ends (e.g., certain knowledge, understandings, skills, attitudes or behavior changes). And these, in turn, were designed to lead to the ability to engage in further activities. It was anticipated that this cluster of multiple activities linked to other actions would ultimately lead to the fulfillment of the program's broad goals or outcomes. Process evaluation focused on program mechanisms seeks to examine the effectiveness of these linkages. You will want to know: Did the anticipated *linkages* in the program's logic model hold up? Did they *make sense* in practice? Did conducting a particular activity lead to certain understandings, which, in turn, allowed another activity to take place efficiently? (Why not reexamine Figure H.2 to see a depiction of the implied program mechanisms for a portion of this book?)

➢ **Question:** How do you as the evaluator begin to understand this? Answer: With great difficulty. It requires selecting particular linkages in the logic model and gathering data about the results and consequences of an activity to determine whether the specific contribution had been achieved. Clearly, there are far too many conceptual linkages within the logic model to examine all of them. Moreover, some may be so complex that measuring attainment would be extremely difficult. Thus you as evaluator might only select several of them for examination based on their importance within the logic model. In doing this, consider which activities and linkages are presumed to be most important.

RECAP—SECTION O
Process Variables: What to Look At

- Program Elements
- Personnel
  - Number of staff
  - Appropriate personnel
  - Understand program
  - Staff attitudes
- Materials
  - Delivered on time
  - Are they used?
- Clients
  - The right clients (number and characteristics)
  - Retained in program
- Organizational Structure
  - Intended activities
  - Administrative procedures and information
  - Appropriate facilities
  - Appropriate budget
- Program Mechanisms
  - Program theory making sense

GAINING ADDITIONAL UNDERSTANDING
Case Study Exercise

Why not look at the RUPAS case study and list the potential implementation issues involved? I suggest that you use the Recap provided in this chapter as the headings for your listing.

Further Reading

After the program is put in place, you will proceed to examine various process variables. In essence, you will then be determining whether the program was implemented properly. The notion of *implementation evaluation* is implicit within this section. Implementation evaluation is an important topic. I believe that examining some additional readings would be beneficial. Here are some of my favorites:

King, J., Morris, L., & Fitzgibbon, C. (1987). *How to assess program implementation.* Thousand Oaks, CA: Sage.

This short monograph describes how process elements are used in examining whether programs have been properly implemented.

Saunders, R. P., Evans, M. H., & Joshi, P. (2005). Developing a process-evaluation plan for assessing health promotion program implementation: A how-to guide. *Health Promotion Practices, 6,* 134–147.

This journal article provides a framework for developing a comprehensive process evaluation plan using the case study of a health promotion intervention.

P

What Is the Evaluation Plan (Outcome Measures)?

In this section I discuss evaluation designs focusing on outcome measures. That is, how do we answer evaluation questions related to the measurement of outcomes? In Section O, I used the term "design" to refer to the description of how the evaluation would be conducted. This included the selection of individuals and instruments. It also included how data would be collected and analyzed. Designs for outcome measures can be complicated. Researchers talk about a variety of sophisticated ways for designing studies involving outcome measures.

I think it would be helpful to simplify what we'll be looking for in developing these evaluation designs. A friend and colleague of mine, Michael Patton, called my attention to a very nice quote from Rudyard Kipling about the six honest serving men of evaluation:

> I keep six honest serving men.
> They taught me all I knew:
> Their names are What and Why and When
> And How and Where and Who.

Let me consider these generic questions as the basis for describing what is included in an evaluation design. I have left off the "where" for convenience, since typically it would occur on site.

I choose to start with *why*. The evaluation design is based on the question of "why." We have a question and we want an answer. This is very important. The why of the design is based on finding an answer to a question. That is the reason I have spent so much time talking with you about what is the question—the real question.

Next, consider *what*. In this case, I will let the "what" refer to the data. What data is potentially available for answering the question? What measure can we use so that we have an answer to the question? What is the concept to be measured? The what refers not only to the concept to be measured—the measure—but also to how these data will be acquired. Will we give a test? Perhaps administer a questionnaire. Possibly observations. It could be that we will conduct interviews. The means of data acquisition, along with the concept to be measured, need to be specified.

If there is to be some data collection—that is, acquiring data—*whom* will it be obtained from? Will we be getting data only from clients of the program? Will we be getting data from other groups who are similar to those in the program being evaluated? Perhaps even from groups that have been selected in some particular way? Will we be asking for information from those who staff and administer the program? If we are concerned about the impact of the program on the community, will we be gathering data from community stakeholders?

Depending on the question that is asked there are a variety of times *when* data might be acquired. We might want to know clients' initial understandings of information to be presented within the program, thus data collection would begin when clients begin the program. We might want to know what progress clients are making, thus data would be collected at multiple intervals. Consider the necessary time schedule for measuring that progress. Are we concerned about the outcomes of the program—namely, what do clients know at the end of the program? These are "when" questions.

At this point I ask you to consider the *how*. How will the data that has been collected be aggregated? That is, will we summarize it? Will we submit it to some statistical analysis? Will we provide very detailed qualitative description? (Evaluators sometimes refer to this as "thick description.") Also, how will we decide what these aggregated or described data mean? Can we discern that the question has been answered positively, for example? This is the valuing component, and standards must be established as a part of the evaluation design that enable us to make these judgments.

AN EXERCISE TO ASSIST US

I think it might be helpful to consider some sample evaluation questions, and as we do, I ask you to examine the implications of each question for the "what," "who," "when," and "how" issues discussed above. In order to do this, I briefly describe a situational example that could provide a context for our subsequent discussion. Christina Christie and I developed a monograph for the journal *New Directions for Evaluation* that included a description of what we referred to as the Bunche–Da Vinci Learning Partnership Academy. A slightly modified and briefer version of the Bunche–Da Vinci situation follows (the full case can be found in the above journal as listed at the end of this section).

THE BUNCHE–DA VINCI PROGRAM DESCRIPTION

The Bunche–Da Vinci program is located in an elementary school in a primarily blue-collar suburb in Southern California. There's a partnership between the school district (specifically the Bunche Elementary School) and a nonprofit educational company called the Da Vinci Learning Corporation. Space does not allow for the full description of the school context, but suffice it to say that it is characterized by students with a high transiency rate, high numbers of non-English-speaking students, and a relatively inexperienced staff with high turnover. Moreover, there is a substantial discipline problem with students lacking interest and being referred to the principal's office. The Da Vinci Corporation provides the curriculum, schedules, and class size requirements. However, the program is conducted by school district staff. The curriculum consists of traditional school subjects along with an elective program. Instruction is heavily reliant on technology. As noted, many of the students are not fluent English speakers, with a little more than half of these participating in regular classes and the remaining students enrolled in a Structured English Immersion program. Student test scores at Bunche have consistently been among the lowest in the school district.

The kinds of questions that we might ask can be thought of as either "causal" or "descriptive." Causality implies that the procedure demonstrated that the intervention (the program) was responsible for the attained outcomes. Descriptive means that results or attainments are presented, but we do not know whether other factors may have been partially responsible for obtaining the results. It is exceedingly difficult to prove causality—that is, I repeat, that a program intervention was *solely* responsible for changes in the outcome. Consider for a moment the following simplistic question.

QUESTION 1: Does the Da Vinci model work?

Well, what do I mean by "work"? One must presume that the intent of the question is that the outcomes attained are meritorious or worthy and the Da Vinci program was responsible for this positive result. Namely, that the Da Vinci model caused the positive result. But I will come back to that issue. Let us first consider the issue of the positive results. We want to know whether the outcome results were valuable. How do we know what is valuable? We might look at student scores and notice that they have increased. And so this question might be rephrased.

QUESTION 2: Does the Da Vinci Program produce improved student outcomes?

But if the outcome scores are higher, does this prove that these improved outcomes were due to the Da Vinci model? Not really. Consider what else might have led to changes in outcomes. Researchers talk about various factors that weaken an evaluation design. These are factors that in some way make the intent of the design less certain. One of these is referred to as *maturation*. This is the notion that there is a natural growth in the program participants. They are getting older; they may be socially and psychologically maturing, and this improved score might be related to this maturation. There may also be other events occurring in a student's life or in their social context generally that were providing knowledge and insights that might have partially accounted for the change in outcomes. Researchers and evaluators refer to this factor as *history*. That is, students at Bunche might be participating in an after-school program that in some way enhances their learning. Or perhaps a major community event provided insights into some aspects of the curriculum. A third factor that might weaken the case for arguments of success is referred to by researchers as the *testing effect*. Simply stated, students become more test-wise. This is particularly true when they have been given a pretest.

TOWARD STRONGER CAUSAL MODELS

And so how might we compensate for these factors that potentially weaken the simplistic design that we intended? One way is that we could have two *comparison groups*, with the idea being that the same maturation, history, and testing factors would affect each of them equally. One would receive the Bunche–Da Vinci program and the other group would receive the existing program. (Note in some instances comparison groups might receive no program at all. That is not possible in Bunche School.) However, in this example, we could have the Da Vinci program implemented in some classrooms at Bunche but not in others.

What is the danger here for not being able to make causal statements? Obviously, the problem is that not all classrooms are the same. The Da Vinci classrooms might have more high-achieving students (or lower-achieving students). One solution is to give each of the classrooms a pretest in which we attempt to determine their initial status and then try to control for differences statistically. And so in this design we could have a *comparison group* that may not be exactly equivalent, and we give a pretest to see the initial differences in the group (pretest) and subsequently a test at the end (posttest). (*Pretest–posttest comparison group design.*) Now let us look at our focus questions for design analysis. Consider the following for an answer to Question 2 using a pretest–posttest comparison group design.

QUESTION 2

What data are needed?

- Academic achievement measures
- Attained through school testing

Who will the data be obtained from?

- Students in Da Vinci classrooms
- Students in comparison classrooms at Bunche

When will data be acquired?

- Beginning of school year for Da Vinci and comparison classrooms
- End of school year for Da Vinci and comparison classrooms

How will these data be analyzed?

- Statistical analysis of differences

This is a better solution, but still not a perfect one. The small number of classrooms would make statistical controls difficult. Well, then, we possibly could administer the Da Vinci program to all Bunche students and find some schools similar to Bunche to use as a comparison. I think you see what the difficulties might be here. How will we get schools that are exactly comparable? And if we could find them, imagine the difficulty of getting them to agree to have their students tested without the potential benefits of the Da Vinci program or some other compensation. Moreover, doesn't the fact that they are different schools, no matter what comparable qualities they share, ensure that some characteristics will differ?

Let's think some more about what would be a better alternative for suggesting that the Da Vinci program (and *only* the Da Vinci program) led to the improved outcomes. Researchers suggest that a design called "the posttest-only control group design" provides the strongest assurance of causality. In this design there is the necessity for random selection of participants. That is, each of the students at a grade level in Bunche would have an equal opportunity to be selected for the Da Vinci instruction or for the regular instruction. Classrooms would be filled in that manner. This design would be called a *randomized controlled trial* (RCT). This provides a better answer to Question 2. In essence, the previous response to question 2 is improved with the addition of randomization, as shown below:

R Da Vinci Classrooms → M

R Regular Classrooms → M

In this depiction, randomization takes place (as designated by the capital R); one group receives the Da Vinci program and the other the regular program. Following instructions, each group is measured on the same outcome indicator. Using this procedure eliminates the design threat of maturity. (Students in each group *presumably* mature in a comparable way.) And we partially eliminate the design threat of testing effect since no pretest is given. However, in this situation we continue to potentially face the evaluation design threat of "history," as mentioned earlier. Will students and teachers in the control classrooms not be aware of what is happening in the Da Vinci program and possibly incorporate aspects of it into their own instruction? It does not appear, then, that focusing solely on the Bunche school, even with randomization, allows us to definitively ascribe causality to the Da Vinci undertaking.

However, most of the above-mentioned design possibilities are nonetheless potentially valuable in providing insight into what is happening at the school and provide *a strong case for suggesting causality.*

Another kind of question seeks to examine progress over time or trends in particular outcomes. This is referred to by researchers as an *interrupted time-series design.* When this approach is used with a comparison group it provides causal insights. Consider the following:

QUESTION 3: Are discipline problems among Bunche–Da Vinci students declining?

This kind of question is best answered when existing data are available prior to the implementation of the program, which it would be in the Bunche case. The question is addressed by examining the trend changes over time. See, for example, Figure P.1.

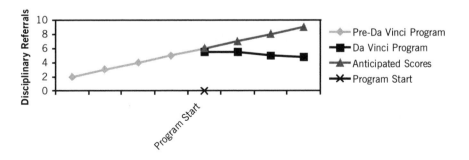

FIGURE P.1. Interrupted time-series data.

As seen in the graph, a high level of disciplinary referrals occurred prior to the start of the program. I have shown a trend line depicting the level of discipline problems prior to the start of the program. (In essence this is a line that best fits the assembled data—it fits best.) The dotted line shows the expected continuance of the trend based on pre-program data. Then I considered the number of disciplinary referrals in Da Vinci classrooms at 6-month intervals after the implementation of the program. Depicted in the graph is the variation from the established trend line. Showing the dataset would provide a visual indication of the possible impact occasioned by the implementation of the Da Vinci program versus the comparison program. Statistical procedures are available for providing a quantitative analysis of such data.

Now, why don't you fill in the chart for Question 3?

QUESTION 3

What data are needed?

- Your thoughts?

Who will data be obtained from?

- Your thoughts?

When will data be acquired?

- Your thoughts?

How will these data be analyzed?

- Your thoughts?
- (See end of section for answers.)

An offshoot of any of these questions or of many of the descriptive questions that follow might address the differential impact on different subgroups (e.g., males vs. females, different ethnic groups). This, of course, would require a focus on data about the subgroup and might have a variety of "what," "when," and "how" answers depending on the specification of the question.

Let me provide a *final* note on the issue of causal designs. Michael Scriven, a noted evaluator/philosopher, has suggested that causation can be directly seen in numerous other ways. He advocates for the systematic application of logical thinking, involving the consideration of alternatives, specification of likely causes, and careful elimination of those that do not ring true. (My words, not his.) See his article in the Further Reading of this section.

DESCRIPTIVE DESIGNS

Another question that might be asked of the Bunche–Da Vinci program is the following:

QUESTION 4: Is a greater percentage of students performing at grade level or above in reading after 1 year of the program compared with the prior year?

This is an infinitely easier question to answer. The intent of the question is not to show causality, but to *describe*. As differentiated from causal questions, the design to answer this question and others are *descriptive designs*—they describe status.

Now, back to considering this question. In this instance we have established a *standard* for judging whether the outcome is satisfactory. An examination of the percentage of students who were performing at grade level at the end of the prior year is compared with the percentage performing at or above grade level at the end of the program year. Similar questions that involve standards might stipulate different expectations related, perhaps, to the mean grade-level performance or to other specifically stated standards. For example, did students know more about technology at the end of the year than at the beginning? Did 80% of the students learn how to access and use the Internet?

Read the above question and provide answers to our "working people" questions.

QUESTION 4

What data are needed?

- Your thoughts?

Who will data be obtained from?

- Your thoughts?

When will data be acquired?

- Your thoughts?

How will these data be analyzed?

- Your thoughts?
- (See end of section for answers.)

The following is another situation entailing questions that we might want to ask about the Bunche–Da Vinci program. This also may be considered as a descriptive design.

QUESTION 5: Do students, parents, teachers, and administrators believe that the program is performing in a satisfactory manner?

If students are dissatisfied with the program this is important to know. Perhaps the heavy technical engagement in the learning of mathematics is making students more math-phobic. Do parents believe that their child is benefiting from the program? Do they feel that their child is more (or perhaps less) interested in school? Similar questions could be asked about teachers and administrators. In essence this is a *one-time snapshot* of some outcome of interest. For this question, you would want to employ surveys, interviews, or possibly focus groups. Obviously, not everyone would be interviewed or participate in a focus group, and so careful selections would need to be made.

QUESTION 5

What data are needed?

- Your thoughts?

Who will data be obtained from?

- Your thoughts?

When will data be acquired?

- Your thoughts?

How will these data be analyzed?

- Your thoughts?
- (See end of section for answers.)

You will note in the above example that there was no standard set, as in the previous question. That is, the basis for judging whether the program was "performing in a satisfactory manner" was not specified. The evaluation design simply referred to describing status and did not imply a basis for making a judgment.

This kind of question, which describes but does not set a standard for judging, is also typical for what I have described earlier as short term, or interim outcomes (remember that term from the table in Section O). A program might have a great number of potential interim outcomes, and the evaluator and program staff would be hard pressed to prejudge acceptability.

Let us now consider another kind of design. To do so I draw from (and slightly modify) the question posed by Jennifer Greene in the *New Directions of Evaluation* volume, related to the Bunche–Da Vinci case.

QUESTION 6: How well are the particular needs of children eligible for Title I, special education, and English language instruction being met by the in-class model of integrated services?

Greene proposed to investigate this question by an *intensive case study design.* Case studies are intended to describe something in great depth. They demand a careful examination of the situation with a full understanding of the context and the use of multiple perspectives. Typically, multiple qualitative methodologies are employed in order to obtain these understandings. Thus a case study design might use observations, interviews, focus groups, or existing datasets. Occasionally, quantitative data help in gaining a fuller understanding of a particular case. Causal designs and some other descriptive designs are more easily depicted and provide more straightforward answers to questions.

The intensive case study conducted by Jennifer Greene was primarily a qualitative design. Such designs seek to holistically comprehend the variety of stakeholder perceptions and experiences. Case studies provide more in-depth understanding and a fuller, more complete and complex picture of the situation. Qualitative instruments provide the basis for developing detailed and rich descriptions of the situation being studied.

So, for the question above, let us refer again to the four essential questions that define a design. Descriptions are less easily depicted for qualitative designs because qualitative practitioners view the design as "emerging"—continually open to modification. (I personally believe that the notion of openness and possibility of modification is, or should be, a characteristic of all descriptive designs, as the evaluator seeks to be relevant and useful.) And so the "what," "who," "when," and "how"— the "working people" of evaluation—for qualitative designs may only be stated tentatively and be subject to change as the evaluation progresses. Rather than put these answers in a "box," I discuss them more fully in narrative style.

Of these "working people," perhaps the most important to consider here is the "who." In most respects, all qualitative studies are case studies. The investigation may be an expansive case study, as proposed by Greene, or smaller, less intensive cases. Moreover, all case studies consist of subcase studies embedded within them. If there are interviews to be conducted, *who* is to be interviewed? If there are observations, then the "who" may refer to groups (grammatically, that is a "which"). So perhaps the major question for qualitative evaluations is related to the selection of cases (or subcases) to be studied.

A FEW WORDS ABOUT SELECTION

I pause here to reiterate a few comments on how individuals or groups might be selected. A technical aside, so to speak. In selecting individuals or groups, you must again be guided by the question along with the political/social context that surrounds the question. You want to select cases that will yield the most information related to your question. In some situations, having a great deal of heterogeneity will help to capture themes that cut across all individuals or groups. Perhaps your question deals with how particular subpopulations are engaging in the process or performing, and so you would be guided by this. Perhaps it is important to provide a single case in very rich detail, and focusing on a "typical" case would be most helpful. Possibly, to be convincing to potential users of the evaluation report, it is important to focus on politically important or otherwise critical cases. Another selection procedure sometimes employed is called snowball sampling (think of a snowball rolling downhill). The idea here is to have the *most* information. Each respondent is asked to suggest others who know a lot about the topic of interest. These are but a few suggestions related to case selection strategies. Ultimately, you must be guided in your thoughtful selection by the concern for the issue that is to be addressed and what evidence will be persuasive.

And now to return to the *who*. In this case, my variation of Greene's study, I might recommend interviewing teachers, administrators, and parents. The teacher group would be a sample representative of the diversity of faculty in experience, education, race, and ethnicity. The number of administrators at the Bunche School is quite small, so all of them might be interviewed. Parents might be interviewed in focus groups consisting of five to 10 parents each. Each group would be relatively homogeneous, especially having groups of parents with children in Title I, special education, or not having English fluency. Of course, the students who are the "who" in this case are those eligible for Title I, special education, and lacking English fluency. Another kind of "who"—although not really "who"—is the classes to be observed.

What is *what*? That is, what data are to be acquired? From teachers and administrators we might seek their perceptions of the effectiveness of the program for the school's population, generally, as well as for the targeted student groups. From parents we might focus on perceptions about their child's learning experiences. For students, we might want test scores by subgroup and by special skill area, over time. For classrooms, we may choose intense observation of one representative class per grade level to note such things as character of services provided, time allocated to different subject areas, and engagement of different kinds of children in the curriculum.

When? Interviews should take place some time between the mid- and end-of-school year. Classroom observations would be made about once a week for half of the school day during the months of October, November, February, and April. Test score analysis will take place after the return of year-end test results.

How? How analyzed? Data analyses are of various types. A full description of applicable procedures for quantitative and qualitative data analysis are presented in Sections Q and R. But briefly, in the case of observation data, systematic evaluation of field notes will provide a portrait of what goes on in classrooms. Interview data will be carefully scrutinized in order to determine descriptions by stakeholders, in their own words, of what transpires in the program. These will be synthesized into persisting themes. Test scores will be examined to identify strengths and weaknesses of the various subgroups of students.

MIXED METHODS

Evaluators have recently given prominence to a concept called "mixed methods." The reasoning behind mixed methods is straightforward. It starts with the notion that there is *no single design* for most evaluations. There may be different designs related to specific evaluation questions and not a single design for all questions. Second, the idea of mixed methods proposes that any question might require *multiple methods* of different types.

Consider the first of these. Designs should match the question, the information needs of stakeholders, and the possibilities of the program context. Because an evaluation consists of multiple questions to be answered, a program evaluation may consist of many traditionally thought-of designs, each concerned with answering a specific question. Moreover, it is possible that one basic design may apply to multiple questions.

Furthermore, answering a single evaluation question may require multiple measures. For example, when a concept embedded within a question is complex, or difficult to measure, then multiple complementary approaches might be employed to examine the various facets of the question. In doing so, the evaluator would gain the required understanding needed to respond properly to the question.

You as the evaluator should be guided by our four questions. For example, many times I have used a questionnaire to acquire a general overview of views and perceptions of a particular stakeholder group. Then, armed with insights provided by the survey about ambiguities, disagreements, or less-than-fulfilling understandings, I engaged in conducting interviews on specific topic areas. Sometimes, instead of interviews, focus groups were used. Possibly quantitative or documentary records added further insight.

The simplistic message related to mixed methods that I wish to convey to you is this: (1) an evaluation does not typically have to have a single design; (2) individual questions are guided by a design based on the four design attributes (what, who, when, how); (3) moreover, a single question may require multiple designs and certainly multiple measures. This is not a difficult message for you who have been reading this book. It captures what I have been preaching throughout. The reason why the topic of mixed methods arises in the evaluation profession is because there are many experienced evaluators who approach the field with a particular paradigm preference that they find difficulty escaping from; that is, "I do experimental studies," or "I am a great fan of qualitative methods." See, aren't you glad that you are new to evaluation, so that you can start out with a fresh look!

SUMMARY

I have taken great latitude in the traditional descriptions of designs in order to make them more accessible. I believe that I have presented a correct representation of traditionally discussed designs. To recap, I presented several of the more commonly used causal designs, including a brief discussion of what is called the interrupted time-series design. Furthermore, I have suggested several situations where descriptive designs are applicable. Then I commented on the case study procedure, which I choose to call another design type. Finally, I indicated that you might answer questions more ably by using mixed methods. Each question might require its own method, and some questions might require multiple approaches.

RECAP 2—SECTION P
Evaluation Design

- Guiding Principle (What, Who, When, How)
- Some Causal Designs
  - Pretest–posttest comparison group
  - Posttest-only control group
  - Interrupted time-series design
- Some Descriptive Design Situations
  - For example, a specified standard to be met
  - For example, one-time snapshot (i.e., attitudes)
- Intensive Case Study
- Mixed Methods

> *My Advice:* Where do you go from here? You certainly may refer to further readings at the end of the section for more in-depth knowledge—and I would encourage that. However, most evaluations that you might do will be descriptive; in small-scale program evaluations you will probably not be seeking to determine causality. As a general rule, I urge you not to get caught up in design titles. At this time, I suggest that you direct your attention to thinking about design as focused on "why" (to answer questions) and then be guided by the four design questions: what, who, when, and how.

———— ANSWERS TO QUESTIONS 3–5 ————

Reference: Bunche–Da Vinci program

Alkin, M. C., & Christie, C. A. (Eds.). (2005). *Theorists' models in action* (New Directions for Evaluation, No. 106). San Francisco: Jossey-Bass.

QUESTION 3: Are discipline problems among Bunche–Da Vinci students declining?

What data are needed?
Disciplinary referral rate.

Who will data be obtained from?
Bunche–Da Vinci students.

When will data be acquired?

Eight different points in time.

How will these data be analyzed?

Comparing data after start of program with trend line.

QUESTION 4: Is a greater percentage of students performing at grade level or above in reading after 1 year of the program compared with the prior year?

What data are needed?

Percent of students performing at grade level or above in reading.

Who will data be obtained from?

Bunche–Da Vinci students.

When will data be acquired?

Scores at end of program year and end of prior year.

How will these data be analyzed?

Direct comparison of percentages.

QUESTION 5: Do students, parents, teachers, and administrators believe that the program is performing in a satisfactory manner?

What data are needed?

Attitude measure related to satisfaction with program.

Who will data be obtained from?

Sampling of students, parents, teachers, administrators of Bunche–Da Vinci program.

When will data be acquired?

Any specified time (most likely middle or end of program year).

How will these data be analyzed?

Summary of data by group. Examination of individual items.

──── GAINING ADDITIONAL UNDERSTANDING ────

Case Study Exercise

In the Section O case study exercise, you looked at those questions that dealt with process. Now turn to those questions from Sections I and N that focused on outcome measures. Write each question down and for each of them answer the "working person" questions: What? Who? When? How?

Further Reading

Caracelli, V. J., & Greene, J. C. (1997). Crafting mixed-method evaluation designs. In J. C. Greene & V. J. Caracelli (Eds.), *Advances in mixed-method evaluations: The challenges and benefits of integrating diverse paradigms* (New Directions for Evaluation, No. 74, pp. 19–32). San Francisco: Jossey-Bass.

Caracelli and Greene provide a well-rounded and accessible discussion about mixed methods and evaluation designs at the conceptual and applied levels.

Cook, T. D. (2006). Describing what is special about the role of experiments in contemporary educational research?: Putting the "gold standard" rhetoric into perspective. *Journal of MultiDisciplinary Evaluation, 3*(6), 1–7. Available at *evaluation.wmich.edu/jmde/JMDE_Num006.html*.

Tom Cook has played an important role in the development of experimental and quasi-experimental methods. This article helps to put some of the current discussion of the role of experiments in perspective.

Mark, M., & Henry, G. T. (2006). Methods for policy-making and knowledge development evaluations. In I. F. Shaw, J. C. Greene, & M. Mark (Eds.), *Sage handbook of evaluation*. Thousand Oaks, CA: Sage.

While mentioning noncausal models including case studies, this chapter focuses on a complete description of causal models.

Scriven, M. (2008). A summative evaluation of RCT methodology: An alternative approach to causal research. *Journal of MultiDisciplinary Evaluation, 5*(9), 11–24. Available at *www.jmde.com*.

This is a marvelously complete discussion disputing many of the claims that are made for RCTs.

Q

What Is the Evaluation Plan (Procedures and Agreements)?

In the previous two sections we talked about the evaluation design and recognized that it is a portion of a total evaluation plan. The evaluation plan in its totality is intended as a description of how the evaluation will be conducted. In part, this description reflects evaluation activities that have already been completed in preparation for developing the design. In part, also, it specifies and anticipates aspects of the evaluation yet to come. This is fully depicted in Figure Q.1. In the evaluation plan, you will need to provide some general insights into how these activities will take place.

EVALUATION ACTIVITIES: PAST, PRESENT, AND UPCOMING

As can be seen, the different evaluation activities take place at various stages throughout the process of conducting the evaluation. Activities 1, 2, and 3 are primarily conducted in the preplanning stage of getting acquainted with the program, its context, and its stakeholders. This is indicated by the word "primary" in the preplanning column. Attention also is paid to these activities subsequently, as indicated by check marks.

Activities 4–7 primarily occur during a "getting started" phase of the evaluator's work. This is indicated by the word "primary" in that column. I have presented details related to Activities 1–7 in our previous discussion.

Activities 8 and 9, pertaining to this section and the prior two, are devoted to writing the plan down. In Activity 8 (Sections O and P), I discussed with you the technical aspects of the evaluation design. I focused on the collection of process measures and on the general methodology for considering outcome data to be collected (what), from whom the data will be collected (who), the schedule for data collection (when), and how data will be analyzed and valued (how). In this section, I follow up by suggesting how activities to be subsequently conducted (such as data analysis) are to be previewed within the evaluation plan. The full discussion of data analysis will be presented in subsequent sections, but it is necessary to provide an indication within the evaluation plan of how that might take place. In this section, too, I will deal with some of the procedures of conducting the evaluation, including agreements to be reached.

Activities 10–13, analyzing the data continuing through to the activity of helping the stakeholder to use the results, are only anticipated at this stage of the plan development. The evaluator's job is to describe how each activity *might* take place. As indicated in Figure Q.1 (previously presented in the overview), these activities primarily occur in the "executing the plan" phase of the evaluation.

Three further listings in Figure Q.1 describe the aids to getting it done properly. One of these refers to the evaluation standards, which is discussed in Section X. It is important that the evaluation plan be constructed in a manner consistent with the standards of the profession. Section E, which we have already discussed, indicates the importance of maintaining positive stakeholder relationships. Another item listed in the "aids" section refers to managing the evaluation. Indeed, an important part of the evaluation plan is the description of the management concerns related to conducting the evaluation—including the various interactions, requirements, and responsibilities.

One additional evaluation option is presented. This is an evaluation activity that might or might not be a part of the evaluation. I refer here to a cost analysis study. I have listed this as taking place primarily in the "executing the plan" phase, but if it indeed takes place, it should be discussed in the evaluation plan.

Evaluation activity	Section in which it is discussed	The evaluation plan stages			
		Preplanning stage	Getting started on the plan	Writing the plan down	Executing the plan
1. Identifying Stakeholders	Section D	Primary	✓	✓	✓
2. Gaining Understanding of the Organizational/ Social/ Political Context	Section F	Primary	✓	✓	✓
3. Describing the Program	Section G	Primary	✓	✓	✓
4. Understanding the Program	Section H		Primary	✓	✓
5. Developing Initial Evaluation Questions	Section I		Primary	✓	✓
6. Considering Possible Instrumentation	Section J Section K Section L Section M		Primary	✓	✓
7. Determining Evaluable Questions	Section N		Primary	✓	✓
8. Finalizing the Evaluation Plan (Design)	Section O Section P			Primary	✓
9. Determining Procedural Aspects of the Plan	Section Q			Primary	✓
10. Analyzing Data	Section R Section S			✓	Primary
11. Answering Evaluation Questions	Section T			✓	Primary
12. Reporting Evaluation Results	Section U			✓	Primary
13. Helping Stakeholders to Use the Results	Section V	✓	✓	✓	Primary
Aids to getting it done properly					
Maintaining Relationships with Stakeholders	Section E	✓	✓	✓	✓
Managing the Evaluation	Section W		✓	Primary	Primary
Abiding by Appropriate Evaluation Standards	Section X	✓	✓	✓	✓
Additional evaluation option					
Conducting a Cost Analysis	Section Y	✓	✓	✓	✓

FIGURE Q.1. Evaluation activities by stage.

THE WRITTEN EVALUATION PLAN

In the previous sections I discussed the evaluation design. Now it is time to add to this design the procedural aspects of the evaluation review. Some of these we have already talked together about, but now it is time to *write them down*. Let us examine the various issues that need to be considered and incorporated into the evaluation plan. Please examine the following list:

Procedures and Agreements

- What is the time frame of the evaluation and the resources available?
- Yet again, are the questions and design appropriate?
- What are the implications for an appropriate time line?
- What staff resources will be required to conduct the evaluation?
- What space will be needed?
- What equipment and materials will be needed?
- What is the schedule for reporting and the required products?
- What are the organization's administrative procedures?
- What are the responsibilities of the program and of the evaluator?
- How will differences be resolved?
- What are the standards for judging the evaluation?

Perhaps the first thing to do is to make sure that there is agreement about the *time frame* of the evaluation and the *resources* available. When does the evaluation begin? When does it end? What financial resources are available? In many instances the evaluation would have begun prior to the development of the evaluation plan. The evaluator might have been hired based on a program proposal, which was subsequently subject to revision. Or the evaluator might have been hired with the idea that a part of the evaluation process involves the development of evaluation questions and the evaluation plan. Presumably also, the designated amount of financial resources available should have been agreed upon. But this needs to be clarified.

You have engaged the program's primary stakeholders in a process of (one hopes) constructing a logic model and (certainly) the development of evaluation questions presumed to be evaluable. And you have developed an evaluation design appropriate for acquiring answers to those questions. One further double-check is not inappropriate. Do a *final review* of *questions* and the *design* selected for answering those questions. Is this what they really want? Engage the primary stakeholders in considering the shortcomings and strengths of the methods for answering the evaluation questions. Better now than to be criticized later. This may seem redundant, but its importance bears further repeating.

In considering the design, determine what an appropriate *time line* would be for accomplishing each of the evaluation tasks. Are there instruments that need to be further developed? When will this take place? When will data collection take place related to each of the questions? How much time will be required for data analysis, valuing, and writing a final report? What modifications need to take place in order for everything to be accomplished by the end of the contract year? An example or prototype time line is to be found in Section W, "How Are Evaluations Managed?" After all, a time line is the device you will use to manage—to know that you are on schedule.

Now that you have an idea of a potential time line, it is important to consider further the *evaluation staff resources* that will be needed to conduct the evaluation. You probably have already engaged staff, or at least thought about it. But the development of the time line may point out the necessity for extra staff at some point. It may demonstrate the need for certain staff capabilities. Furthermore, will you need additional staff to assist in data collection?

What *space* will be necessary to accomplish the evaluation? Presumably, you have some office space available for staff to work comfortably on the project. This should be discussed and included in the plan. But will you need physical space at the program site?

What *equipment and materials* will be needed for the evaluation? Will you need computers or equipment for administering tests or questionnaires? Will these need to be available and easily accessed? You should consider whether you have necessary access to computers and computer programs to perform the appropriate quantitative or qualitative analyses. Don't forget materials. Test instruments might need to be purchased. Who will bear the cost? Think now of what other materials might be required.

You need to consider and reach agreement on *report requirements* and *required products*. What reports are expected and when? Is there a specific report format that is anticipated? Who is responsible for printing written reports? How, and to whom, will they be distributed? What are the dates when reports, of all types—written or oral—are expected?

A very important element in the proposal relates to the program's *administrative procedures*. Many an evaluation has been unsuccessful because the evaluators did not determine ahead of time what administrative procedures would be required in order to conduct various activities within the evaluation. Whom do you report to? Who authorizes data collection? How will scheduling take place? Are there administrative constraints that might cause impediments to the evaluation?

It is extremely important to clarify the *responsibilities of the program* as well as the *responsibilities of the evaluator*. This is not an issue that you want to have to negotiate during the process of collecting data. Will program staff members schedule the required interviews, for example? Will the staff members or administrator of the program be responsible for assuring that program participants are available during data collection periods? Generally, will the primary stakeholders and others cooperate with the evaluation and provide necessary assistance? Other matters that I have referred to earlier also pertain here. Who will print reports? Will space be provided at the site?

As the evaluation proceeds there may be a need to modify elements of the evaluation. Perhaps the data collection will become too time consuming. Possibly, also, there will be dropouts from the program that in some way affect the design. There may be differences of opinion about who has what responsibility. A procedure for considering *how disputes will be resolved* is an important element of the evaluation plan. Admittedly, as careful as you are to be inclusive, whatever is written will not completely address the resolution of differences. But some attempt at addressing this issue is worthwhile.

When you do an evaluation, you obviously want to do a job that is considered "well done." What *standards* will the program client employ in making *judgments* about the evaluation? I refer not to the standards for judging program outcomes, but the standards for judging you and your work. What will it take to get a pat on the back and a statement "job well done"? Actually, it doesn't quite happen that way, but you get what I mean.

The evaluation plan is an agreed-on prescription of what you will do in the evaluation, what others will do, and how a successful evaluation can be achieved. In lieu of a recap of what we have discussed, see the list earlier in this section. Read the list and test yourself on how much detail you can remember!

THE CONTRACT

The evaluation usually needs to be formalized by agreement on a contract. The full evaluation plan specifies what you will do in the evaluation. Although many of the issues discussed above may simply be handled by a memorandum of understanding or in other ways agreed on verbally, there is a need for a *formal contract*. To the extent possible, many of these above issues could be included in that contract. The contract also would include a detailed *budget*. This is discussed further in Section W. Other items of the program plan should also be recognized as having been agreed on. One way to do this is to refer to the program plan within the contract. This assures that the content of the plan, including the evaluation design, is acknowledged and affirmed by both parties to the contract.

One other issue that needs to be raised relates to the timing of obtaining a contract for the evaluation. Indeed, the process might have been quite different from the way I have detailed it in this book. You might have written a program proposal in order to have been selected to do the evaluation. That is, there may have been an earlier program proposal. A contract may have been written based on that earlier proposal. And what might be required at this point would simply be an *updating* of that *earlier contract* based on your further understanding of the program. Modifications might also be merited based on program stakeholders' better understanding of their program and the importance of questions to them. (Thanks to your good work.)

> ➤ *My Advice:* Many evaluators insist on the creation of ponderous contracts that seemingly cover everything. I do not concur. Of course, when you are dealing with a governmental agency they usually have a required contract form. In such instances, reference should be made to the evaluation plan. For small projects, I prefer minimal contracts and greater flexibility. *Trust is important.* If you do not feel that those you are dealing with are trustworthy, don't do the evaluation.

GAINING ADDITIONAL UNDERSTANDING

Case Study Exercise

Examine the evaluation design issues posed in Sections O and P. Also, consider the potential procedural issues that need to be addressed for this RUPAS evaluation. Consider what might be necessary issues on which you need to gain agreement in doing this evaluation. The case description and your prior case exercise work might not provide you with as much information as you would like, but try listing some of these issues. You might use the items noted in the list earlier in this section as a starting point.

Further Reading

Stufflebeam, D. L. (2004). Evaluation Contracts Checklist. Kalamazoo, MI: Evaluation Center, Western Michigan University. Available at *www.wmich. edu/evalctr/checklists.*

Daniel Stufflebeam has done an incredibly complete job developing this checklist for evaluator contracts. In my opinion, it's "over the top," but use it as a general guide.

Stufflebeam, D. L. (2004). Evaluation Design Checklist. Available at *www. wmich.edu/evalctr/checklists.*

This is an excellent checklist addressing issues at all phases of the evaluation, but particularly helpful for this section of the book.

SECTION

R

How Are
Quantitative Data Analyzed?

Okay, I know that you're already thinking about the "S" word. Statistics! But don't worry; there will be no formulas in this section, and *statistics* is not a nasty word. Here, I provide you with some general understandings about statistics and explain a few terms and talk with you about how to get started and how to think about handling quantitative data. And finally, I provide some general guidelines for what kinds of analyses are appropriate, given different types of data. For the serious "heavy" stuff, you will need to consult the references at the end of this chapter or take a statistics course (or both).

Now to get started. By now you should know what I am about to say in the next sentence. *You must be guided by the questions* to be answered—what are you trying to find out? You need to consider how the data that you have acquired might be examined so that they will shed light on those questions. What are the outcomes that you want to examine (*dependent variables*)? What are the activities or predictors that you believe contributed to the attainment of those outcomes (*independent variables*)? Clearly, you should have considered these issues prior to collecting the data.

First, however, a little explanation about some statistical terms is necessary.

TYPES OF DATA

What kind of data do you have? The kind of data analysis that will be possible is determined by the kind of data that you have. So let's talk about three different levels (or kinds) of data. The three levels that I will discuss are *nominal* data, *ordinal* data, and *interval* data. Another level of data is referred to as *ratio data*. Ratio data are similar to interval data, but are distinguished by having present a 0 on the scale. A 0 indicates the complete absence of a the construct being measured. For purposes of this analysis, I will not make the distinction between interval and ratio data.

Nominal data means that the data are named; they constitute a category. For example, a questionnaire that asks ethnicity and provides response possibilities of Caucasian, African American, Hispanic, and so forth is creating nominal data categories.

Ordinal data implies that the data follow some order—a rank order. Remember again the Likert scale that I mentioned in an earlier section. There is a ranking or an order implied. "Strongly agree" is more agreeable than "agree," which in turn is more agreeable than "neutral." While there is an order, a rank order, to these data, there is no equal distance implied. For example, how much better is a "strongly agree" response than "agree"? Is it the same amount of "betterness" as "disagree" is to "strongly disagree"?

Interval data share the notion of rank order with ordinal data, but in addition create equal intervals. That is, the distance between comparative points on the scale is the same. The distance between 75 feet and 80 feet is the same as the distance between 85 and 90 feet. A temperature of 90° is 5° warmer than 85°, as is 80° as compared to 75°. Not surprisingly, these data are sometimes also called *numerical data*.

A FIRST ACQUAINTANCE WITH THE DATA

The first step in understanding and describing data is to make them more accessible. This can be done by listing the data in order. For example, if the data are nominal (e.g., ethnic categories), then each of the categories can be listed, and you might tabulate how many times each category occurs in the data. If the data are interval, then each of the numbers would be listed with an indication of how many times each had occurred. You would be creating what is called a *frequency table* (i.e., how frequently each response was made).

For interval data, it is also helpful to look at the *relative position* of scores in a frequency distribution. A person's relative position in a group may be portrayed by indicating what percentage of the people in a group has a score less than him/her (assuming that more is better). This is referred to as the *percentile rank*. Relative position might also be indicated by *deciles* (think 10) and *quartiles* (think 25). In essence, being in the first decile means being in the first (or lowest) 10%. And the third quartile means being somewhere between 50% and 75%.

MEASURES OF CENTRAL TENDENCY

In statistics, measures of central tendency are a way of telling what category is most frequently listed, or what category is average, or what category is in the middle of the distribution. For nominal data, the best descriptor of central tendency is what is called the *mode*. Mode simply is another way of saying "style" or "typical." For example, when we say "pie à la mode" we simply are saying pie in the prevailing fashion or style—namely, with ice cream. And so a question about mode for nominal data is, "Of the categories depicting ethnicity for participants, which one is most frequently represented?"

Now, what about a measure of central tendency for ordinal data? Think, for example, of an ordinal variable that consists of five categories from "strongly agree" to "strongly disagree." Clearly, we could describe the frequency distribution in terms of the mode—the most frequently mentioned category. But we are able to go beyond that. We could find the *median*. Median simply means middle (think of the median on a highway). What is the middle score? If responses were collected from 35 people on the "strongly agree" to "strongly disagree" scale, what was the 18th highest score?

Interval data introduce additional possibilities because they create equal intervals—these are numbers, and numbers is where statistics really get going. Of course, a mode or a median can be found for an array of interval data. But with interval data it is possible to calculate a *mean*. A mean is simply an average. What is the average grade in the class? A mean is calculated by adding all of the scores together and then dividing by the number of participants.

MEASURES OF VARIABILITY

What about *variability*? The question here is how much the scores are dispersed or spread out. Not much can be said about variability related to nominal data because they are distinct categories. On the other hand, ordinal data can be looked at in terms of their *range* (i.e., what is the lowest response and the highest response). "Oh, the scores ranged from strongly agree to strongly disagree." But that doesn't really tell you much. To get a better sense of the entire dataset's distribution, you might consider looking at the *interquartile range*—the distance between the first and third quartiles. This will tell you where the bulk of the data lie.

The range of interval data does provide some meaningful information. It provides an indication of the numerical distance from the highest score to the lowest score. However, a better indicator of variability for interval data is a statistic called the *standard deviation*. This is a number representing the spread of the scores around the mean. This statistic is important in understanding the data and subsequently calculating the probability that the results shown are real and not attained simply by chance. Given the assumption of a *normal distribution*, approximately 68% of the scores will fall within the interval encompassed by one standard deviation on each side of the mean, and 96% within two standard deviations (see Figure R.1, below).

GETTING FURTHER ACQUAINTED WITH THE DATA

Let's stop for a moment and talk about these words *normal distribution*. A normal distribution is found when the data form a bell-shaped curve, as found in Figure R.1. The reason why normality is important is because most statistics are based on assumptions of normality. Remember the undergraduate courses where the professor "graded on the curve"—so many percent "A," so many percent "B," and so on? Note that in a normal distribution, the mean, median, and mode are the same. Non-normal distributions typically are caused by the presence of *outliers* in the dataset. These are data points that stand too far off from where all others are clumped. Leaving outliers in the database in your analysis might lead to results that are *skewed*—results that appear to be higher or lower than what is actually present. For example, in Figure R.2, where the distribution is negatively skewed (or skewed to the left), the most typical score (mode) is greater than the middle score (median) and the average score (mean). On the other hand, in Figure R.3, where the distribution is positively skewed—that is, skewed to the right—the mode is less than the median and the mean. These results might be caused by outliers—scores that are vastly different from the rest of the data.

Understanding the distribution of the data, including whether data are normally distributed, is essential. If it is a *small dataset* (one that you feel that you can handle manually), then you can look at the

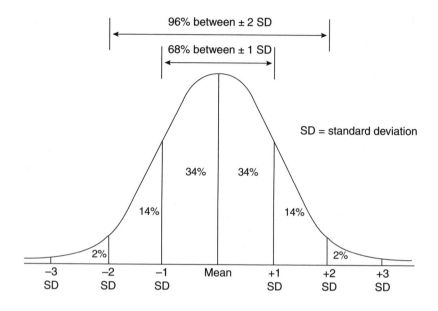

FIGURE R.1. Normal curve.

responses. Are there some data that clearly don't make sense? If there are "outliers," their presence can lead to a non-normal distribution. You might want to go back and check on whether the outliers are typographical mistakes. Suppose that your population (the group of people from whom you collected the data) were high school students and you see a data item that lists an age of 10, or an age of 32; clearly, these are incorrect data. Are there other responses that simply don't make sense? If you can bring clarity to a particular data response, then do so; otherwise, you may need to delete that response.

Another kind of problem is determining how to deal with missing data. That is, perhaps a respondent failed to answer one question. Researchers suggest several approaches to handling this. One of them is simply to assign the average response, across all subjects, to that location. Another is to not consider the response.

These activities are referred to as "cleaning the data." You are simply getting the data in a form that is more workable. Are there surprises in what you have observed so far? Are the surprises sufficient to lead you to question the data? If so, see what else you can do to clarify the data on hand.

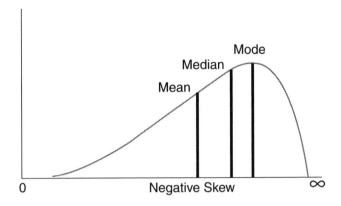

FIGURE R.2. Negative skew.

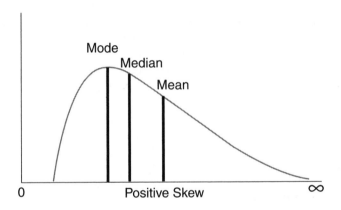

FIGURE R.3. Positive skew.

If it is a *large dataset*, then instead of dealing with the data manually, you will want to enter it into a computer database for ease of subsequent handling. There are a number of options that you might then use. *Microsoft Excel*, for example, provides a way to handle most of the simple statistics of data manipulations. Specialized statistical programs are needed for more complicated analyses (e.g., SPSS, Stata).

First, you will want to determine disparities in the data. You might start by looking at how people typically answered the questions you asked. You will want to calculate the mean and standard deviation in order to determine whether the data are normally distributed. You will check outliers, as above. Before taking those outlier data points out, you want to go back and check whether any were actually typographical mistakes.

DESCRIPTIVE AND INFERENTIAL STATISTICS

Now it is important to consider whether the data were acquired from the total population or a sample of the population. If the *total population* (all participants) constitutes the dataset, then it is adequate to use various descriptive methods of depicting or describing what the program looks like. In this case, simple tables showing the number of responses in each category of nominal or ordinal data can be appropriate. Or if you are trying to show the relationship between datasets, you can use tables called *cross-tabulations*. This will allow you, for example, to depict the number of females who reported one of the categories from "strongly agree" to "strongly disagree" in relation to the number of males at each of those same ordinal levels (see Table R.1).

Another option is to determine the *correlation* between two variables; that is, the strength and direction of their relationship. This, of course, requires two variables that have *numbers*—interval data. If two variables have a strong positive correlation, then one increases in value as the other increases, as in Figure R.4. On the other hand, if two variables are negatively correlated, then as one variable increases in value, the other decreases (see Figure R.5). Finally, as illustrated in Figure R.6, if two variables are not related in any way, then this is called a zero correlation.

These different values and ways of displaying data are called *descriptive statistics*. Again, if you have data from a total population, simply describing the data using descriptive statistics may be the appropriate way to proceed. If the data are interval, then you might

TABLE R.1. Cross-Tabulation

Scale	Gender	
	Male	Female
Strongly agree	20	25
Agree	15	10
Disagree	15	15
Strongly disagree	50	50

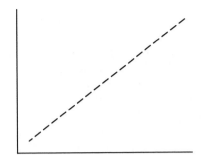

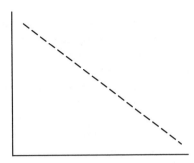

FIGURE R.4. Strong positive correlation.   **FIGURE R.5.** Strong negative correlation.

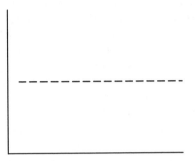

FIGURE R.6. Zero correlation.

want to provide the mean or median, for example. And you might want to provide the standard deviation as a descriptor of variability.

ARE THE RESULTS SIGNIFICANT?

In some instances, you might want to *infer* that the findings from your study are generalizable—that is, that they apply to other populations in other places. You will need to use statistical procedures that allow you to make such inferences. In that case, you might need to use what is referred to as *inferential statistics*.

Even if you are not seeking to generalize your findings to other contexts, as would be the case in most formative evaluations, it might be appropriate to use inferential statistics. Suppose, for example, that you were unable to give a test or a survey to everyone from the larger population at your program site. Instead, you used a sampling procedure—an appropriate sampling procedure—to obtain data from a small group of people (a *sample*) whom you think represent the larger group. Then you would need to statistically determine whether you can infer that the results obtained from the sample would apply to your entire program (the *population*). You want determine that data from the sample adequately reflected the total site population.

Not surprisingly, the methods appropriate for determining whether differences are *statistically significant* depend on the level of data and the nature of the comparison that you seek to make. Thus you might want to examine a single item and determine, for example, whether the differences between the number of people "satisfied" is statistically different from the number "dissatisfied." Is it appropriate to suggest that the differences found in the sample are sufficiently large so that you can say with assurance that they apply to the total population? You want to determine the statistical probability that the differences did not occur simply by chance. You might, for example, say that you would not accept the results as "significant" unless there was a 5% or less probability that it was a chance occurrence.

Or you might want to look at multiple sets of values and examine whether, for example, satisfaction from "strongly agree" to "strongly disagree" differs statistically between students at different grade levels. Is the pattern of "satisfaction with school" different for high school seniors than freshmen? Each of the combinations of nominal/ordinal/interval variables will trigger, in combination with your research questions, particular statistical techniques that might be appropriate. Moreover, whether one or more independent and dependent variables are to be included will lead to different statistical techniques that are to be used.

APPROPRIATE STATISTICAL TECHNIQUES

As always, we start with the *questions*. Imagine that you are doing an evaluation. Table R.2 shows some questions that you might need to answer in doing an evaluation. Now I want you to examine each of the questions in Table R.2 thoroughly before reading what else I have to say about each question. (*Stop now* and just read each question—the first column only.) Furthermore, it is important before you proceed that you fully understand the distinctions between nominal, ordinal, and interval data. If you need to review, please refresh your memory.

Let's take a look at Question 1 in Table R.2: What are the independent and dependent variables? We want to know whether there is a dif-

TABLE R.2. Examples of Appropriate Statistical Techniques

Questions	Independent variable(s)	Dependent variable	Statistical test[a]
1. Do participants in the program being evaluated and the comparison program differ in their participation in after-school programs (participant or not)?	Nominal	Nominal	Chi square
2. How does extent of program participation (high, middle, or low) compare to attainment (high, middle, or low)?	Ordinal	Ordinal	Goodman and Kruskal's gamma
3. Do participants in the program being evaluated and the comparison program differ in their achievement scores (numbers)?	Nominal (1 variable, 2 groups)	Interval	t-test
4. Do participants of different cultural backgrounds differ in their achievement scores?	Nominal (1 variable, multiple groups)	Interval	Analysis of variance (ANOVA)
5. Do high scores on the attitude survey (numbers) predict high scores on the knowledge test?	Interval	Interval	Linear regression
6. How are pretest score, age, and number of sessions attended related to end-of-program achievement score?	Interval (more than 1)	Interval	Multiple linear regression

[a] A description of each of these tests is found in the Jaeger listing in "Further Reading."

ference between programs in terms of participation—whether people in the programs participated or not. This is the nominal, dependent variable. The question suggests that we want to know whether there is a difference between kinds of programs—the program that was evaluated and the comparison program—so this is a nominal, independent variable. To analyze the data at this level, we would have to construct a cross-tabulation table and conduct a chi-square test. This statistical test and others mentioned are found in the statistics texts like those found in the Further Reading.

What about Question 2? Our variables are "extent of participation" and "level of attainment," and both are measured on the ordinal scale, but which affects the other? Given the way the question is worded, we clearly want to know the effect of participation on attainment, so the former is the independent variable while the latter is the dependent variable. To analyze this kind of data, we would need to calculate Goodman and Kruskal's gamma.

Let's do one more—Question 3. Again, given the question, what are the independent and dependent variables? It looks as though we want to compare achievement scores of participants who are in the program being evaluated and those who are not. So achievement scores are the interval, dependent variable. The nominal, independent variable refers to participants who are in each evaluated program.

Now, you try examining the remaining questions by looking at Table R.2. Notice in Question 4 that "different cultural backgrounds" is a nominal variable and that there are multiple groups. In Question 5, both the independent and dependent variables are interval data. And finally, in Question 6, observe that there are multiple independent variables and that each qualifies as interval data.

I want you to understand that in this section we reviewed only a few examples of appropriate statistical techniques. Other statistical tests mentioned on the tables are linear regression, where independent and dependent variables are both interval, and multiple linear regression, where there is more than one independent variable. Some researchers might employ different tests to answer the questions above. To assist you, there are several computer programs available for performing the various statistical analyses, including the Statistical Package for the Social Sciences (SPSS), Stata, and SAS. Other statistical techniques are more complex, such as MANOVA, MANCOVA, path analysis, and hierarchical linear models (HLMs). These are well beyond us at this time.

Now, you might be wondering why we are talking about data analysis, particularly if you are doing formative evaluations. Isn't this discussion better suited for summative evaluations? This may initially appear to be the case, but actually, the kinds of data and data analysis techniques that I have mentioned are often used in summary formative evaluations as well. Evaluators need statistics to get a firm sense of what is happening in programs. Evaluators need statistics to be confident that differences are not chance occurrences.

> *My Warning:* Now, you clearly cannot consider yourself statistically capable based on this chapter. However, if simple statistics are helpful and easily understood by stakeholders then perhaps you could do that. If not, it is best to consider getting statistical assistance.

RECAP—SECTION R
Analysis of Quantitative Data

- Types of Data
  - Nominal
  - Ordinal
  - Interval
- Looking at a Frequency Distribution
  - Percentile ranks
  - Decile and quartiles
  - Interquartile range
- Central Tendency
  - Mode
  - Median
  - Mean
- Variability
  - Standard deviation
- Further Issues
  - Normality
  - Outliers
  - Missing data
- Descriptive Statistics
  - Frequency distribution
  - Central tendency and variability
  - Cross-tabulations
  - Correlation
- Inferential Statistics (Determining Significance)
  - See Table R.2

────GAINING ADDITIONAL UNDERSTANDING────
Case Study Exercise

Consider now the questions you addressed in the Section P RUPAS case study exercise. Some, *but not all*, might have been answered using quantitative data. (You might, for example, have decided to employ qualitative methods to examine some of these outcomes.)

For those questions using quantitative methods, identify in each question:

- The independent variable.
- The dependent variable.
- For each of these, note whether they were nominal, ordinal, or interval.
- For each, indicate whether there was one or multiple identified groups of the independent variable.
- For each, consider whether there was one independent variable (or more than one).

Now, consult Table Q.2 and determine an appropriate statistical test for each question.

Resources

Excel—*office.microsoft.com/excel*

Statistical Package for the Social Sciences (SPSS)—*www.spss.com*

Stata—*www.stata.com*

SAS—*www.sas.com*

Further Reading

Fitz-Gibbon, C. T., & Morris, L. L. (1987). *How to analyze data.* Thousand Oaks, CA: Sage.

This booklet provides a basic introduction to a variety of elementary statistical techniques, including those for summarizing data, for examining differences between groups and for examining relationships between two measures.

Jaeger, R. M. (1990). *Statistics: A spectator sport.* Beverly Hills, CA: Sage.

Richard Jaeger has written the easiest to read short textbook on statistics. A complete description, clear explanations, and no equations. Well worth reading.

May, H. (2004). Making statistics more meaningful for policy research and program evaluation. *American Journal of Evaluation, 25*(4), 525–540.

This is a somewhat technical paper on how to communicate statistical findings in ways that are more understandable. I include it in this section because, in my view, statistical analyses that are to be conducted should be guided by whether they can be described in a form that is useful to those who will receive the evaluation report.

Newcomer, K. E., & Wirtz, P. W. (2004). Using statistics in evaluation. In J. Wholey, H. P. Hatry, & K. E. Newcomer (Eds.), *Handbook of practical program evaluation* (2nd ed., pp. 439–459). San Francisco: Jossey-Bass.

This is a very nice overview of procedures for selecting appropriate statistical techniques. It is a further expansion of what is discussed in this section.

S

How Are Qualitative Data Analyzed?

For qualitative data, it is particularly difficult to *separate the tasks* of choosing an instrument, selecting the appropriate sample as part of the design, dealing with the logistics of collecting the data, and, finally, analyzing the data. Qualitative analysis is an iterative process. In fact, analysis of data is an ongoing activity, part of data collection. At each stage, the researcher reexamines data and searches for meaning.

REFINING THE DATA

In Section L, I talked about the process leading up to the construction of *field notes*. Now what does the evaluator do with these field notes consisting of descriptive materials that were recorded along with the observer comments depicting evaluator opinions, reflections, and potential biases? First, as in the analysis of quantitative data, you should consider the questions that need to be answered. Are you clear about what the question is and how you hope to answer the question based on the evaluation? Do you have enough information to adequately address the questions? Do you still have some issues that you are quite unclear about and feel that more information would be helpful? If time permits, attempt to gather such data. You are ready to proceed when you are satisfied with the completeness of your field notes—usually when comments seem to be repeating themselves (or when time and/ or money have run out).

Let us not forget that you might have obtained documents and other materials that also offer qualitative insights. These too will yield qualitative notes along with the field notes based on the data that you personally collected. Recall, however, that you have less familiarity with these documentary materials and how they were collected/ obtained and by whom. Try to consider the perspectives and potential biases within these materials before attempting to incorporate them into your dataset.

Now you are ready. You have before you a massive amount of information—perhaps overwhelming. What to do? You are trying to find patterns in the data that will lead to understanding and interpretation related to the evaluation question or issue. Keep focused. The first step is getting the data into a manageable form. Let's call this *data reduction*, a process commonly referred to as *coding*. This is a process that involves thinking about how you could divide all of the information that you've collected into neat, coherent chunks. Let's call these chunks *codes*. These categories consist of a word or a short phrase describing something in the field notes that is relevant to your question.

How do you begin considering these codes? First, you can learn much by respecting the *insider perspective*, the views and thoughts of those within the program. How do *they* view their world? In your observations or interviews, it may have become clear to you that insiders seem to have their own typology—their own way of categorizing their world. One starting point in determining codes is to begin to understand the meaning of the labels that insiders use to describe people or human events. What do their labels for people or events or interactions mean? Try to understand them. That may be an initial step in developing codes.

Other data are also available for potentially expanding your ideas. Codes may emerge from your own *intensive examination* of field notes. This is the hard part. First, you want to look at what information is actually present and try to create labels for each important piece. A large part of it is simply (not really simply) examining the field notes and attempting to give names to topics that appear to be present. Read through all of the field notes and make some comments to yourself— indicate the names or categories in the margin. What kinds of labels or categories appear to be present and repeating across field notes? Perhaps then read through your field notes again to identify additional codes that might have been missed on a prior reading. Were these new codes? Test them against your prior interpretations. Perhaps they suggest a variation in a previous code—sometimes an expansion of the code, sometimes breaking it into multiple codes. You should read and reread field notes to refine the code book and to settle on patterns emerging from the data. This code refinement process is one of the ways that the qualitative researcher ensures rigor.

A substantial amount of work is involved in sorting through data, listing these codes on a sheet, and cataloging where they occur in the various field notes. In essence, you are engaged in the act of preparing an *index* (like a book index). This tells you where to find different concepts within your field notes. Consider also where relevant quotes are to be found.

There are computer programs that assist in the organization and compilation of this index once codes are partially developed. Two computer programs that are especially helpful for analyzing qualitative data are called NVivo and Atlas.ti. However, one problem in using software programs for qualitative analysis is that there can be a reliance on "autocoding." This is very dangerous because it assumes that specific constructs are addressed in the field notes in the exact same way. Software programs should *never* be used as a substitute for carefully reading the data. However, qualitative software programs are especially helpful when conducting longitudinal studies; data are housed in one convenient place. But if one is inclined to use computer programs, an especially powerful procedure that allows active participation by the evaluator is Many Eyes. This visual display program allows you to graphically represent qualitative data such as interview transcripts and program descriptions. One could, for example, analyze transcript notes and derive patterns related to frequencies and associations.

When possible, I personally prefer to not use computer programs. I like to "feel" the data. I like to personally "touch" each piece of the data and feel involved in getting acquainted with the data. I prefer this to the anonymity of a computer doing its work.

Looking carefully at the exact nature of these codes and their interrelationships is a major part of the data analysis process. In essence, the approach is a combination of summarizing codes and examining similarities and differences between and within codes. You also will want to look at the extent to which codes overlap. In doing this, you will begin to develop *themes*. In essence, you will be looking for commonality in codes. A particular comment or observation may in fact be potentially applicable to multiple codes and may help you see overarching themes.

Once you have discovered these themes or patterns, what are you to do with them? What roles do they play in analysis? For example, are the cross-cutting themes highlighting any particular relationships? If there aren't any consistent patterns, then that itself is a finding and you should appropriately describe the inconsistencies as well. Based on these descriptions, you can begin to compare relationships within and between groups and add depth to understanding the data.

At this point, you may be wondering what should be done if you begin to notice conflicting information across themes. First, review your data and ask yourself whether it is accurate. Does it really reflect what happened in the field? Then consider recoding the data, but not in an effort to change the results; rather, only to help you make better sense of it. If, after recoding, you still come up with conflicting information, then you have the option to go back into the field to collect more data or to describe and report the inconsistencies. While collecting more data will be costly in terms of time and other resources, it may be necessary in order to obtain accurate information and to substantiate your preliminary findings. As you can see, qualitative analysis is an iterative process. You look, and then you look again.

TESTING THE VALIDITY OF THE ANALYSIS

Once you believe that you have arrived at an appropriate understanding of the themes, it is important to further test the validity of your assertions. Engaging in a kind of validation process helps to strengthen your analysis and its findings. One method of testing whether what you have produced makes sense is to be a "naysayer." Say to yourself, "I wonder whether what I found is *not* true." Consider *competing explanations*. How might the data have been organized differently? And if you do so, what alternative or competing explanations could then have been derived? Consider a new scenario: Suppose I described the themes in this way; if I did, would the data that I have fit those themes better? Discounting the adequacy of alternatives helps to validate your findings.

Furthermore, consider the *outliers*—negative cases that appear to lead in a different direction than your findings. In the previous section, we discussed quantitative outliers. Here we are considering qualitative outliers—data that differed substantially from the other qualitative information. For example, there could be opinions of people who completely disagree with the rest of the group, and they seem to be alone in their positions. How much credence do they have? Say to yourself, "If I reread the field notes with the negative cases in mind, do I gain a new perspective?" Including and considering the handful of outliers gives you more information that could potentially explain the trends that you are seeing. Doing so gives you a more accurate understanding of people's perspectives and experiences while testing the assumptions you have made.

Another means of testing the validity of your analysis is by *triangulation*. Triangulation of data really means looking at the information in multiple ways. We talked about this concept earlier. Triangulation is not easy to do when focused on qualitative data. Findings from observations may differ from those generated by interviews. But the differences may be attributable to a different focus for each of these investigations. Another consideration: Were there differences in the perception of multiple evaluators or data collectors? Did the data from observations or interviews change over time? It is helpful to try to bring together multiple data sources to increase the validity of your qualitative findings. Indeed, triangulation is a hallmark of qualitative analysis since significance testing is impossible. The claims that you make will have greater validity when they are based on consistent patterns across multiple data sources.

Another kind of validation procedure involves what researchers call *member checking*. This involves talking with informants (e.g., those who had been interviewed) to determine whether your notes, and otherwise recorded data, were appropriately understood and interpreted. Did you properly capture their thoughts? Are your interpretations reasonable?

You as the evaluator could also try out brief preliminary data summaries and possible themes with selected larger groups of stakeholders to obtain their input. I have always believed that it is helpful to gain stakeholder input on the validity of an evaluation. I talk more about that in both the valuing section of this book (Section T) and the reporting section (Section U). The insight provided by sharing initial data and interpretations may prove to be helpful in validating or potentially modifying the findings. However, be careful. The selection of informants might introduce a new source of bias to the data and, moreover, it could be politically disruptive.

A final validity test relates to *you*. In qualitative evaluation, you as the evaluator are as much the instrument as the interview or the observation protocol. Consider your biases, your points of view. Reexamine your field notes and, in particular, your evaluator observation notes. Are there ways in which these views—your views—might have had an undue influence on the categories that you have indicated? Pay heed to, and be warned by, the old adage, "If you are a hammer, everything looks like a nail."

RECAP—SECTION S
Qualitative Data Analysis

- Refining the Data—Data Reduction
  - Insider perspective
  - Intensive examination
  - Coding
  - Defining themes
  - What are the patterns or relationships across themes?
- Testing the Validity of the Analyses
  - Competing explanations
  - Triangulation
  - Member checking
  - You and your biases

──── GAINING ADDITIONAL UNDERSTANDING ────

Case Study Exercise

Consider now the questions you stipulated in the Sections O and P case study exercise that might have involved the acquisition of qualitative data. It may be difficult, given the information we have, for you to examine the data reduction steps for RUPAS. Assume that you had analyzed the data. Speculate on some of themes and findings that emerged.

Resources

Many Eyes—*manyeyes.alphaworks.ibm.com/manyeyes*

NVivo—*www.qsrinternational.com*

Atlas.ti—*www.atlasti.com/de/index.html*

Further Reading

Becker, H. S. (2009). How to find out how to do qualitative research. *International Journal of Communication, 3,* 545–553.

The noted sociologist Howard Becker critiques two National Science Foundation conference reports. In doing so, he posits that better understanding of qualitative practice can be attained by "inspecting recognized exemplary works and seeing how they did what made them exemplary." Remember that this article refers to doing qualitative *research* (the researcher sets known questions). Nonetheless, it offers fascinating insights, particularly as to the iterative nature of qualitative work.

Mabry, L. (2003). In living color: Qualitative methods in educational evaluation. In T. Kellaghan & D. Stufflebeam (Eds.), *International handbook of educational evaluation* (pp. 167–185). Norwell, MA: Kluwer Academic Publishers.

This is an excellent, easy-to-read discussion of the qualitative data collection and analysis process.

Patton, M. Q. (1987). *How to use qualitative methods in evaluation.* Newbury Park, CA: Sage.

This comprehensive small book is a part of the Center for the Study of Evaluation *Program Evaluation Kit.*

Patton, M. Q. (2003). Qualitative evaluation checklist. *Evaluation Checklists Project.* Available at *www.wmich.edu/evalctr/checklists/qec.pdf.*

This is an excellent checklist of things to think about in qualitative evaluation.

Olney, C. A., & Barnes, S. (2006). Collecting and analyzing evaluation data. *Planning and Evaluating Health Information Outreach Projects.* Available at *nnlm.gov/evaluation/booklets/booklet3/booklet3_whole.pdf.*

Booklet 3 of this Outreach Project focuses on collecting and analyzing evaluation data. I particularly recommend pages 19–29 for a simple discussion.

SECTION

T

How Do Analyzed Data
Answer Questions?

In the previous two sections, I talked about how to analyze quantitative and qualitative data. In that discussion, I focused on the presentation of data related to individual questions. Is that enough? Some evaluation writers would say, "No!" Their view is that findings alone need to be supplemented with a *specific answer* of "good" or "bad." They would ask about the bottom line related to the data findings in each question—not just what did you find, but was it good or bad, acceptable or not? Such evaluation writers, moreover, would insist that data about individual questions alone do not suffice. The essential issue, they would maintain, relates to judging the merit and worth of each outcome and of the program as an entity. Their view is that the evaluator has the personal responsibility for providing a final judgment of merit and worth (e.g., the program is good or the program failed).

DIFFICULTIES IN VALUING

Aside from the issue of the appropriateness of this theoretical stance, let me ponder with you some of the difficulties involved in "valuing." How positive do the particular findings of a question have to be in order to warrant a statement of "good"? Or, conversely, how negative to be "bad"? Are criteria sufficiently well established to be able to make such judgments? What if the answers to some of the questions is "good" and to some the answer is "bad"? How are judgments to be made about the total program, given these diverse values? Are some questions more important than others? How much more important? Does the evaluator decide? How is this decision made?

These are daunting questions indeed, and at this point I raise the further issue of the conditions under which making value judgments about the program are, in fact, *necessary*. Moreover, I ask you to consider differences in the nature of value judgements between formative and summative evaluations. Summative evaluations generally are designed to answer questions that lead to "go/no-go" decisions. That is, they provide the answer to whether the program is good or bad—what is its merit and worth? Typical questions include: Was the program successful? Is this program worth keeping? Should the program be re-funded? Should the program be expanded to other locations?

Formative evaluation, on the other hand, is designed to provide information for potential program improvement. It is anticipated that the program will continue and the evaluation is designed to provide insights into what is working and what is not, in order for modifications to be made. Formative questions also might seek to answer whether specific program activities had been implemented and, if not, what program modifications or changes might be appropriate. Or, more broadly, a summary formative evaluation would seek to take stock of the program's current status at some defined point in time (e.g., end of year) in order to determine areas in need of further improvement.

I believe that most of what we engage in as evaluators are formative evaluations. They may be formative implementation evaluations or summary formative evaluations. In the total scheme of things, there are very few real summative evaluations conducted—and certainly not very many when we are considering evaluation in small local programs. And so my view is that these programs do not necessarily require that a valuing judgment be made, and if so, it is different from summative valuing.

At this point, you might ask:

"Marv, I seem to remember that in Section A, you talked about how you and your wife approached the purchase of a house. You came up with criteria that would be important. You had weightings that you attached indicating the relative importance of criterion. Judgments were made about each of the house candidates, for each of the criteria. Thus, while you asked separate questions (e.g., number of bedrooms, quality of bathroom), you managed to come up with a *single judgment of merit and worth* for the objects being evaluated. How is this different from the kinds of evaluation situations in which I might be involved?"

Good question. But you see, that was really a summative question. My wife and I were trying to decide, "Shall we buy or not?" In fact, it was a summative evaluation (nonprofessional) because we were comparing different alternatives about which we would make a summative decision. We were going to decide *which* house to buy. Formative evaluations related to the house situation would generally relate to gaining understanding of the status of various aspects of the house. What things are working and which are not? Is the paint getting shabby looking? These are formative appraisals unlike a decision to buy or not to buy the house.

VALUING IN A FORMATIVE CONTEXT

So what kind of valuing, if any, takes place in formative evaluation situations? Let's take this one step at a time. First, given the nature of formative evaluation, a judgment about the goodness of the program as a total entity is not required. It is often superfluous. The question of aggregating value judgments related to individual questions is not necessary.

What, then, is appropriate? Some evaluation writers maintain that even attempting to come to a final judgment about individual questions is inappropriate. They say that the values to be found within the data related to a question are subject to the individual perspectives of multiple stakeholders. They would maintain that we all see value from our own frame of reference. They would prefer that data related to questions be provided in expansive description (they would say "thick description"). In that way, stakeholders should be able to make up their own minds based on this thick description. Thus valuing from that theoretical perspective is not the job of the evaluator, but honors the subjective judgments of multiple individuals. There are further variations within that perspective, but I will not do that fine-tuning.

I don't go that far, and that is not the tone of this book. Rather, I view the evaluator's role as much more facilitative and enabling in the valuing process. I want to establish a *framework for judging results*. Please recall that in Sections I and N, I suggested that you work with primary stakeholders in getting them to depict more fully the parameters of acceptability related to each question. That is, what were their views (before any data were collected) as to what would be an acceptable set of findings for each question? Valuing was in large part performed by primary stakeholders before they might be biased by examining actual findings. As you might recall, I asked you, the evaluator, to introduce scenarios of possible findings to determine acceptability from the perspective of these stakeholders. Where qualitative instrumentation is likely to be used and in other situations and where quantitative pre-valuing is not applicable, I tend to inquire as to what they think a successful program will look like. A qualitative or descriptive statement might be used as a basis for subsequent comparisons. I try to help them to write up a description of what success would look like.

Am I fantasizing? In part, yes. This is an ideal-world description, which is only infrequently met. It is difficult to get stakeholders to sit down and engage in this process. But I try, and sometimes I succeed.

And so in many instances I settle for complete description and the best possible descriptive answers to the specific questions. While I view complete description as important in potentially enhancing the ability of stakeholders to improve their program, that is not enough. I believe that description does not obviate the role of the evaluator in summarizing data and indicating patterns that are clearly found. Summary findings are not value judgments; they simply enhance the possibility of determining whether values previously specified had been met. Where means of judging value were not previously specified, summary findings enhance the ability of stakeholders to determine the value for their program. Moreover, I like to guide the primary stakeholders' valuing by offering alternative conclusions that might be warranted by the findings. These are presented as questions for their consideration.

However, there are some situations where it is possible and appropriate for the evaluator to make judgments (good/bad statements). In those instances, questions might have been asked so specifically that the evaluator is able to answer the question in a yes/no (attained/not attained) fashion. An example of this is when the question itself had indicated a specific standard for judging (e.g., success as indicated by a score of 23 on the XYZ test). Alternatively, standards might have been preestablished for some questions answerable by using a standardized test. In that instance, the determination of "good" might have specified a particular norm level to be achieved.

There are perhaps more "sophisticated" ways in which valuing might take place. Typically, they are not warranted in formative evaluations. For example, evaluation in a summative context most frequently would involve demonstrating value by showing the statistical significance of differences between outcomes of a program and its comparison program. (You might want to reexamine the discussion in Section P about causal models to note the complexity of selecting appropriate control groups.)

If, however, you had conducted such a randomized control trial then significant differences between the two programs might provide a satisfactory indication of *merit*. Note, however, that *worth*, the second aspect of value, is not necessarily demonstrated if the costs of the two programs were different. In essence, the program differences, while *statistically significant*, might not be *practically significant*.

In Section Y, I provide a detailed example of how cost considerations can be examined in programs with multiple outcomes. You may think of this as a much more detailed and professional version of the weighting system that I used in my house purchase example provided in Section A.

➢ *The Bottom Line:* Valuing based on data from RCTs may be of great value for summative evaluations. This is particularly true when this "significance" data is combined with a weighting system for considering multiple outcomes. However, for formative evaluations within a use-oriented framework, standard-setting by primary stakeholders is the appropriate method for valuing. As previously noted, this stakeholder standard-setting is informed by evaluator representations of value positions of underrepresented stakeholder groups.

"VALUING" REDEFINED

It is clear to me that, despite the initial description of valuing presented in Section A, there is no single way to portray the role of the evaluator in valuing. There are many evaluator approaches and each carries with it different implications for how valuing transpires. Evaluators can be engaged in valuing by guiding stakeholders in the process of reaching conclusions about value. Evaluators can be engaged in valuing by acting as a social conscience in reflecting on the meaning of findings. Evaluators can assist in valuing by providing stakeholders with the opportunity to actively engage in evaluation and, in that process, themselves determine the worth of an enterprise. And yes, evaluators can perceive their role as personally making a decision of merit or worth. Based on what we have now seen, let me redefine the role of the evaluator in valuing. It is my view that *the role of the evaluator in valuing is to activate, be engaged in, and contribute to the process of determining merit or worth.*

➤ *A Final Note:* Have I ever done valuing (of the determining good/bad variety) in a formative evaluation? Well, yes. Let me explain. Many years ago, I was conducting an evaluation of the educational programs at all of New Mexico's juvenile detention camps. My value judgment at one of those facilities was, "This is an educational disaster area." I would say that was a value statement that went well beyond simply saying "bad."

Now, how did I get there? This small facility, housing about 25 youths, was located on the highest mountain in southern New Mexico. It had one classroom and was allocated one teacher. When I arrived at the facility there had been no teacher obtained and the classroom was not in operation. The staff had done nothing to compensate for these deficiencies. The juveniles mostly hung around the large lodge-like building all day. When staff were questioned about any kind of educational program or learning activities that might be available, none were mentioned. One staff member mentioned, hopefully, that they sometimes let the youths go out to chop wood. Obviously, the state's newspapers had a field day with my "disaster area" quote. Fortunately, before the criticism got out of hand, an influential member of the state legislature who had come along as an observer seconded my value judgment. So when it comes to whether I assign values in an evaluation, I can never say "never." In this situation, the evidence was so incontrovertible that I, as evaluator, was thrust into making a value statement. Might it happen again? Possibly.

RECAP—SECTION T
Valuing

- Traditional View of Valuing
- Difficulties in Valuing
  - Formative/summative differences
- Valuing in a Formative Context
  - Developing a framework for judging results
  - Summative valuing solutions explained—not warranted
  - Bottom line
- Valuing Redefined
- A Final Note

━━━ GAINING ADDITIONAL UNDERSTANDING ━━━

Case Study Exercise

Examine again the evaluation questions you considered in Section I and subsequently refined in Section N. How did you propose to consider the questions (Sections O and P) and the analytical procedures that you might have employed (Sections R and S)? Now, for each question reflect on how you might have challenged primary stakeholders to provide valuing guidelines when each of the questions was initially framed. Look at the questions and consider what you might have said.

Further Reading

Cousins, J. B., & Shulha, L. (2008). Complexities in setting program standards in collaborative evaluation. In N. Smith & P. Brandon (Eds.), *Fundamental issues in evaluation* (pp. 139–158). New York: Guilford Press.

Cousins and Shula do an excellent job of describing the role of stakeholders in establishing a basis for valuing evaluation results. They demonstrate how standard-setting must precede data collection.

Stake, R., & Schwandt, T. (2007). On discerning quality in evaluation. In I. Shaw, J. Greene, & M. Mark (Eds.), *Sage handbook of evaluation* (pp. 404–418). Thousand Oaks, CA: Sage.

This chapter goes into great depth about ways of thinking about how quality is discerned. Judging quality is a major component of the valuing process.

Norris, N. (2005). Validity. In S. Mathison (Ed.), *Encyclopedia of evaluation* (pp. 439–442). Thousand Oaks, CA: Sage.

Norris maintains that "one of the defining problems of the field of evaluation remains the validation of evaluation judgments." The diversity of evaluation approaches leads to multiple ways of validating.

U

How Are Evaluation Results Reported?

Evaluation has, as an ultimate purpose, the improvement of the program being evaluated. This is especially true for formative evaluation. When evaluation results are reported, it helps to ensure that relevant information is available for potential program improvement. Thus it is necessary to pay heed to how you report to stakeholders. However, first let me point out the relationship between reporting and communicating.

COMMUNICATION

Evaluation reporting typically means reporting findings. These findings can either be presented as the program proceeds and the evaluator acquires data, or at intermittent points throughout the evaluation—particularly at the end of the program year. But reporting is part of a larger entity, the act of communicating. This occurs throughout the evaluation. Indeed, the very act of conducting an evaluation involves communication at every stage—two-way communication. This, surely, must be obvious at this point in your reading of *Evaluation Essentials*.

Evaluators identify stakeholders and engage them in order to determine their information needs. Stakeholders communicate their views and their concerns. Evaluators communicate as well. Often, the communication and information provided by evaluators help stakeholders to properly identify their most salient information needs. Developing

an evaluation plan involves a good deal of communication as evaluators inquire about stakeholders' needs and indicate what is possible. A
simple reading of all of the preceding chapters provides abundant evidence of an active communication process that encompasses all stages
of the evaluation. Continuous communication of all types is an essential part of the evaluation process.

REPORTING

Now, "evaluation reporting" refers to the specific set of information-
disseminating activities by which evaluators communicate what they
have learned about the program based on their systematic study. Even
this reporting can be thought of in several segments: reporting that occurs
throughout the process of the evaluation and reporting that occurs at the
end of the program year or at other designated points in time.

Ongoing Reporting

Let us deal with the first of these—ongoing reporting. During the
course of the evaluation, you undoubtedly will gain insights about the
program. Such insights might, for example, relate to the extent to which
the program is being operated as it was intended. You as the evaluator
might note, for example, that some activities have not taken place or
have taken place in a very poor manner. Or, in conducting interviews
or observations, you might begin to develop insights into negative attitudes that have been arising toward the program. I believe that it is
inappropriate in most instances to allow the program to proceed on a
course toward inevitable failure. I feel that you as the evaluator have an
obligation to report such interim findings as they occur. Let me caution,
however, that there is a fine line to be drawn in making these decisions about when to report. There are hazards involved in providing
extensive information prematurely, which may not be accurate. In such
instances, you should state the tentative nature of this reporting.

There are many ways in which interim evaluation findings are
reported. You might prepare written "mini-reports" describing what
has been learned to date. Or there can be more casual reporting, including such things as e-mails, oral reports, telephone reports, or visual
presentations.

Let me restate the broader issue involved: I view continued
engagement with stakeholders (particularly primary stakeholders) as
a key part of the evaluation process. Thus ongoing reporting of your
observations and impressions is essential. This is especially true for

those evaluators who focus their evaluation orientation toward organizational learning and evaluation capacity building.

Reporting Final Results

Even final results can take on a variety of formats. Reporting must consider stakeholders—their needs and their preferences—when deciding the reporting format. Of course, this would have been determined and agreed on when developing the evaluation plan (particularly in Section Q). The main issue here is considering multiple stakeholder groups and their needs. Do some groups require reports presented in a language other than English? Are there diverse communities that are not normally part of the information network for which particular reporting should be devised?

Then there is the question of the extent of detail that is appropriate in a report. Perhaps reports need to be presented at multiple levels of detail. I believe so, but this can often be accomplished by proper formatting of the evaluation report (see discussion below).

Stakeholder preferences may also be a factor. Some people find certain kinds of reports or formats more comfortable and more easily understood. There are a variety of reporting formats that seasoned evaluators might employ: multimedia, electronic reports, websites, storytelling, and sociodramas, to name but a few. And, of course, there is a written report.

Most end-of-evaluation findings involve a written report; however, that is not always the case. Some evaluation authors have questioned the cost effectiveness of written reports. That is, would the program stakeholders want to use the funds that would be necessary to produce a written report in another manner: for program activities or for additional evaluation work. Report writing is a very labor-intensive activity. Would a less costly presentation to all relevant stakeholders be equally effective at a substantially lower cost? Perhaps such a presentation could be videotaped so that many others could have access to this report. Will the ongoing reporting that is to occur suffice? Nonetheless, written reports are the most common form of final reporting. (Please note that when I talk about final reports, much of what we have to say also refers to other scheduled reports, such as a midyear report.)

THE FINAL WRITTEN REPORT

So let us now turn to the discussion of a final written report. I will summarize my discussion in two categories: the format and structure of the report, and the nature and quality of the writing itself.

Format of the Report

With respect to the first of these, I view a typical report as consisting of: an *executive summary*, a *brief description* of the program, the discussion of the evaluation *procedures or methodology*, the *findings*, and, finally, an *appendix* consisting of notes or attachments. Some evaluation writers add recommendations to this section or include the recommendations within the findings section. I discuss my views of the appropriateness of such an inclusion (in either form) later.

Let the end be the beginning. Confused? I strongly believe that the *executive summary* should be the very first part of the report. We as evaluators must, at the very outset of the report, succinctly address the stakeholders' concerns: What did you find? This executive summary should provide a brief description of the program that was conducted. Next, a brief description of the methods and procedures used by the evaluator to acquire understandings about the program. Finally, and most important, the questions and the main findings associated with each question need to be briefly summarized.

I believe that the executive summary provides an introduction to the report that allows readers to first gain the full picture very quickly, which often is the only thing busy administrators will read anyhow. The individual sentences, or the brief paragraphs, in the executive summary should provide an appropriate overview of the findings. Each major finding should be accompanied with a page number indicating the location in the report where that particular finding will be addressed more fully (see Figure U.1). Thus some readers may only read the executive summary and from that gain a general understanding of the findings—the bottom line. Other readers of the executive summary will note the page references and be motivated or inspired to read, in greater detail, about the findings that are of special interest to them. More determined readers will desire to read the whole report, including program description and methods. Technically astute readers also will avidly consume the appendix to the report.

Following the executive summary I would place a *description of the program* itself. Simply stated, what was the program that was implemented? What were the goals of the program? What major activities were pursued in an attempt to accomplish those goals? If the program details are quite complex, then I suggest that they be summarized and readers then be referred to an appendix.

Next is the discussion of the evaluation *procedures and methods*. These would have been fully explicated in the evaluation plan that you developed with stakeholders. That plan can be summarized here. However, procedural/methodological changes may have arisen during the conduct of the evaluation. These changes should be noted. In

Program

_____

_____ See pp. ____ to ____

Methods

_____

_____ See pp. ____ to ____

Results
Question 1: _____
Findings: _____
_____ See pp. ____ to ____

Question 2: _____
Findings: _____
_____ See pp. ____ to ____

Question ___ : _____
Findings: _____
_____ See pp. ____ to ____

Unintended consequence/overlooked area: _____
Findings: _____
_____ See pp. ____ to ____

FIGURE U.1. Executive summary.

describing procedures it is important that you remember that a part of
the procedure includes the process you went through in developing
a logic model and in framing the decision questions. While research
reports tend to require substantial discussions of methodology within
the body of the report, evaluation reports are different. I feel that in
a decision-oriented situation such as an evaluation, where users have
been involved from the outset, it is not necessary to encumber readers
with overly extensive detail of procedures as a part of the main body
of the report. This section should provide adequate detail so that the

reader can understand the evaluator's approach. However, all of the complexity does not need to be described. A further description of particular aspects of the methods, along with copies of instruments used, should be placed in the appendix.

And now to the *findings*. The findings constitute the bulk of the report. Findings, of course, should be keyed to the particular questions or issues that were determined in the plan as being important to relevant stakeholders. That means that the questions should be the foci of each portion of the findings section. Data for answering a question may have come from a variety of data sources—both quantitative and qualitative. The evaluator's job is to integrate these data into sensible answers to questions. Data should be presented by question. A brief summary of data derived from each particular instrument and the analysis of these data could initiate the findings section. Then, however, the focus must turn to answering stakeholders' questions. What is the case being made by the data? What does the full dataset mean? Do different subsets of data (qualitative and quantitative) provide corroborating or contradicting findings? Often, qualitative data are an effective means of elaborating and exemplifying quantitative findings.

Frequently, issues emerge which were not a part of the initial question set—they were *overlooked*. These might be questions or issues that later were felt to be of interest by the primary stakeholders. In that instance, they should be considered along with the initial questions. Sometimes, however, the evaluator is confronted with data indicating *unintended consequences*—either positive or negative. These should be duly noted and addressed within the findings section. As noted in Figure U.1, these are included in the executive summary as well.

Needless to say, despite our best intentions, not all questions are able to be answered. Or at least, not all questions are able to be answered definitively. Evaluators cannot, and should not, go beyond the data that they have. Findings need to be well substantiated and where they cannot be—say so. You can only report what you know—what you have learned. Do not go beyond that.

Furthermore, not all findings are positive. Clearly, you as the evaluator must resist the temptation to provide pleasure (good news) when it is not warranted. Bluntness, on the other hand, is not necessary. There are judicious ways to communicate *unfavorable findings*. Information to stakeholders imply suggestions for improvement. Thus framing negative findings as opportunities for improvement is fruitful behavior. Also, to the extent to which you have established nonthreatening relationships with stakeholders throughout the evaluation, negative findings are more easily accepted. You, one hopes, would have become a trusted advisor. Needless to say, none of the above should be done in a way that damages your integrity. Presenting findings in a sensitive manner is important, but an evaluator's integrity must be preserved.

Do I advocate making *recommendations* a part of the findings? Or not? Many evaluators view recommendations as an inherent part of an evaluation. I take issue with that point of view. (However, feel free to disagree and go the way of the majority.) Now, let me justify my point of view. I believe that findings point out either strengths or deficiencies. If the findings are positive, the implication for program continuance in its current form might thus be implied. (However, that is not necessarily so.) Furthermore, if the findings are positive, but also show particular tendencies that might lead to potential modifications or enhancements of the program, then there are choices to be made. What is the best possible way to do this? For example, let us say that Activity A seemed to have a particularly positive impact. Should the program do more of it? How much? At what cost? These are decisions that I believe are administrative in nature. The evaluator is an expert in systematically collecting, acquiring, synthesizing, and helping to value data. Evaluators are not necessarily expert in the content of the program; many, if not most, of the relevant stakeholders are. Evaluators usually know less about the content and goals of drug prevention programs, welfare-to-work programs, or mathematics programs than the stakeholders. Can the evaluator assist in discussing possible alternative recommendations? Can the evaluator assist in explaining what the data have to show or imply about each of these potential courses of action? Sure and sure. I frequently pose several possible courses of action. These are presented in order to stimulate thinking about what might be feasible and appropriate.

I, however, like to *assist* in the recommendation process *up front.* Up front? Yes, way up front. When the evaluation questions of importance are being determined and I ask whether stakeholders really want answers (remember that earlier section?), I like to put forth the issue of "What difference would it make? What would you do given this, that, or another set of findings?" In essence, I am asking primary stakeholders to consider what recommended courses of action might be implied given particular future findings. I am asking for a consideration of future recommendations given possible outcome results. The examination of potential recommendations is part of the evaluation focusing and planning (particularly in Sections I and N).

Now, finally, let us turn to the last portion of the written report and consider the *appendix.* I have indicated at previous points in this discussion the various materials that might be placed in an appendix or attachment to the report. The intention is to keep the report within a reasonable page limit and to enhance its readability. The compulsive stakeholder, or perhaps the more sophisticated stakeholder, will want to read everything. And, as noted, there are intermittent stages for those who want only a summary of the findings (the executive summary), the findings with additional detail about how those findings were reached. And then, of course, there is the man or woman who wants it all. The appendix is the place to provide all of the substantiation of the report. If statistical methods were used, detailed discussion of the analysis procedures and the more esoteric analyses find their home here. Copies of instruments rest here as well.

RECAP 1—SECTION U
Communication and Reporting

- Communication
- Reporting
  - Ongoing reporting
  - Final reporting
    - Executive summary
    - Program description
    - Procedures and methodology
    - Findings
    - Appendix
  - Questions about findings
  - Overlooked questions
  - Unintended/unfavorable findings
  - Recommendations

NATURE AND QUALITY OF WRITING

I have discussed previously in this section how the way in which the report is formatted might serve the needs of *multiple audiences*. Furthermore, in distributing the evaluation report, you as the evaluator might plan for it to be distributed in pieces, providing only those sections appropriate to each audience. Thus there might be many copies of executive summaries distributed to various stakeholder groups and only a limited number of the full report, including the technical appendices. There might also be the possibility that reports are presented in other languages. These are issues to be resolved with the primary stakeholders.

While content is important, it must be communicated in a way that is understood and persuades. The first thing to be said about quality of writing is that evaluators must write for the audience. Who are they? What would be readable? In my writing, I like to think about a moderately informed but not fully knowledgeable stakeholder. I then picture this reader and, as I write the report, ask whether that individual would understand what I am saying. When I say something that I think might be difficult to understand, I explain it again in another way or give an example. Think of a person you know and imagine that you are talking to that individual.

For a report to be readable, it must have a *clear and accessible style*. What do I mean by "accessible"? You should write without an abundance of complex syntax. The writing should not be convoluted. Simple sentences without a lot of "add-on" thoughts are preferred. I may be guilty of violating this rule in the current volume (since I seem to be very fond of semicolons and dashes). The evaluator might also want to vary the length of sentences to avoid monotony. Sentences all of the same length, style, and tone are not interesting to read.

Let us, jointly, take a moment to reflect further on one of the most serious problems with professional writing—*jargon*. By jargon I mean primarily the technical language of evaluators—the terms that I have tried to avoid throughout this volume (and which are far more profuse in most other evaluation texts). Evaluators too often feel the need to explain things in technical terms when they could be explained more simply. I suppose this applies to everyone and to all situations. Some technical terms may be necessary. If you must use them, explain each simply upon first use.

One can indicate technical details and still do so in writing that has pleasing *verbal quality*. Writing style that is mechanical or plodding does not add to readability. And the aim of a report is to be convincing. People cannot be convinced by something that is boring, and they end up not having the patience to read to its end. Think of the novels that you have started reading and put down uncompleted because they were too boring. You were not convinced that the author had anything to say. You want the readers of your evaluation report to be convinced that you have something worthwhile to say.

Furthermore, it is important to *guide the reader* in understanding what you are about to say. You want the reader to understand the flow and sequence of the argument to be presented. Executive summaries, as we have discussed them earlier in the section, provide an overview of the full report and help the readers get into it and to understand its structure. Your next job is to guide the reader in dealing with the content in the body of the report. Guiding paragraphs that set the framework for a section are helpful. They introduce the reader to what is to come. You may also guide the reader in reading individual paragraphs. Many writing specialists maintain that the initial sentence of a paragraph is important because it sets the tone and structure for what is to be further detailed within that paragraph. Often, a well-written report can be roughly summarized by simply reading the first sentence of each paragraph.

Carefully chosen *illustrations* help, for example, to demonstrate the point being made within a paragraph or portion of a report. Perhaps it is simply noting a striking statistic or repeating memorable quotations from the qualitative data. Possibly, you might use an example from another more easily understood domain of the concept being addressed. Sometimes metaphors help people to understand the message being conveyed. Metaphors are persuasive. The one caveat to be noted is that illustrative examples generally should represent the general trend of the data and not the outliers.

Finally, *graphic devices* could be valuable aids to reader understanding. This would include tables, charts, and other graphics. Of course, they must be used judiciously in ways that add to, rather than detract from, the report. Overly abundant, overly complex tables are not helpful. If detailed tables are available from the data collected, but not essential, consider a simplified version within the body and the detailed table in the appendix.

I have provided some guidelines to good writing, some of which have been detailed. But *writing is also an art*. Practice it, criticize yourself, and let others comment. Listen to comments, but your writing should reflect you and what you are comfortable saying and the way in which you are comfortable doing so. That is a key to successful evaluation reporting.

Finally, a simple suggestion—value clarity above all other elements of style.

RECAP 2—SECTION U
Quality of Writing

- Serve needs of multiple audiences
- Write in a clear and accessible style
- Avoid jargon

- Use pleasing verbal quality
- Guide the reader
- Use illustrations where appropriate
- Use tables, charts, etc., where appropriate
- Developing your writing skills—writing is an art
- Value clarity

GAINING ADDITIONAL UNDERSTANDING

Case Study Exercise

Who might be the recipients of a RUPAS final evaluation report? Would you anticipate that a single evaluation report will suffice, or will multiple versions be necessary to accommodate different stakeholder groups?

Further Reading

Alkin, M. C., Christie, C. A., & Rose, M. (2006). Communicating evaluation. In I. Shaw, J. Greene, & M. Mark (Eds.), *Sage handbook of evaluation* (pp. 385–403). Thousand Oaks, CA: Sage.

This is a complete discussion of the evaluator's role in communicating to stakeholders. This includes informal communication, interim reports, and formal reports.

Grob, G. F. (2004). Writing for impact. In J. Wholey, H. P. Hatry, & K. E. Newcomer (Eds.), *Handbook of practical program evaluation* (2nd ed., pp. 604–627). San Francisco: Jossey-Bass.

This is a very persuasive piece about "how to write compelling evaluation reports that convince readers of the findings and promote taking action in response."

V

What Is the Evaluator's Role in Helping Evaluations to Be Used?

In this section I provide some explanation about the nature of what I mean by "evaluation use" and the many forms that it takes. Furthermore, I discuss later in this section what you as an evaluator can do to enhance evaluation use. I consider this section extremely important because of my view that evaluation is not simply some kind of intellectual exercise resulting in a report. Frequently, such reports are received, smiles and thanks are given, and the report sits on the shelf. I don't want that. Reports, like books, are meant to be read. I hope that your evaluation reports will not only inspire, but also lead to changed thinking and actions within programs that you evaluate.

Greater methodological rigor alone does not lead to increased use. As we have noted throughout this book, methodological appropriateness is important. But beyond that, there are many things that you as an evaluator can do to foster evaluation use. You must play an active role in assuring that use will take place.

In that sense, this is not really the fifth-to-last section of the book. In fact, preparation for utilization starts at the *beginning* of an evaluator's engagement. To repeat yet again, the first step in helping to assure evaluation use—that the evaluation has an impact—and that your work does not go for naught, is to establish relationships with stakeholders and for you to think about and focus on evaluation use throughout the process.

A WORD ABOUT "USE"

You now, perhaps, have an intuitive sense of what I mean by evaluation use. Before I provide a more precise definition, I would like to set two boundaries on this discussion. First, when I talk about use, it is in relationship to a *particular program*. The concern that you must have, as an evaluator, is whether your stakeholders are in a position to use the evaluation to improve their program. The second boundary that I want to establish relates to *intent*. I am more concerned about use that was intended; that is, instances where you believe that there is a possibility that particular evaluation information will benefit stakeholders. There is often use that occurs that is incidental, unintended, not anticipated, or far away in another program. These kinds of use, while worthwhile, are less under the control of the evaluator. They are more the fodder of evaluation researchers and theorists who like to talk about such things. I want to focus on actions within the grasp of the evaluator that might lead to use.

WHAT IS USE?

Evaluation use refers to how the evaluation process and information obtained from an evaluation affects the program that is being evaluated. By this, I am referring to such things as the following: Did the evaluation generate a new understanding of certain aspects of the program? As a consequence of the evaluation (or partial consequence), were changes made in the program? Did program staff acquire new skills and insights during the course of an evaluation that were attributable, or partially attributable, to the evaluation?

There is a great deal of research and other writings about evaluation use. Indeed, it may be the area of evaluation that has been most thoroughly researched. When discussing evaluation use, evaluation writers tend to make the distinction between "instrumental use" and "conceptual use." *Instrumental use* refers to situations where evaluation information has been used to influence direct action such as making particular decisions about a program. That is, evaluation information was a direct instrument for making change. *Conceptual use* describes situations where no direct decision has been made, but where particular conceptual understandings about aspects of the program have been modified based on the evaluation information.

Evaluators also refer to situations where evaluation is employed to justify a prior decision. In these instances, the purpose of the evaluation was not to answer a question, but rather to ratify an action already taken. I do not consider this an instance of real use. This kind of "symbolic" use will not be part of our discussion.

Instrumental and conceptual use may result from two different aspects of the evaluation. Most thoroughly examined within the literature on instrumental and conceptual use is the use of *evaluation findings*. Indeed, evaluation use may occur as a consequence of such findings. That is, does the evaluation report eventuate in instrumental changes or conceptual modifications? When you as an evaluator conclude an evaluation and provide a final report, does that report influence potential changes/improvements in the program? Please note, as I have reminded you throughout this volume, that findings from interim reports may also be used.

Throughout this book, I have also discussed the importance of engaging the primary stakeholders—and to some extent, all stakeholders—in the process of evaluation. We have talked about the role of stakeholders in developing logic models. We have addressed the role of stakeholders in selecting questions to be examined. On a somewhat less active level, stakeholders may have observed (or participated with) the evaluator in developing instruments, conducting interviews, collecting data, and so forth. These kinds of engagement and observation of the evaluation process may also lead to evaluation use. Stakeholders have learned something from being a part of the evaluation process. What they learn may influence what they now know about the program, changes they might make, or how they now think about the program. Engaging in the evaluation process may also increase their appreciation for evaluation—and future receptivity to other program evaluations. It might also increase their knowledge of evaluation. Evaluation writers refer to these kinds of use as *process use*—use as a consequence of engaging in the evaluation.

Thus let me summarize. I ask you to think of evaluation use as occurring either conceptually or instrumentally related to the findings of the evaluation. Evaluation use may also occur because of engagement in the process. This use also may be either conceptual or instrumental.

WHAT CAN YOU DO?

There is an extensive literature on the factors associated with increased evaluation use. For simplicity, I consider these factors in three categories. First, there are fixed characteristics of the program and evaluator situations that, when they are present, are more likely to lead to evaluation use. Think of these as the *preconditions*. The second category relates to the actions that you as the evaluator might take *during the conduct of the evaluation* that are likely to increase evaluation use. Finally, I believe that there are evaluator activities at the *end of the evaluation contract* (and even beyond) that are a part of the evaluator's responsibility for enhancing use.

Preconditions

Let us consider first the *preconditions* that, if present, are more likely to lead to evaluation use. Clearly, some of these are not controllable. Others are potentially modifiable. The first, and perhaps most important, of these relates to *you* and who you are and what you believe. Use is more likely to take place if the evaluator is perceived as a credible source of information. If you are viewed as credible, your evaluation will be more respected. This *credibility* initially is based on prior reputation and initial stakeholder perceptions. A part of credibility, obviously, is the evaluator's technical capabilities and understanding of evaluation. But take heed, credibility is not only based on perception at the outset of the evaluation. Evidence strongly suggests that credibility is, in large part, acquired. Changes in credibility may come about when evaluators demonstrate their abilities and skills in the conduct of the evaluation and provide evidence that they listen, they care, they are nonpartisan and unbiased.

Another aspect of evaluator characteristics is their *personal commitment to use*—commitment to attempting to enhance use. You need to strongly believe that evaluation is important. You need to want to really make a difference. I have talked about this within this book and hope that you have already acquired that commitment to use. I sincerely hope that this chapter further convinces you of the importance of having this commitment.

Another set of evaluation use preconditions has to do with *stakeholders' previous evaluation experience*. In many instances, prior evaluations may have been an unpleasant experience. Perhaps a prior evaluator did not seek stakeholder engagement and, while conducting a technically sound evaluation, missed the mark on what stakeholders wanted and needed. Perhaps the findings of the evaluation were quite negative and were presented in a manner that did not enhance receptivity. Your job is to attempt to alleviate this negative perception of evaluation and evaluators by stakeholders. You are providing a new kind of evaluation, one that is more stakeholder sensitive and concerned about providing assistance rather than simply judging. Let them know this.

During the Evaluation

An issue associated with evaluation use is the extent to which *stakeholders* have an *interest in this evaluation*. Do they even want an evaluation conducted? Is it being forced upon them? Is this something that they perceive as a rite of passage associated with the acceptance of a program development contract? If so, on any of these, they are not likely to be highly interested in the evaluation or its potential use. These are, in part, preconditions of the situation. But your role in fostering interest in the evaluation is an important part of conducting the evaluation. You want to get stakeholders to understand that this evaluation is different. This evaluation seeks to be of help to them in improving something that they care about—their program. In part, this is accomplished by the process that we have described in this volume, starting with the development of questions that are relevant to stakeholders.

In the past, I have had contracts to do evaluations of programs that were externally funded. In those instances, I encouraged stakeholders to consider what is minimally necessary to satisfy the evaluation requirements of the contracting agency. Then, having satisfied that, I attempted to turn the evaluation into something that focused on primary stakeholders' real evaluation concerns. In short, I sought to increase their interest in evaluation and its use.

Evaluation works best and has the greatest likelihood of being used when it is elevated to the status of *valued norm* of the organization. That is, the stakeholders with authority as well as others in the organization make evaluation a part of their *modus operandus*. It is the way that things are done. People look to evaluation as what we do and what we consider valuable. Obviously, this is a very hard goal to reach. But keep it in mind as a part of what you want to reinforce throughout the process of conducting the evaluation.

I will bore you now by repeating what I have perhaps said a hundred times in this volume: *Active participation of primary stakeholders* is an essential part of the evaluation. Active participation increases stakeholder interest in the evaluation and it increases their commitment to its use. It leads to the potential for the evaluation being considered as a valued norm, an important part of the way the organization operates.

I talked earlier about the importance of evaluator credibility and how credibility accrues throughout the process. I mentioned technical expertise and, of course, communication. Another aspect associated with building credibility and, in turn, enhancing use is *timeliness*. It is essential for you as the evaluator to respond quickly to administrative requests and to provide information and reports in a timely fashion. Attitude changes take time to sink in. Changes in program operation do not occur instantly. Give stakeholders the time to digest evaluation findings so that action can take place. The extent to which the evaluator's behavior and actions are timely has impact on use.

The Endgame:
Teaching Stakeholders to Use Evaluation

Use of findings frequently occurs at the end of the evaluation, after the presentation of the final report. (Remember again that use may occur based on interim findings or based on the evaluation process.) In the previous section of this book, I spoke of how to more effectively present evaluation reports. I spoke of the evaluator's credibility earlier in this section. Evaluations also may have credibility. Accordingly, an *evaluation report must be seen as credible*. In part, this report credibility is a function of the evaluation procedures employed and the extent to which they are communicated in an understandable fashion. Credible evaluation reports are more likely to be used.

The final area on which I will comment is related to how you as an evaluator may foster use through active involvement in *teaching stakeholders how to use information*. Thinking about how to use evaluation information is not really a part of most stakeholders' world. Sure, they may think about large summative decisions, but digging into the data and sorting out the implications is more difficult. At this point, I ask you to reflect on my previous comments with respect to making recommendations as part of the evaluation report. I generally "don't do" recommendations. I prefer that courses of action be determined by the stakeholders. And this is where you as the evaluator play an important role. Your guidance in understanding the meaning and potential implications of findings is vital.

But getting to the point of evaluation use often requires group action. Evaluator skills in helping stakeholders to engage in the process of considering possible use are often necessary. In a study of effective evaluation use that I coordinated, one of my professional colleagues noted that "school administrators, teachers, and parent . . . often do not have group process skills and decision-making skills. They must be given assistance in how to read, analyze, and make decisions based on evaluation data." The effective evaluator that my colleague studied had outlined a planning and decision-making process in which the evaluator listed the specific steps sequentially, the data that were available to inform the decisions, and the specific decisions that could be made. Another professional colleague in that same study identified an evaluator who regularly encouraged stakeholders to use evaluation data by giving them information on a related task or problem. In essence, this evaluator trained stakeholders to use data in making program decisions by giving them practice with the process. The bottom line: Engage stakeholders in activities designed to focus their attention on the multiple ways that evaluation information might be used.

RECAP—SECTION V
Evaluator Actions in Obtaining Use

- The Preconditions
  - Credibility
  - Evaluator commitment to use
  - Stakeholders' prior evaluation experience
- During the Evaluation
  - Stakeholder interest in this evaluation
  - Valued norm
  - Active participation
  - Timeliness
- The Endgame
  - Effective reports
  - Teaching use to stakeholders

GUARD AGAINST MISUSE

I have talked about the importance of your actions in helping evaluation use to occur. Of equal importance is your responsibility for guarding against misuse. Misuse occurs when stakeholders modify, misstate, or inappropriately excerpt from the evaluation report. You have an important responsibility for assuring that your evaluation is conveying the information that you intended and not being misapplied in ways not justified by your evaluation. Misuse may start with stakeholders taking your report and simply modifying sections of it. This is inappropriate. Misuse may occur by stakeholders summarizing elements of the report in ways that are not consistent with what you stated. This is inappropriate. Misuse may occur by stakeholders when they injudiciously excerpt portions of the report consistent with their beliefs, but not with the tone of the report. This is inappropriate.

And so I ask you to consider use; do all that you can to foster appropriate use. However, be alert to potential misuse.

GAINING FURTHER UNDERSTANDING

Case Study Exercise

As before, the case study provides opportunities for further learning. Consider the RUPAS case:

- Who might use the evaluation findings?
- Assume that Amy Wilson will be a user. She had no prior evaluation experience. What might you have done to foster a greater inclination for her to use the evaluation? What might you do to engage in "teaching use," as I have discussed it, to Amy or to others?
- In what ways might you as the evaluator have established and maintained your credibility as a precondition to enhancing use?

Further Reading

Alkin, M. C., & Taut, S. M. (2003). Unbundling evaluation use. *Studies in Educational Evaluation, 29*(1), 1–12.

This journal article describes the "landscape" of evaluation utilization—namely, the different kinds of utilization, with an emphasis on those that can be influenced by the evaluator.

Cousins, J. B. (Ed.). (2007). *Process use in theory, research, and practice* (New Directions for Program Evaluation, No. 116). San Francisco: Jossey-Bass.

This journal volume provides an excellent introduction to process evaluation. Pay particular attention to Chapter 1, pp. 5–8, for a discussion of the historical evolution of the term *process use.* Also see Chapters 3 and 7 by Jean King and Michael Patton, respectively.

Forss, K., Claus, R. C., & Carlsson, J. (2002). Process use of evaluations: Types of use that precede lessons learned and feedback. *Evaluation, 8*(1), 29–45.

This article focuses on the kind of evaluation use associated not with findings but with the process of conducting the evaluation.

Hofstetter, C. H., & Alkin, M. C. (2003). Evaluation use revisited. In T. Kellaghan & D. Stufflebeam (Eds.), *International handbook of educational evaluation* (pp. 197–222). Boston: Kluwer Academic Publishers.

This book chapter summarizes the context, stakeholder, and evaluator factors associated with attaining a high level of evaluation use.

Patton, M. (2007). Misuse of evaluations. In S. Mathison (Ed.), *Encyclopedia of evaluation* (pp. 255–256). Thousand Oaks, CA: Sage.

This is an excellent short description of misuse. For a more complete discussion examine the Alkin and Coyle article that Patton cites.

W

How Are Evaluations Managed?

Many of the administrative, or management, activities have been discussed in conjunction with other sections. However, I think it is helpful to summarize those various isolated comments and, where appropriate, extend their discussion. I discuss management activities in this section in four parts, which are labeled: *acquiring the evaluation, contract/ agreement, budget,* and *operational management.*

ACQUIRING THE EVALUATION

Evaluations are commissioned in a variety of ways. As we earlier noted, some evaluations can be categorized as *internal* evaluations— that is, within the organization itself. In such instances someone within the organization is asked to evaluate the program with which they are familiar. Ideally, that individual has some evaluation expertise. Perhaps that person is you, and I hope that this book will help you carry out that assignment. Where the individual who will be performing the evaluation is a member of the program staff, there will be fewer written documents. That is, there might be no need for a contract, but you should have an agreement stipulating what is to be done and perhaps the additional resources that will be necessary for the conduct of the evaluation.

Sometimes internal evaluations are conducted by individuals not specifically within the program to be evaluated, but from the larger organization that encompasses that program. Let's call this *internal–external*. For example, a school district might have an evaluation unit consisting of one or more individuals whose responsibility is evaluating the various programs within the district. In that case, the resources for the conduct of the evaluation might already be within the evaluation unit, or some portion of it might be provided as a supplement by the program itself. The nature of the relationship and the necessity for formality in agreements will differ from case to case.

Most evaluations, however, are *external*. That is, they are conducted by a party outside the organization who has been specifically commissioned for this activity. This is where I focus my attention with respect to the process of acquiring the contract or agreement to perform the evaluation. External evaluations take on several forms. In some instances, the program personnel are aware of an evaluator whom they believe to be competent and will approach him or her about potentially conducting the evaluation. In the evaluation literature, this is referred to as a *sole-source* evaluation—that is, just one person is contacted. In more instances than not, the evaluation report commissioners have a fixed dollar amount in mind and are simply asking the potential selected evaluator to indicate what he or she might do in the evaluation within that particular cost constraint. Sole-source evaluation normally requires a simple agreement that I describe below.

Usually a program will allow *multiple potential evaluators* to *compete* in acquiring the evaluation. This might be done informally by simply contacting a number of individuals or agencies that are known to conduct evaluation. Sometimes this selection from multiple evaluators is done at a more formal level. In that instance, a *request for proposal* (RFP) is employed and distributed broadly so that individuals can decide whether they want to be part of the competitive process.

The Proposal

Typically, several factors are considered in the selection of an external evaluator based on the proposal. To put it simply, we might consider the three components as: the *evaluation objectives and plan* presented by the evaluator; the *budget*; and the *competency* of the evaluators. There are great variations in how these components are presented and are emphasized. Some RFPs provide fairly elaborate descriptions of the evaluation that is desired and seek cost estimates from competitors along with an indication of staff competency. Some RFPs provide a maximum bid cost and a minimally developed plan, asking the potential evaluator to provide a detailed indication of how the evaluation might be conducted. As you can see, such a way of commissioning the evaluation eliminates some of the important steps in constructing an evaluation that I have outlined. The evaluation bidder must intuit the principal stakeholder's important questions, as well as the logic model and other preparatory items that I have noted. In many cases, the evaluator might be able to modify the contract based on his or her subsequent active engagement with primary stakeholders.

CONTRACT/AGREEMENT

Some evaluation writers are absolutely adamant that every evaluation should have a formal contract with all of the "i"s dotted and all of the "t"s crossed, so to speak. This is certainly sound advice if the evaluation is large enough. Large evaluations with costly budgets, many tasks, and numerous personnel deserve to have the understandings between evaluators and contractors very well stipulated. Unfortunately, if a project is small, a relatively substantial amount of energy, evaluator time, and implicit financial costs are expended in negotiating a complex contract. It simply makes no sense.

However, there must always be a "meeting of the minds" between those who contract for the evaluation and the evaluators. Some kind of written agreement is always necessary—this helps in avoiding potential future conflicts. For smaller evaluations, a letter from the evaluator stipulating the various terms and understandings is appropriate. This should be accompanied by a confirmation letter from the contracting agency agreeing to those terms. The degree of completeness and formality will vary based on the size of the program (and of the evaluation).

But if there is a formal contract, what needs to be stated? What needs to be agreed to? What is the essence of a contract or even of an informal agreement? Many of the aspects to be included within the formal contract have already been discussed in previous sections (particularly in Section Q). Clearly, the contract must stipulate the individuals to be involved in the conduct of the evaluation. And accompanying the names of the individuals who will be involved, there should be information about their capability, experience, and their cultural competence. Moreover, there should be an indication of the time commitment of each of the key professional personnel. In simple agreements, this might be a rough estimate of the percentage of time to be devoted to the evaluation effort. In more complex contracts, time might be stated as number of days of effort or, even further, expressed in terms of time to be devoted to each of the designated tasks required for accomplishing the evaluation.

As noted earlier in this section, contracts and agreements may be reached and agreed on at various points in time. Assume for a moment that the contract (and we will use this term to mean both contracts and agreements and everything in between) had been signed based on an RFP competition. In that instance, you as the evaluator would not have had the opportunity to gain full understanding of the program, its logic, and the development of finalized questions to be addressed. That being the case, the evaluation contract should specify some general understanding about the nature of the program to be evaluated, because further detail had not yet been pursued. The contract should indicate the initial understandings about the goal of the evaluation, initial preferences stated about kinds of data to be collected, and to the extent possible, the kinds of analysis procedures to be employed.

The contract also should address the issue of evaluator reporting responsibilities. Will there be a final evaluation report? As I noted in Section U, some evaluators maintain that a final written evaluation report is not always necessary. I believe that written evaluation reports are usually necessary. Thus it is important that the evaluator reach an agreement about the reporting time line with the stakeholders. When is the final report due? Are there to be other interim written reports as well, and on what schedule? If oral reports are to be provided, there should be agreement on when that is to occur.

A bit of an editorial aside is in order at this juncture. I note that some evaluation writers talk about the need to establish *ownership* of the data and the report. One concern that they state is the right of the evaluator to unilaterally decide to publish the evaluation findings (e.g., in a journal). I do not feel great concern about this matter because of my strong commitment to the relevance of the evaluation for the particular program site being evaluated. If there is something in the evaluation that is sufficiently generalizable and of interest to a broader audience, it is the client's right to determine whether that will be allowed.

Please note, however, that the right of ownership does not extend, in any way, to modifying the evaluator's report. In my view, instances of doing so, or of use of inappropriate or misleading quotes from the report, authorize evaluators to make their public voice heard.

Clearly, if you as the evaluator had provided a plan upon getting the contract, it would not have been as detailed as what I have described in Sections O–Q. You would not have had the same level of familiarity with the program. Under those circumstances, the plan as described in the contract might undergo change as you help the primary stakeholders to define their questions and examine potential evaluability. Such changes, if made, should culminate in a written agreement about revisions.

BUDGET

The budget constitutes an agreement with the client on an *established dollar amount* that may be made available for the conduct of the evaluation. Sometimes the dollar amount is fixed and the limits are impermeable. Other times, as discussion takes place in general terms about what might be accomplished within the stipulated dollar limits, the amount of the evaluation budget can be negotiated upward (or perhaps in very unusual cases, downward).

The budget document, which should be viewed as a part of the contract, may also vary in complexity depending on evaluation size. At a minimum, in instances of a fixed-price contract, that dollar amount should be stipulated along with the *schedule* indicating when *payments* will be made and under what conditions. By this, we mean that the contract amount might be paid at scheduled intervals (e.g., monthly) or tied to completing stipulated activities in the evaluation plan (e.g., reaching agreement on a logic model, conducting the implementation evaluation, collecting evaluation data).

The *basic budget* has as its prime components the costs associated with evaluation personnel, including salaries and employee benefits. Also included is a breakdown of various supplies and materials, equipment, travel, and consultants. A final category of most simple budgets is "indirect costs." This latter item depicts those costs that cannot be specifically stipulated; for example, the cost of office rental space. An evaluation consultant may have several projects so there is the need to prorate the cost of the space among the different projects. This basic budget is depicted in Figure W.1.

A somewhat more complete and formal budget will provide even greater detail. In this case, the basic budget (shown in Figure W.1) would be supplemented by a budget justification document. This is simply a listing of the various budget items and an explanation of how each was calculated. Thus personnel are named, their salaries indicated, and the percentage of time they will be working indicated. The basis for determining employee benefits is also described. In some cases, the organization might have a specific health and benefits policy, which should be described. Furthermore, where travel is an item, policies such as reimbursement rates should be indicated as well as the justification for travel.

More substantial and complex budgets indicate the cost by task (activity categories of the evaluations). For each evaluation task, evaluation staff members are listed with an indication of the time and the salary benefits associated with performing the various evaluation tasks. This is depicted in Figure W.2.

January 1, 20___–December 31, 20___

I. Direct Costs

    A. Salaries and Wages $_____

    B. Employee Benefits   _____

    C. Supplies and Materials   _____

        1. Office Supplies $_____

        2. Equipment Rental   _____

        3. Telephones   _____

        4. Mailing   _____

        5. Printing   _____

    D. Equipment $_____

    E. Travel   _____

    F. Consultants   _____

    Total Direct Costs $_____

FIGURE W.1. Sample budget.

Task #/ Personnel	Salary	% Time	Task salary	Benefits	Total personnel cost	Task total
Task 1: Develop logic model						
• Mr. Jones	_____	_____	_____	_____	_____	_____
• Ms. Gonzalez	_____	_____	_____	_____	_____	
Task 2: Agree on questions						
• Mr. Jones	_____	_____	_____	_____	_____	_____
• Ms. Gonzalez	_____	_____	_____	_____	_____	
. . .	_____	_____	_____	_____	_____	_____
						Grand Total _____

FIGURE W.2. Personnel costs by task.

OPERATIONAL MANAGEMENT

There are a variety of tasks associated with managing an evaluation. Beyond the contractual obligations (or at least agreements) that need to be fulfilled, and developing a budget, there are many other management matters to be considered. There are evaluation personnel to be hired and coordinated. There are relationships to be maintained. Let us consider some of these management tasks—although you will certainly think of many others that need to be examined.

Evaluation Tasks and Their Sequence

The evaluator must delineate the evaluation tasks, determine how long each will take, and the necessary deadlines for each. Much of this may already be partially specified as a part of the evaluation plan developed in Section Q. The sequence of tasks will more or less coincide with the order presented in the sections of this volume. Furthermore, there is a need to indicate which evaluation personnel will be involved in each task. Finally, there is the matter of keeping track of all of this to see that it is proceeding as planned.

But it is not all that simple to determine when each task will take place. The sequence suggested in this volume is of some assistance. However, there are contingencies. Some evaluation tasks must be completed before others can commence. Why not list all the tasks that need to be accomplished and then consider which ones precede others? Be especially alert to contingency activities. That is, Activity X might need to be done before Activity Y can be started. Be aware of these prerequisite activities.

Now you might prepare a chart showing the time line for the project, which depicts the sequence of activities that must occur. In doing so, you must consider the amount of time required for each task, the general sequence of tasks, and the contingencies. Perhaps you might construct a chart as noted in Figure W.3.

As an example, Figure W.3 provides a general *evaluation time line*. Notice that I have not provided dates for the accomplishment of each of the evaluation tasks, nor have I indicated the amount of evaluation personnel time (or days) to be allocated to each task. This is intentional, since I believe that each evaluation has its very own idiosyncrasies. Some evaluations may start with an RFP and a proposal, which might correspond to what I have designated as "evaluation plan" on the time line. Alternatively, a full proposal might have to be written to obtain the evaluation contract (not shown in Figure W.3). Furthermore, some other programs to be evaluated might already have a logic model and

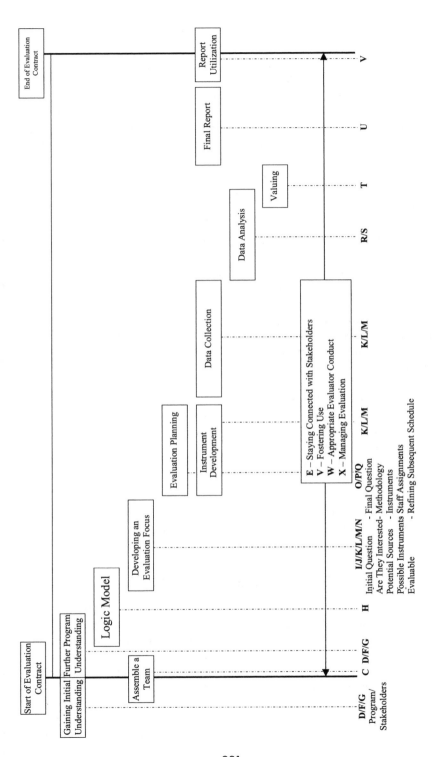

FIGURE W.3. General evaluation time line.

221

will not need to have evaluator assistance on that action. In other programs, primary stakeholders might adamantly refuse to engage in the logic model exercise. Some evaluations might require a vast amount of instrument development while others might use mostly existing instruments. Some evaluations might have been operating for some period of time and have already gathered substantial process data for determining program implementation. I think you get the point. Evaluations are different. Thus I ask you to consider this general evaluation time line as simply a stimulus to your own thinking as you engage in an evaluation.

As you will note from this general time line I have specified several items not typically found on evaluation time lines. Two of these precede the start of the evaluation contract, one of which is "gaining initial understandings" of both the program and the stakeholders. The second, "assembling a team," begins prior to the contract, but continues thereafter. At the end of the time line, an activity appears that is listed as beginning during the contract period and extending beyond the end of the evaluation contract. With respect to that task, I believe that "assisting the program in utilization" is an important part of the evaluator's job, even if beyond the end of the contract.

To a great extent, the general time line presented in this chart follows the sequence of sections presented within this volume. I have paid heed to the natural dependencies between tasks—which tasks must precede others. Furthermore, I have noted instances where a task may commence prior to the start of another task on which it depends, but will continue subsequently (see, e.g., the "data analysis" task). Finally, I so value the importance of the evaluator maintaining appropriate relations with the stakeholder that I have designated this as a task that continues throughout the full program contract.

Please note the key below the time line chart to see which sections of this volume deal with each task.

Selecting Appropriate Staff

Another management task associated with the time line that you may now have constructed is determining the skills necessary for performing each evaluation task. Your initial selection of staff members for accomplishing the evaluation should reflect what you believe to be the needs of the evaluation. After completing the evaluation plan, you will gain a better understanding of the specific evaluation tasks that need to be conducted. Thus it will be important to consider anew the staff requirements for fulfilling those requirements. Another management task at this point might be the need to recruit additional evaluation staff. But you also should consider staff already on board to determine whether they have the appropriate skills—technical, social, and cultural. Examine accurately and forthrightly your own skills as well.

You must understand your staff skills well enough so that evaluation personnel can be assigned most appropriately. In some cases, you as an individual evaluator, or as a member of a small team of evaluators, might feel that you do not have sufficient competency to properly accomplish particular tasks. Staff training may be necessary. Furthermore, consider the places where appropriate short-term consultants might be needed.

Maintaining the Schedule

So you have completed a schedule of activities and personnel assignments (including your own evaluation responsibilities). What next? Accomplish it! It is important that you are attentive to *maintaining* and adhering to that *time line*. Check progress on a very regular basis, and if you are falling behind, do something about it. Reasons for not maintaining the schedule are many. Sometimes program staff have changed the schedule and you have not obtained proper access for data collection. Possibly, implementation difficulties have caused delays not only in the program schedule, but also in the completion of the evaluation tasks. Program-caused delays should be discussed promptly with the administrator in charge of the program (and the individual responsible for the contract, if different). Delays in communicating are not helpful. Decide jointly about what can be done and whether modifications in evaluation responsibilities are necessary.

Other difficulties in maintaining the schedule may be attributable to failures of the evaluation team. Have there been staff losses and is there a need for more evaluation assistance? Did the plan underestimate the amount of time required to complete some evaluation tasks? Were there computer failures that slowed data analysis? The possible problems are endless. The evaluation plan and time line should have built in a little "cushion" so that minor difficulties can be handled with relative ease. Anything beyond that might require that the evaluation team provide the additional resources needed or renegotiate the budget if possible (usually not).

Communicating, Relating, Communicating

Finally, a very important management responsibility is maintaining contact with primary stakeholders and keeping an ear open to the thoughts of the larger stakeholder audience. Update and inform primary stakeholders. Be available to listen to their concerns (although surely all of them cannot be alleviated). As I have repeated countless times throughout this volume: Maintaining positive relationships with stakeholders is essential.

RECAP—SECTION W
Managing the Evaluation

- Acquiring the Evaluation
  - Internal evaluation
  - External evaluation
    - Sole source
    - Request for proposal (RFP)
- Writing the Proposal
- Obtaining the Contract or Agreement
- Developing the Budget
- Managing Operations
  - Time line
  - Staff skills required
  - Maintaining the schedule
  - Communicating, relating, communicating

GAINING ADDITIONAL UNDERSTANDING

Case Study Exercise

What are the skills and attributes likely to have been required in conducting this evaluation?

- Would funding such a staff have been difficult?
- Given the RUPAS context, what factors might have imposed the most difficulty in adhering to the time line?

Further Reading

Bell, J. B. (2004). Managing evaluation projects. In J. S. Wholey, H. P. Hatry, & K. E. Newcomer (Eds.), *Handbook of practical program evaluation* (2nd ed.). San Francisco: Jossey-Bass.

This chapter cover a wide range of issues, including many that have been discussed in prior sections of this book. You should pay particular heed to the topics of proposal development, staffing concerns, and time line monitoring.

Horn, J. (2001). *A checklist for developing and evaluating evaluation budgets.* Available at *www.wmich.edu/evalctr/checklists.*

This is another in the series of checklists available through the Western Michigan University site. Horn's checklist provides a guide for developing budgets.

Stufflebeam, D. L. (1999). *Contracting for evaluations.* Available at *www.wmich. edu/evalctr/evalcontract.pdf.*

This checklist related to contracting for evaluation is very complete— perhaps too complete. Use it as a general guideline.

Stufflebeam, D. L. (2000). Lessons in contracting for evaluations. *American Journal of Evaluation, 21,* 293–314.

Stufflebeam reflects on some personal experiences in contracting for evaluation.

What Are
the Evaluation Standards
and Codes of Behavior?

B y now, you have a sense of what constitutes a good evaluation. That is, you have some understanding of the standards that might be used to *judge whether an evaluation is well done*. I would like you to reflect for a few minutes now about what you have read in this book. What do you think might be the five major themes that emerge for making that judgment? Stop now. Don't turn to the next page quite yet. Think about it. Remember there is no single right answer. What characteristics make a good evaluation? *Think about it!*

JUDGING AN EVALUATION

Let us jointly consider what we have conversed about in this book. First, you undoubtedly have noticed a continued discussion on the topic of *evaluation use*. We talked about doing meaningful evaluations that can be used by primary stakeholders in order to improve their programs. We highlighted the importance of identifying appropriate audiences—stakeholders. Furthermore, we considered the questions to be examined in the evaluation and emphasized the selection of questions that stakeholders really want answers to, answers that will be useful to them. We considered the topics of report clarity and appropriate dissemination.

In Section C, we considered the issue of who does evaluations—what an evaluator looks like. In that section, I highlighted the importance of the evaluator having a use orientation. Perhaps one of the most important things leading to potential evaluation use is an attitude and a belief on the part of evaluators that it is important.

And so we see that one potential *standard* for judging evaluations reaffirms the importance of seeking evaluation use. The goal is evaluation use. When judging the evaluation itself this means that it should have *utility*—that is, the ability and characteristics that make it potentially useful.

What else? Clearly, an evaluation cannot be conducted if the evaluation plan and projected evaluation procedures are not realistic or practical. One can create exotic evaluation designs that may be totally inappropriate for the context. Evaluations have to be organizationally, politically, and financially feasible. I have addressed some of these topics within sections of this volume. We jointly considered the organizational, social, and political context and how it enables or constrains the evaluation. And we looked at whether the questions being considered were evaluable, taking into consideration these organizational, social, and political elements as well as cost considerations. That is, we were trying to assure that the evaluation to be conducted was *feasible*.

In several places throughout the volume we talked about ethical issues. We considered ethics from the point of view of the evaluator in terms of disclosing potential conflicts of interest. I also stressed the necessity that the evaluator not be compromised in the presentation of evaluation reports. The evaluator also has to deal with stakeholders in a manner that respects their rights and their points of view.

Furthermore, at various junctures within this volume I indicated the need to go into the community and try to understand "where people are coming from." I noted the need to get the broad stakeholder views that could be injected into the discussion with primary stakeholders. I indicated the need for respecting the rights of human subjects and respectfully dealing with people. I commented on the concern for the evaluator to be aware of the legal constraints surrounding the evaluation, including the kinds of mandated reporting that would be required. Let's give a name to this assortment of legal, ethical, and personal interaction elements and call it *propriety*—the condition of being proper, fitting, or suitable.

Of course, what is an evaluation if it is not technically correct—technically accurate? We have talked about evaluation as being a systematic procedure for the collection, analysis, and valuing of information. And indeed, *accuracy* must be considered as one of the standards for judging a good evaluation. This whole volume deals with conducting a technically correct and adequate evaluation. I maintain that the first element of accuracy is getting it right—asking the right questions. We certainly have explored that issue in many, many sections. Identifying the appropriate information sources is another element of accuracy. Developing an evaluation plan with defensible information sources keyed to the evaluation questions is yet another step. Appropriate collection and analysis of data—valid and reliable data—are likewise important. Finally, reaching informed conclusions is an essential element of accuracy.

THE PROGRAM EVALUATION STANDARDS

I CHEATED. The above discussion, while absolutely true and reflecting the issues discussed within this volume, identifies four of the five major concepts in the book *The Program Evaluation Standards*. The book was produced by the Joint Committee on Standards for Educational Evaluation. A few words of description are in order here.

The Joint Committee was initially formed in the late 1970s. The committee consisted of representatives from 16 major professional associations. Their work engaged hundreds of persons in deliberations, writing, field-testing, and the like, in order to develop agreed-on standards for the conduct of evaluation. The first publication of *The Program Evaluation Standards* was in 1981, with subsequent editions in 1994 and now in 2010. The embracing concepts of *utility, feasibility, propriety,* and *accuracy* have formed the basis for the *Standards* since its initial publication. Within each of these concepts, the Joint Committee has derived between three and eight specific standard statements.

In the 2010 edition, a fifth concept was added: *evaluation accountability*. In essence, this refers to the importance of systematic reflection and examination of the extent to which an evaluation is accountable. That is, did the evaluation fulfill the expectations of the *Program Evaluation Standards*? I tend to think of accountability more broadly. The standard on accountability refers to a responsibility to stakeholders to obtain a systematic review of their evaluation to provide assurance that the evaluation was done well. I believe that the activity called meta-evaluation, which forms the basis of the accountability concept, is one part of an evaluator's actions to evaluate his/her own efforts in order to improve. I discuss the need for learning more about evaluation and for improving evaluator skills in Section Z. The *Program Evaluation Standards* summary is presented in Table X.1. It would be helpful as you read the specific standard statements to reflect on the ways in which each of them has been dealt with in this volume. You will notice that there are sometimes conflicts between specific standard statements.

TABLE X.1. The Program Evaluation Standards

Utility standard statements

U1 Evaluator Credibility	Evaluations should be conducted by qualified people who establish and maintain credibility in the evaluation context.
U2 Attention to Stakeholders	Evaluations should devote attention to the full range of individuals and groups invested in the program and affected by its evaluation.
U3 Negotiated Purposes	Evaluation purposes should be identified and continually negotiated based on the needs of stakeholders.
U4 Explicit Values	Evaluations should clarify and specify the individual and cultural values underpinning purposes, processes, and judgments.
U5 Relevant Information	Evaluation information should serve the identified and emergent needs of stakeholders.
U6 Meaningful Processes and Products	Evaluations should construct activities, descriptions, and judgments in ways that encourage participants to rediscover, reinterpret, or revise their understandings and behaviors.

(cont.)

TABLE X.1. *(cont.)*

Utility standard statements *(cont.)*

U7 Timely and Appropriate Communicating and Reporting	Evaluations should attend to the continuing information needs of their multiple audiences.
U8 Concern for Consequences and Influence	Evaluations should promote responsible and adaptive use while guarding against unintended negative consequences and misuse.

Feasibility standard statements

F1 Project Management	Evaluations should use effective project management strategies.
F2 Practical Procedures	Evaluations procedures should be practical and responsive to the way the program operates.
F3 Contextual Viability	Evaluations should recognize, monitor, and balance the cultural and political interests and needs of individuals and groups.
F4 Resource Use	Evaluations should use resources efficiently and effectively.

Propriety standard statements

P1 Responsive & Inclusive Orientation	Evaluations should be responsive to stakeholders and their communities.
P2 Formal Agreements	Evaluation agreements should be negotiated to make obligations explicit and take into account the needs, expectations, and cultural contexts of clients and other stakeholders.
P3 Human Rights and Respect	Evaluations should be designed and conducted to protect human and legal rights and maintain the dignity of participants and other stakeholders.
P4 Clarity and Fairness	Evaluations should be understandable and fair in addressing stakeholder needs and purposes.
P5 Transparency and Disclosure	Evaluations should provide complete descriptions of findings, limitations, and conclusions to all stakeholders, unless doing so would violate legal and propriety obligations.

(cont.)

TABLE X.1. *(cont.)*

Propriety standard statements *(cont.)*

P6 Conflicts of Interests	Evaluations should openly and honestly identify and address real or perceived conflicts of interests that may compromise the evaluation.
P7 Fiscal Responsibility	Evaluations should account for all expended resources and comply with sound fiscal procedures and processes.

Accuracy standard statements

A1 Justified Conclusions and Decisions	Evaluation conclusions and decisions should be explicitly justified in the cultures and contexts where they have consequences.
A2 Valid Information	Evaluation information should serve the intended purposes and support valid interpretations.
A3 Reliable Information	Evaluation procedures should yield sufficiently dependable and consistent information for the intended uses.
A4 Explicit Program and Context Descriptions	Evaluations should document programs and their contexts with appropriate detail and scope for the evaluation purposes.
A5 Information Management	Evaluations should employ systematic information collection, review, verification, and storage methods.
A6 Sound Designs and Analyses	Evaluations should employ technically adequate designs and analyses that are appropriate for the evaluation purposes.
A7 Explicit Evaluation Reasoning	Evaluation reasoning leading from information and analyses to findings, interpretations, conclusions, and judgments should be clearly and completely documented.
A8 Communication and Reporting	Evaluation communications should have adequate scope and guard against misconceptions, biases, distortions, and errors.

(cont.)

TABLE X.1. *(cont.)*

Evaluation accountability standards

E1 Evaluation Documentation	Evaluations should fully document their negotiated purposes and implemented designs, procedures, data, and outcomes.
E2 Internal Meta-evaluation	Evaluators should use these and other applicable standards to examine the accountability of the evaluation design, procedures employed, information collected, and outcomes.
E3 External Meta-evaluation	Program evaluation sponsors, clients, evaluators, and other stakeholders should encourage the conduct of external meta-evaluations using these and other applicable standards.

Note. From Yarbrough, Shulha, Hopson, and Caruthers (2010). *The Program Evaluation Standards* (3rd ed.). Copyright 2010 by Sage Publications. Reprinted by permission.

AMERICAN EVALUATION ASSOCIATION GUIDING PRINCIPLES

There's another set of guidelines used by evaluators. The American Evaluation Association (AEA) created a task force to consider guiding principles for evaluators. It is important for us to differentiate between the *Program Evaluation Standards* and the *AEA Guiding Principles*. As you noticed in the prior discussion, the *Evaluation Standards* focus on the characteristics of an evalua*tion* that make it a good evaluation. On the other hand, the *Guiding Principles* have as a primary focus the actions that the evalua*tor* should (or should not) take. The first focuses on evaluations; the second focuses on evaluators.

The five major categories of the *AEA Guiding Principles* are: *systematic inquiry, competence, integrity/honesty, respect for people*, and *responsibilities for general and public welfare*. Table X.2 shows the actions expected of evaluators.

TABLE X.2. American Evaluation Association Guiding Principles

A. *Systematic Inquiry. Evaluators conduct systematic, data-based inquiries, and thus should:*

1. Adhere to the highest technical standards appropriate to the methods they use.

2. Explore with the client the shortcomings and strengths of evaluation questions and approaches.

3. Communicate the approaches, methods, and limitations of the evaluation accurately and in sufficient detail to allow others to understand, interpret, and critique their work.

B. *Competence. Evaluators provide competent performance to stakeholders, and thus should:*

1. Ensure that the evaluation team collectively possesses the education, abilities, skills and experience appropriate to the evaluation.

2. Ensure that the evaluation team collectively demonstrates cultural competence and uses appropriate evaluation strategies and skills to work with culturally different groups.

3. Practice within the limits of their competence, decline to conduct evaluations that fall substantially outside those limits, and make clear any limitations on the evaluation that might result if declining is not feasible.

4. Seek to maintain and improve their competencies in order to provide the highest level of performance in their evaluations.

C. *Integrity/Honesty. Evaluators display honesty and integrity in their own behavior and attempt to ensure the honesty and integrity of the entire evaluation process, and thus should:*

1. Negotiate honestly with clients and relevant stakeholders concerning the costs, tasks, limitations of methodology, scope of results, and uses of data.

2. Disclose any roles or relationships that might pose a real or apparent conflict of interest prior to accepting an assignment.

3. Record and report all changes to the original negotiated project plans and the reasons for them, including any possible impacts that could result.

4. Be explicit about their own, their clients', and other stakeholders' interests and values related to the evaluation.

5. Represent accurately their procedures, data, and findings, and attempt to prevent or correct misuse of their work by others.

(cont.)

TABLE X.2. *(cont.)*

6. Work to resolve any concerns related to procedures or activities likely to produce misleading evaluative information, decline to conduct the evaluation if concerns cannot be resolved, and consult colleagues or relevant stakeholders about other ways to proceed if declining is not feasible.

7. Disclose all sources of financial support for an evaluation, and the source of the request for the evaluations.

D. *Respect for People. Evaluators respect the security, dignity, and self-worth of respondents, program participants, clients, and other evaluation stakeholders, and thus should:*

1. Seek a comprehensive understanding of the contextual elements of the evaluation.

2. Abide by current professional ethics, standards, and regulations regarding confidentiality, informed consent, and potential risks or harms to participants.

3. Seek to maximize the benefits and reduce any unnecessary harms that might occur from an evaluation and carefully judge when the benefits from the evaluation or procedure should be foregone because of potential risks.

4. Conduct the evaluation and communicate its results in a way that respects stakeholders' dignity and self-worth.

5. Foster social equity in evaluation, when feasible, so that those who give to the evaluation may benefit in return.

6. Understand, respect, and take into account differences among stakeholders such as culture, religion, disability, age, sexual orientation, and ethnicity.

E. *Responsibilities for General and Public Welfare. Evaluators articulate and take into account the diversity of general and public interests and values, and thus should:*

1. Include relevant perspectives and interests of the full range of stakeholders.

2. Consider not only immediate operations and outcomes of the evaluation, but also the broad assumptions, implications, and potential side effects.

3. Allow stakeholders' access to and actively disseminate evaluative information, and present evaluation results in understandable forms that respect people and honor promises of confidentiality.

(cont.)

TABLE X.2. *(cont.)*

4. Maintain a balance between client and other stakeholder needs and interests.

5. Take into account the public interest and good, going beyond analysis of particular stakeholder interests to consider the welfare of society as a whole.

Note. From the American Evaluation Association. (2004). *Guiding Principles for Evaluators.* Available at *www.eval.org/Publications/GuidingPrinciples.asp.* Copyright 2004 by the American Evaluation Association. Reprinted by permission.

───────── **GAINING ADDITIONAL UNDERSTANDING** ─────────

Case Study Exercise

What have you learned about the *Standards* and codes of behavior? Again, consider the RUPAS case and reflect on some of the difficulties that might have inhibited adherence to the *Evaluation Standards.*

Which of the activities that you considered conducting seemed to be in compliance with the *Standards*? Which may not have been appropriate?

Consider, also, ways in which you as the evaluator might not have been sufficiently mindful of the *Guiding Principles.*

Further Reading

Mertens, D. M. (1995). Identifying and respecting differences among participants in evaluation studies. In W. R. Shadish, D. L. Newman, M. A. Scheier, & C. Wye (Eds.), *Guiding principles for evaluators* (New Directions for Program Evaluation, No. 66, pp. 47–52). San Francisco: Jossey-Bass.

In this chapter Donna Mertens explores the implications of the *Standards* with respect to recognizing differences among participants in such things as culture, religion, gender, and ethnicity.

Morris, M. (2003). Ethical considerations in evaluation. In S. Mathison (Ed.), *Encyclopedia of evaluation* (pp. 303–328). Thousand Oaks, CA: Sage.

Michael Morris has written extensively on this topic and provides a nice overview here.

Morris, M. (2008). *Evaluation ethics for best practice.* New York: Guilford Press.

This book presents a series of case studies in which evaluators comment on how they would deal with the ethical issues implicit in each. This provides further insights into the *Guiding Principles.*

Sanders, J. R. (1995). Standards and principles. In W. R. Shadish, D. L. Newman, M. A. Scheier, & C. Wye (Eds.), *Guiding principles for evaluators* (New Directions for Program Evaluation, No. 66, pp. 47–52). San Francisco: Jossey-Bass.

James Sanders examines the differences between the *AEA Guiding Principles* and the *Evaluation Standards.*

Simons, H. (2006). Ethics in evaluation. In I. Shaw, J. Greene, & M. Mark (Eds.), *Sage handbook of evaluation* (pp. 243–265). Thousand Oaks, CA: Sage.

This chapter provides a very complete discussion of the variety of issues implicit in conducting an ethical evaluation.

Yarbrough, D. B., Shulha, L. M., Hopson, R. K., & Caruthers, F. A. (2010). *The program evaluation standards: A guide for evaluators and evaluation users* (3rd ed.). Thousand Oaks, CA: Sage.

Approved by the Joint Committee on Standards for Educational Evaluation, an ANSI member, this is the full description of the standard statements with clarifying examples.

Y

How Are Costs Analyzed?

Evaluations rarely include a cost analysis. In many ways this is unfortunate because understanding the costs of a program relative to its benefits or effectiveness is important. But cost analyses of various types can be very difficult to do. And, indeed, you might ask: Is a cost analysis of a program as part of an evaluation worth the cost?

Let me provide an example to simply show the difficulties of performing an analysis of just the costs of a program. To do this and stick to the familiar, I will select as an example a product evaluation instead of a more complex program evaluation. Assume, for example, that you are thinking of buying a home theater system. The first question you might ask is what such an entity costs: What is the *cost*? This is a seemingly simple question. It is not. You might indicate that the answer is to be found by simply checking a few technology or large appliance stores and seeing what price they are charging. However, that is not the real cost. Determining the real cost of a program (in this case, a product) is a very difficult enterprise. Think, for example, of the cost of traveling to the stores or of setting the system up at home, or the cost of express shipping from an online merchant. There are other personal costs as well. However, I will not get into that now, but will defer discussion of "costing" to the end of the section.

COST-EFFECTIVENESS ANALYSIS

One kind of cost analysis question is, "Where can we get the best deal?" Imagine that you are considering two stores, Target and a local appliance chain. Each has a home theater system of interest to you. The old story of "comparing apples and oranges" may come into play here. There are two ways in which a comparison might be done. The simplest is if they have the same system, and if it is one that you desire, then you can compare prices. To make it simpler at this point, we will think of the price the store charges as the total cost—but keep in mind this will be shown to be an incomplete accounting of the real cost. At this point, and with no added considerations, you might choose the cheaper system as your most cost-effective option.

On the other hand, if each store has a different system but at the same price, then you can compare them on the capability—such as most volume without distortion on your favorite CD. You would have an easy way to choose. But because you may have several qualities of a system, such as volume and number and types of ports for accessories, a decision will require a matter of personal judgment in *weighting* the relative importance of the various quality or outcome measures.

In either case, considering the same product at different prices, or differing products at the same price can benefit from cost-effectiveness analysis. You are comparing two items on the basis of their costs and their effectiveness (in the above example, effectiveness is their capability).

Let's apply this framework to a health program. Performing a cost-effectiveness analysis of a drug treatment program, for example, requires that you have a competing program. Moreover, if that competing program is of the same cost, then you can compare the accomplishments or outcomes of the programs. Which program keeps addicts off of drugs for the longest period of time may be the central outcome—or some other appropriate outcome measure.

The alternative condition that allows the conduct of a cost-effectiveness evaluation is to find a competing drug treatment program that perhaps uses different methods, but has the same specific goal and the two programs attain that goal equally. For example, 75% or more of the participants complete the program. Assume that two competing programs meet that goal. In that instance you can compare their costs. You can see from this example how difficult it is to find two programs with such comparability in order for a cost-effectiveness analysis to be completed.

As I have noted, the major impediment to the conduct of cost-effectiveness evaluation is the necessity of restricting the analysis to a single benefit measure. Cost-effectiveness can only be done if two programs have equal costs—then differences in outcomes are examined. Or if a single outcome (benefit) is the same in each program, then costs are compared. This is, indeed, a major dilemma; most social programs have multiple desired outcomes.

COST-BENEFIT ANALYSIS

Another kind of cost analysis procedure, even more sophisticated and complex, is referred to as a cost–benefit analysis. This analysis shows the relationship between the costs of a program and the benefits that will be attained. That is, if a program costs $50,000, will the value that will be derived from it equal or exceed that dollar amount? This, of course, requires that the benefit measure be converted to dollars. And so, in the simple home theater example, if you are contemplating the purchase, you will need to determine the actual dollar benefits that might be derived from having a home theater system. Will it provide learning experiences that better prepare you to obtain particular jobs? What will be your additional lifetime income obtained above your current expectations? Will it keep your teenage children off the streets and out of trouble? What kind of possible trouble and how might that affect their future benefits (in dollars)? Wow!!

Consider, also, another program example. Imagine that 85 people complete a drug treatment program. How might you as the evaluator determine in dollar terms the various benefits associated with that program completion? In this program case you might be able to examine societal benefits, not personal benefits. The government has established a program. Is it a worthwhile expenditure for society? Do the benefits exceed the costs? To do this, you will need to investigate what the research evidence says about the cost to society of an individual who returns to using drugs. What about police costs? Social service costs? But there are also personal benefits. An individual who has successfully completed the program may be in a better position to obtain employment, get off of welfare, and contribute to society. In small programs, such as in this example, the extreme difficulty of doing these calculations makes cost–benefit analysis not cost beneficial. (That's a pun.) The cost of the program to have you aggregate the benefits in dollar terms is a very large percentage of the cost of running the program itself. The costs of performing that analysis will surely exceed the derived benefits.

However, cost–benefit analyses have been employed productively on very large-scale social programs. Economists, for example, have calculated the costs and benefits of building a dam. And in doing so, they have looked at costs, including the social displacement of individuals, and benefits from the electricity produced by such a dam, among many, many other costs and benefits.

As we have seen, the dilemma with cost-effectiveness analysis is that we are restricted to a single outcome measure. If we are comparing two programs, they must have the same intended goal—desired outcome, measured in the same way, and we may only do the comparison based on a single outcome. And the dilemma with cost–benefit analysis is that somehow we must find a way to convert all *outcome data benefits to dollar amounts.*

COST–UTILITY ANALYSIS

Some economists talk about a potential way out of these dilemmas. They do so by a modification of cost-effectiveness with subjective judgments used as the outcome measure. The term employed is *utility*, meaning the degree of happiness, the degree of benefit that one *perceives* that has been obtained. Note the word *perceives*. The utility notion comes from the philosophical concept of utilitarianism, an approach to ethics generally attributed to Jeremy Bentham and expanded by John Stuart Mill. The way this concept might be used in a cost analysis framework is in the narrower economic sense of perceived usefulness.

The concept of cost–utility is deceptively simple. Indeed, it is instinctual. You look at the cost of several competing alternatives and then you look at the utility rating or happiness that is to be derived from each alternative. One TV costs $1,000 and another costs $1,500. Will you get more happiness from purchasing the first or the second one? Or suppose you do it more formally. Imagine that you assign utility ratings to each of the TV sets. But, of course, there must be ground rules to guide your utility ratings. Assume that you rate each on a scale of 0 to 10. Furthermore, the scale ratings need to be of equal value. That is, the data are like interval data (see Section R). Actually, given that the data are grounded at 0, they are what is called "ratio data," the data type that we previously did not discuss. If you rate one television as 4, then a rating of 8 is considered twice as good. Having a utility rating for each, you then can make a calculation of cost per utility. This is demonstrated in Table Y.1. And so we see that TV set 2 is superior, that it could be attained at a cost of $200 per utility unit (utile), rather than $250. It costs less per unit of utility or happiness.

Now let me discuss how a cost–utility analysis can be performed at the program level. But first, a few words about the word *utility*. Econ-

TABLE Y.1. The Concept of Cost–Utility

	Cost (C)	Utility (U)	C/U Rating
TV Set 1	$1,000	4	1,000/4 = 250
TV Set 2	$1,500	8	1,500/8 = 200

omists who talk about the notion of utility fret about the near impossibility of obtaining an accurate utility measure. I find that to be a relative nonissue for our purposes. For the most part, they are concerned about large-scale, multisite programs and thus about generalizability issues. They question whether any sample population can truly reflect real societal utilities. I have approached evaluation in this volume as being reasonably site specific and as attempting to meet the needs of a local program. Thus, since generalizability is not an issue, the perceived utility of local stakeholders should suffice quite nicely. We want to consider what those whose program it is, and who live with the program, consider to be of value—to have high utility.

And so we wonder how might you as the evaluator go about doing a cost–utility study in a local context, given the stakeholder participatory mode that I have presented in this book. Let me deal here only with the discussion of the utility component of the cost–utility analysis. Naturally, costs will have to be determined in some systematic manner, as I discuss later in this section.

First, let me make it clear that the utility measures need to be determined prior to any data collection or analysis. We do not want the results, as subsequently perceived by stakeholders, to bias perceptions about the degree of importance of any of the outcome areas. The method that I propose is a more sophisticated version of that used as an example in Section A. In that instance, where I was deciding on a house to buy, I delineated the aspects of a house considered to be important (think outcome measures) and then indicated the relative importance of each aspect. In essence, I was asking the degree of happiness (utility) that might be ascribed to an extra bathroom, for example. In the case of a real evaluation, we will have more accurately defined outcome measures.

Single Outcome

And so let me describe a potential procedure for determining utility where there are several alternative programs, each of which has the same single measurable outcome. Let us say, for example, a test score. Now, the question facing us is how much decision makers are willing

TABLE Y.2. Stakeholder Rankings of Utility

Score	Utility
480 or below	0
490	2
500	5
510	7
520	8
530	9
540 or above	10

to pay per increment of test score increase. For example, if one program receives an average score of 500, how much greater happiness is derived from a score of 510? Would they be 10% happier, or 20%, or 50%? In essence, we need to establish utility rankings for scores that might be obtained. Again, I suggest a 0 to 10 rating. The rankings assigned by stakeholders might look something like Table Y.2.

Seemingly, this chart recognizes an expectation of a score of 500. A score of 490 expresses a degree of dissatisfaction and a score of 480 or below is considered worthless. On the positive side, a 10-point increment above 500 seems like a plausible and achievable goal and warrants a jump to a utility rating of 7. Scores above that have only incrementally larger utility ratings.

Then, dividing the cost of each of the competing programs by its ranking provides a cost–utility ratio. If using the rankings on Table Y.2, one program has a cost of $800 and a utility rating of 8 (which is a score of 520). Then its C/R ratio is 100. A competing program with a rating of 5 (score of 500) and a cost of $750 would have a C/R ratio of 150 (750/5). The latter program has a higher cost–utility ranking.

Multiple Outcomes

A program having multiple outcomes builds upon this procedure. We now know how to calculate the utility for differences in an outcome. The same procedure described above can be used for each of the program's outcome areas. But now the question arises: *Are all outcomes created equal?* The answer is probably not. Primary stakeholders may very well assign a higher utility ranking to an instructional program's average reading score than to student satisfaction as a measure.

Each outcome area can have an importance measure attached to it. It is necessary to stress to the primary stakeholders that they are to provide a utility measure for each outcome on a scale of 0 to 10, where 0 is considered as providing no contribution to happiness, 5 is average, and 10 represents the highest possible contribution. Furthermore, it is important to stress to respondents that they must treat the scale as if it has interval properties. That is, a score of 6 is viewed as having twice the utility as a score of 3.

Now let us look at Table Y.3. We have two programs that I have creatively called Program 1 and Program 2. For each of these programs there are two outcome measures: reading score and student satisfaction. Through a process depicted in Table Y.1, we have determined with stakeholders that reading score is of more importance (has a larger utility weighting) than student satisfaction. Thus reading score received an outcome utility weighting (W) of 6 and student satisfaction a weighting of 4. These utility weightings are listed in column W for each of the programs. Furthermore, outcome scores (R) are assigned a ranking based on the relative value of different scores as I have shown in Table Y.2.

The *outcome utility ranking* (U) is simply obtained by multiplying the R and the W values. The total program utility is obtained by adding the score for reading and the score for satisfaction for each of the programs. Thus in this instance Program 1 has a total program utility of 58

TABLE Y.3. Establishing a Cost–Utility Ratio

Outcome measures		R^a Outcome score ranking	W Utility weighing	U Outcome utility ranking	Total program utility	Cost per participant	Cost–utility ratio
Program 1	A (e.g., student satisfaction)	7	4	28	58	$900	900 ÷ 58 = 15.51
	B (e.g., reading score)	5	6	30			
Program 2	A (e.g., student satisfaction)	8	4	32	56	$800	800 ÷ 56 = 14.28
	B (e.g., reading score)	4	6	24			

[a]As described in the previous example.

and Program 2 has a total program utility of 56. Dividing the cost per participant for each of the total programs by the total program utility score provides us with a cost–utility ratio. In Table Y.1 Program 2, then, is apparently the preferred program.

RECAP—SECTION Y
Cost Analysis Procedures

- Cost-Effectiveness Analyses (Multiple Programs)
  - Determine costs
  - Determine (single-measure) outcomes
  - Same costs—compare on outcomes
  - If same outcome—compare on costs
- Cost–Benefit Analysis (Single or Multiple Programs)
  - Determine costs
  - Determine outcomes
  - Convert outcomes to benefits (in dollars)
  - Calculate ratio of costs to benefits
- Cost–Utility Analysis (Single Outcome)
  - Determine costs
  - Determine outcomes
  - Establish outcome score ranking for each level of outcome
  - Calculate ratio of cost to rankings
  - Convert outcomes to rankings
- Cost–Utility Analysis (Multiple Outcomes)
  - Determine costs
  - Determine a utility weighting for relative worth (or importance) of each outcome dimension (W)
  - Determine ranking score for each outcome measure
  - Assign this ranking score to each attained outcome measure
  - Multiply R x W to determine a measure of utility (U)
  - Add utility ranking of each outcome within a program to determine total program utility
  - Divide total program utility by cost to obtain a cost–utility ratio

AND NOW TO COSTS

What are the program costs? Simple! Can't we just simply look at the budget for the program? No! And No!

The real cost for the home theater that we talked about earlier must include your time in going to the store, the transportation cost, and the installation cost once you get it home. For programs that are to be evaluated, one can only imagine all of the data that need to be aggregated in order to compute a real cost. Calculating costs is a very complex endeavor. Some authors have provided quite detailed descriptions about how to identify and determine the costs for the *ingredients* of programs. We provide a reference in the supplemental readings for this section to those inclined.

Think for a moment. A new program is being introduced. What is required in order for the program to operate? The budget provides some insight but not enough. Of course, there are standard budget items such as a listing of the personnel who will be required to run the program. This may include staff employed to directly deal with clients in operationalizing the program. But it also will need to include administrative personnel.

The program may require various materials or equipment necessary to operate the program—computers, for example. What supplies are necessary? Paper, pencils, or pens? But wait, there are also additional administrative costs. Perhaps clerical help is required for ordering supplies or following up with clients. What about custodial staff for maintaining or renovating the facility? Oh yes, the facility! Space will undoubtedly need to be rented. What about consultants? Possibly consultants are needed for equipment maintenance. Furthermore, will staff training be necessary, and if so, will consultants be needed for this training?

But wait, you might say, what about the space we already have? Furthermore, there is no new administration; people in the larger organization will be providing various administrative backup services. And the facility is already being maintained for the other programs currently taking place. So how do you as the evaluator handle this? The answer: It depends. If two alternative programs are being implemented at the same site, using the same amount of facilities, and comparable staff, then many of the costs that one might want to determine are in essence the same for both programs, and it might suffice simply to look at marginal (or additional) costs that are associated with each individual program. That is, one program might need additional equipment while another might need additional aides. There might be unique travel expenses associated with one program and not with the other. By looking at marginal costs, we would not determine the actual full cost of each program, but would gain understanding of relative cost differences that could be used in a cost analysis (cost-effectiveness analysis, cost–benefit analysis, or cost–utility analysis). If the programs have substantially different cost bases then it may not suffice to only look at marginal costs. In that case, full costing would be required.

HOW TO DETERMINE COST

One influential evaluator has suggested a procedure for identifying all the ingredients of a program that have costs associated with them. I pretty much have alluded to the categories in the previous discussion: personnel, space, equipment, supplies, and services (including consultants).

Perhaps the most straightforward costing takes place in regard to *personnel*. Of course, there is a listed salary for each individual directly involved. Associated with the salary are employee benefits that also need to be determined. The two alternative programs being compared in the cost analysis may have staff employed who have slightly different salaries based on, perhaps, their seniority. But if there are no specific requirements for years of service necessary for participation in the program, then it is important to not allow the biasing effect of particular salaries. Thus it is appropriate to determine a typical salary for that employee category for each of the programs.

A particularly vexing issue is how to deal with personnel who only have a portion of their time allocated to participating in the program. Thus an aide might be assisting in two different programs. Clearly, one needs to determine the portion of the time to be charged to each of the programs. This is also an issue with administrative personnel who may be responsible for a whole organization and who only peripherally supervise the program in question.

Let us next consider *facilities/space*. If what is being examined is a new program for which a new structure will be erected, the issue is particularly complex. Clearly, the building has a life of service. The costs of building obviously are not charged to a single year or even to multiple years of the program included in the evaluation. Economists suggest amortizing the cost of the building over the number of years of anticipated service. By amortizing we simply mean what people do when they buy a house. The cost of a $50,000 loan payable over 30 years with interest has specified monthly payments that would "pay off" the loan.

I suggest a simpler solution. Why not just include as the cost for space what the rental price would be for a facility of the type required? This is not without its difficulties. If the typical space that might be required for operating the program is not available or, if available, would require renovation and restructuring in order to meet the needs of the program, then these particular renovation costs also need to be included. While this remodeling or restructuring might take place in the first year of the program's operation, again you will need to amortize the cost of this remodeling over multiple years.

Another area for which costs need to be determined is *equipment*. Some large equipment might feasibly be rented or leased. However, many small purchases, such as a computer or a printer, are more appropriately purchased. And (I'm sure you hear it coming) this purchase price needs to be spread over the expected life of that equipment.

As alluded to earlier in this section, the program might require *consultants* of one type or another. Some consultant services might be required throughout the program. For instance, there might be the need for an ongoing computer consultant. But in the case where program staff need to be trained or to participate in an off-site training workshop, such training might only be required in the first year of the program, or perhaps every 2 or 3 years. Thus this cost cannot be charged in a single year. (And . . . you know what comes next about how to treat this cost.)

Finally, there might be *travel costs*. Do these occur each year or are they primarily in the first year? The answer will help you to determine how these costs are handled. Furthermore, there certainly are costs associated with maintaining the facility and providing utilities (heat, lighting, telephone, etc.). What about supplies: paper, unique program materials, printing, food to be provided to participants, publicity materials, brochures?

There are also costs to entities other than the program, such as *costs incurred by participants*—perhaps purchases that they need to make, or transportation. Time is a cost. For example, more often than you wish, you might have made the statement, "That meeting just cost me 2 hours." The inference is that time has value. There are other things that might be done using that time. Different programs may require different amounts of client time. Whether one wants to consider this time as a cost is perhaps debatable. It depends on whether you are considering the costs simply from the perspective of the program. Another time cost that certainly must be included is volunteer time. If individuals are volunteering to assist in a program, they are saving personnel costs. Moreover, their volunteer time might well have been coaxed into participating in another program.

The costing elements that I have been discussing and an efficient means for examining them are presented in a book by Levin and McEwan listed in the Further Reading for this section. Full understanding of the cost issue requires greater detail than I am able to provide here.

══════ GAINING ADDITIONAL UNDERSTANDING ══════

Further Reading

Levin, H. M., & McEwan, P. J. (2003). Cost-effectiveness analysis as an evaluation tool. In T. Kellaghan & D. Stufflebeam (Eds.), *International handbook of educational evaluation* (pp. 125-152). Norwell, MA: Kluwer Academic.

This is the definitive discussion on cost-effectiveness, cost–benefit, cost–utility, and cost "ingredients."

Levin, H. (2005). Cost–benefit analysis. In S. Mathison (Ed.), *Encyclopedia of evaluation* (pp. 86–90). Thousand Oaks, CA: Sage.

Henry Levin has produced an easily readable description of cost–benefit analyses in this encyclopedia entry.

Z

How Can You Embark on a Program to Learn More about Evaluation?

I now offer three suggestions for how you can learn more about evaluation and improve your skills as an evaluator. The first reinforces the notion of further learning described at the end of each section of this volume. The second indicates sources of learning that go beyond this book and its suggested readings. And the third anticipates your actions as an evaluator and discusses how you can obtain feedback to improve your skills and your evaluations.

GETTING FEEDBACK ON EVALUATION

One of my favorite lines is from a poem named "To a Louse," by the Scottish poet Robert Burns. The line: "O wad some Power the giftie gie us to see oursels as ithers see us" (as written in the original). We learn by seeing how others view us or the products of our efforts. There are multiple ways in which the evaluator may benefit from the Robert Burns call to action. To me, perhaps, the most important source of such information are the stakeholders. Consider doing a debriefing with *stakeholders*. Ask them: "Were the questions that you asked the right ones?"

"Why weren't they the right ones?" "How might I have pushed you to get to these preferred questions?" "Did you feel that the measures that we used were appropriate?" "Did you feel that there were problems in data collection?" "What were they, and what might we have done differently?" "Were the statistical analyses sufficiently understandable?" "Was the report presented in a fashion that made sense to you?" "How might it have been improved?" "Are there actions, decisions, that you anticipate might be made that have been enhanced through the evaluation findings?" "Do you have a better understanding of your program now?" "Do you have a better understanding and appreciation of evaluation as a consequence of this evaluation?"

Another informal source of more technical feedback than can be learned from querying stakeholders can come from *other evaluators*. Why not consider finding a colleague, preferably a more experienced colleague, and get together for a short discussion about your report? Here the questions might reflect more technical issues. Were each of the instruments used valid? How might they have not captured the intent of the questions? Were the statistical analyses that were used appropriate? Were the qualitative data sufficiently detailed to justify the conclusions? And so on.

A more formal means of getting feedback on evaluation is through what is referred to as a *meta-evaluation*. You will recall that meta-evaluation was included within the fifth category of *The Program Evaluation Standards* detailed in Section X. The procedure for conducting a meta-evaluation at its simplest is to examine whether the evaluation was performed in accordance with the criteria set forth in the *Standards*. Some evaluation writers advocate that each evaluation should have a meta-evaluation conducted by an external evaluator. That is, an evaluation (in accord with the *Standards*) of the evaluation. I personally think that this is overkill and simply not feasible. Typically, we barely have sufficient resources to do an adequate evaluation, let alone establish resources for the conduct of a meta-evaluation. But if resources are available, fine, it is an excellent basis for reassuring stakeholders and providing you with feedback. If not, you might have a colleague at least reflect on your evaluation in terms of the *Standards*.

TAKING FULL ADVANTAGE OF THIS VOLUME

Only a brief discussion of this is necessary. Throughout the volume, I have provided opportunities at the end of each section to gain further understanding of evaluation based on the theory underlying my conception of evaluation. If you responded to my suggestions, you would have engaged in further reading in order to increase your knowledge related to the topic. Furthermore, the RUPAS case study that I presented is a vehicle that I hope you might have employed for applying acquired skills. If you have not been mindful of my invitation to engage in active learning, then let me now present a suggestion. Think about the sections of this book. Go to the outline at the beginning of the book: Which sections are a little hazy? Why not go back and do some further reading?

GAINING EVALUATION EXPERTISE BEYOND THIS VOLUME

How do we learn? We read, we practice, we participate, and we listen. In this book, you have engaged in reading—both within the sections as well as in the additional readings. I have not mentioned other evaluation textbooks—my pride of ownership tells me that they are not as readable as *Evaluation Essentials*. But if you wish to learn more and get another perspective, there are certainly interesting books to read.

We learn also by practice. You have had a simulated opportunity to do some practice based on the case study. That is, you practiced doing, or at least thinking about doing, an evaluation. You might find it worthwhile to examine other evaluation case situations listed at the end of this section. I reference two books that are worth reading for insights into how experienced evaluators say they conducted (or would conduct) specific evaluations.

We learn also by participating. Evaluation is a profession. There are specific competencies that one anticipates evaluators would have (see Further Reading). There are evaluation degree training programs. And there are evaluation professional associations throughout the world. Many of these have annual conferences, which are very helpful. One such conference is the annual conference of the American Evaluation Association. Here you will have the opportunity to hear many very stimulating presentations from leaders in the field. Perhaps, also, you will consider sharing your own evaluation experiences with others. Details may be found online at the website: *eval.org*.

I make it a point each year to attend this conference. Since we are not strangers—indeed, how could we be? We have had a long conversation—feel free to come up and say hello.

GAINING ADDITIONAL UNDERSTANDING

Further Reading

Stevahn, L., King, J., Ghere, G., & Minnema, J. (2005). Establishing essential program evaluator competencies. *American Journal of Evaluation, 26*(1), 43–59.

This excellent article describes the competencies required of an evaluator. I hope that you proceed to gain them.

Stufflebeam, D. L. (2001). The meta-evaluation imperative. *American Journal of Evaluation, 22*(2), 183–209.

Stufflebeam is probably the "father" of meta-evaluation. This is well worth reading.

Studying Cases

I invite you here to learn about evaluation by studying cases. Here are two excellent sources that you might examine.

Alkin, M. C., & Christie, C. A. (Eds.). (2005). *Theorists' models in action* (New Directions in Evaluation, No. 106). San Francisco: Jossey-Bass.

In this monograph, the Bunche–Da Vinci case abbreviated in Section P is presented in full detail. Four different evaluators describe how they would do the evaluation.

Fitzpatrick, J., Christie, C. A., & Mark, M. M. (2009). *Evaluation in action: Interviews with expert evaluators.* Thousand Oaks, CA: Sage.

In this excellent volume, Fitzpatrick and her colleagues provide a brief description of each of 12 different evaluations and then interview the evaluators to answer questions about why they did what they did.

Real-World Experience

Now, perhaps, you are ready to go out and assist on an evaluation. Or, possibly, you might have an opportunity to be an active observer of an ongoing evaluation. Try it!

An Evaluation Lesson

by "Unknown Student"

Get your control group
Make an experimental design
Randomly choose all your subjects
Allow plenty of time

Pretest and posttest
Use accuracy and care
Any unanticipated outcomes
You must declare

Train all your staff
And visit the site
Now the perfect evaluation
Will be done just right

The data are collected
Analyzed with expertise
The report carefully written
Is sure to please

Now you sit back and await
After your tiring escapade
The news from the boss
"Program changes will be made."

You have not long to wait
For the phone quickly rings
Your presence is asked for
To clarify a few things

This poem was written by a student in one of my classes many years ago and given to me as a gift. Unfortunately, the author's name was not included and all attempts to search records have been unsuccessful. I would be very pleased to have the author contact me to get reacquainted and to include her name in subsequent printings.

"It's interesting," you're told
"But not what we need
The goals are different
Than we agreed."

"But, but," you sputter
"It should be done this way
You guys are not in tune
With evaluation today!"

"Sorry sir," you're told
"It is you and not us
We don't need all this data
of T-tests and stuff

The things you found out
Will not help our lot
We need to find ways
To improve what we got.

We can't change our teachers
We can't change our hours
We can't change our SES
We don't have that power.

We called you to help
Evaluate what we're doing
Not judge all our faults
Rather suggest ways of improving."

A comment is made
As you leave the door
That you return to school
And learn some more

Evaluation, they say
Is not research design.
Randomization and control groups
Needn't be used all the time

They said you begin
By first finding out
Who makes the decisions
And what they are about

Next, ask relevant questions
In order to know
Many more things
Than just "go or no"

Find out why they wish
An evaluation done
And who are the people
They think must be won?

You must address, too
In your report
A number of groups—
It's quite a sport!

You should involve yourself
And take a good look
At the actual program
Not the one in the book

Study as a whole program
As well as the parts
Observe, interview, question
It's all part of the art

Don't go blowing whistles
On people or goals
You're not a policeman
For that's not your role

Keep in close contact
With those who asked for advice
And make your report
Helpful, clear, and concise

Don't expect miracles
Because you did a good job
You provided more data
To add to the blob

Utilization will occur
In small little bits
And your evaluation report
Helps decisions better fit

This is just a small part
Of the evaluator's role
Take Dr. Alkin's #460
To learn of your goal

Perhaps you won't be able
The perfect report to complete
But you'll know for sure
How to tackle the feat

You'll learn it's an art
And not just a skill
The evaluator's job
Is more than research drill

"Come back," you're told
"When these things you learn
And if you're serious about evaluation
We'll give you another turn."

Index

About the Author

Marvin C. Alkin is Emeritus Professor in the Social Research Methodology Division of the Graduate School of Education and Information Studies at the University of California, Los Angeles. He has been a member of the UCLA faculty since 1964 and has, at various times, served as Chair of the Education Department and Associate Dean of the school. Dr. Alkin was one of the founders of the Center for the Study of Evaluation and was its Director for 7 years. The Center, established in 1966 by the U.S. government to engage in research on appropriate methods for conducting evaluation of educational programs, continues to be an integral part of the UCLA Graduate School of Education and Information Studies. Dr. Alkin is a leading authority in the field of evaluation. He has published important research studies on the use of evaluation information in decision making and on comparative evaluation theory. His publications include five books on evaluation and more than 150 journal articles, book chapters, monographs, and technical reports. His books include *Using Evaluations* (with Peter White and Richard Daillak), *Debates on Evaluation*, *Evaluation Roots*, and the four-volume *Encyclopedia of Educational Research* (6th edition). Dr. Alkin is currently Associate Editor of *Studies in Educational Evaluation* and co-section Editor of the *American Journal of Evaluation*. He previously had been Editor of *Educational Evaluation and Policy Analysis*. He has also been a consultant to numerous national governments and has directed program evaluations in 14 different countries.